ERITREA

ERITREA

NATIONHOOD AND SOVEREIGNTY

Bereket H. Selassie, ed.

THE RED SEA PRESS
TRENTON | LONDON | NEW DELHI | CAPE TOWN | NAIROBI | ADDIS ABABA | ASMARA | IBADAN

THE RED SEA PRESS
541 West Ingham Avenue | Suite B
Trenton, New Jersey 08638

Cover design: Ashraful Haque

Cataloging-in-Publication Data may be obtained from the Library of Congress.

ISBNs: 9781569028094 (HB)
       9781569028100 (PB)

IN HONOR OF OUR HEROES AND MARTYRS

Time will not erase their memory
Nor will the cruel acts of madness.
And may their suffering illumine the darkness
Imposed by tyranny
And replace it with the bright dawn of Liberty.

--Bereket Habte Selassie

TABLE OF CONTENTS

FOREWORD: ISAIAS AFWERKI'S DECLARATIONS ARE IN VIOLATION OF ERITREA'S SOVEREIGNTY

Bereket H. Selassie

A Mid-Summer 2018 Surprise

With a countenance ablaze with a smile Eritreans had never seen—for they knew him only with a sullen scowl—Isaias Afwerki told a cheering Ethiopian crowd that henceforth there would not be a separate Eritrea and Ethiopia. "We are one people," he was telling them, and anyone who doubts this must have his head examined, he seemed to intimate. This was music to the crowd's ears. Here was what they always thought to be the arch enemy of Ethiopia—the devil incarnate—proclaiming in no uncertain terms that he was one of them—a lost child come home from the cold!

The crowd was delirious with joy.

The declaration of *"Aykessernan" (We didn't suffer loss)* was made in Asmara as the Abiy/Isaias "bromance" was unfolding. The statement "we are one people" was said in Addis Ababa in July 2018.

Isaias did not stop with this astounding proclamation of a new imperial enterprise: he struck a nail on the coffin of the countervailing, anti-imperial liberation experience. The words he used were carefully chosen leaving no room for doubt that his new fealty to the imperial enterprise is unshakable. He said: *Aykesseranan!… AiTef'anan!*

These words might not have meant much to the incredulous Ethiopian crowd, and especially to the new partner, who had after all been a loyal adjutant to his former foe Melles (now departed), playing a crucial role as a military spy even in the so called "Weyane War," between Ethiopia and Eritrea.

I kept wondering how Abiy's evangelical conscience "processed" the heartless *Aykessernan* declaration, given the fact that he knew a few thousand innocent Eritrean youth had been sacrificed as fodder in the so called "Badme War." Perhaps he rationalized it as the war imperative, as did Isaias. But rationalizing is one thing; declaring that we did not lose is quite another.

I am devoting a few lines to this point because Abiy's speech when he was newly elected Prime Minister and especially his release of all prisoners and declaration of peaceful resolution of the tension between Eritrea and Ethiopia was so affecting that he had fooled some of us into hoping that the proverbial millennium was around the corner. He also deceived the international community, which glamorized his image with crowning him with the Nobel Peace Prize in 2018, a decision now regretted by so many including some who lobbied for him to get that symbolic honor at the time.

But such is the manipulative power and insanity driven by imperial ambition that even formerly sane-looking persons can shroud themselves with total masquerade while shamelessly being sucked up into the vortex of imperial yearnings. The imperial bug seems to have stung Abiy, if he hadn't been infected before. Perhaps the royal bug is a more apt metaphor in his case, since he has told us that his mother had told him he would be crowned the seventh king of Ethiopia, one day.

The Insanity of imperial yearnings of Isaias

To the reader who wonders how a once popular Liberation Fighter—a revolutionary—could entertain imperial yearnings, the answer can be found in a combination of medical and historical-cultural context. I have explored this subject in my book, *Desecraters of the Sacred Trust* (2020). As I have explained in the book I just cited, Isaias has had dreams of becoming the Lord and Master of realms beyond puny Eritrea. He even entertained prophetic qualities and some of his admirers (a few living, others departed) had believed he deserves realms far beyond Eritrea. Then why pretend to be a revolutionary and a liberation fighter of Eritrea, you might wonder. And it is a good question. The curious mind seeks to answer this puzzling question even by quoting Confucius. But the answer is simple. It is about ambition, and ambition, to quote Marc Anthony of Shakespear's Julius Caesar, should be made of "Sterner Stuff," the Stuff that is willing and eager to sacrifice thousand souls and declare *Aykessernan* ("We did not suffer loss").

Isaias and the Liberation Fight

So Isaias is willing, though certainly not able yet, to sacrifice Eritrea's sovereignty on the Altar of his imperial project. It should be recalled that fifty years ago (On December 1, 1970), the Ethiopian army committed the most horrendous massacre in Eritrea. Some 1000 innocent civilians were burned alive in the villages of Beskidra and Ona. Today the same army is back in Eritrea, this time at the invitation of Isaias Afwerki, as part of the Isaias-Abiy joint strategy to attack Tigray. The reason given by Abiy for the attack of Tigray with heavy duty armament was the claim that the TPLF leaders had committed crimes for which they must be arrested and made to face justice.

Now while we are on the subject of the war in Tigray, we must in all fairness consider the question of who started the war and why. Abiy's explanation is that the TPLF leaders defied the central (federal) government by deciding to organise an election in their region, following the decision of the federal government to postpone the election because of the Covd-19 pandemic. They went ahead with the election in defiance of the federal government's decision to postpone the election. They held the election and thus presented a *fait accompli*, while the other regional governments agreed with the decision of postponement. It is important to note that the TPLF leaders cited their constitutional right to hold the election and that postponement of the election violated what is ordained in the constitution.

The two sides thus held opposed positions, which leads to the question whether, irrespective of who is constitutionally on the right side, there were genuine efforts to resolve these fundamentally opposed political differences and constitutional interpretations with sagacity and flexibility, and even , perhaps, by including help and counsel from the global community. This is a highly relevant question in view of the fact that war involves unnecessary loss of life and destruction of property. Did the federal government under Abiy devote sufficient time and energy in attempts to persuade the TPLF to negotiate a peaceful solution to avoid war. Abiy says this had been done, including the dispatch of mediators to travel to Mekele to try to convince the TPLF leadership that a peaceful solution is a better option and that the TPLF leadership were not willing to compromise.

The TPLF, on their part contend that the Abiy government had decided to invade Tigray and attack , a strategy that they had been hatching for over a year in consultation with Isaias, who has his own reason for going to war with the TPLF.

Abiy characterized the war campaign involving 100,000 soldiers armed with tanks and heavy artillery as a law-and-order action, as a police operation designed to arrest criminals. The response of the TPLF is that it is war of genocide, aimed at obliterating them and also Tigray as a whole. Whatever the final outcome, it is already clear that the war in Tigray has already cost heavy casualties and devastation of property.

The War in Tigray and Its Consequences

The so-called police operation ended in the capture of Mekele, Tigray's capital. But the object of the operation, namely the arrest of the culprits, was not realized: they were not captured;

they had left town tactically retreating to the mountains. They had reverted to their old mode of guerilla warfare. So Mekele fell under federal authority, having been captured by the Federal Ethiopian forces, minus the "criminal Junta,"that is the TPLF's top leadership, as Abiy's government had dubbed them. Clearly, the capture of Mekele neither ended, nor would end the war in Tigray, reportedly planned and executed under the joint Ethiopian forces and several Eritrean divisions ordered by Isaias to be part of the joint operation.

Another Consequence of the Tigray War
Abduction of Eritrean Refugees

In addition to the vengeance that Isaias secured from the Tigray war, it has also been reported that he used the opportunity of the involvement of Eritrean troops in the Tigray war to score another vindictive victory by abducting (reportedly) some 6,000 Eritreans from the refugee camps of Tigray and taking them back to Eritrea from where they had fled years earlier. Such act, if true, is a serious violation of international law and both Isaias as the perpetrator of the act, as well as Abiy as a presumptive enabler of the abduction, are answerable under international law. Some responsible people from the region and the international community have been calling for a thorough investigation of the abduction by a neutral body under the aegis of the United Nations and the African Union.

The most immediate action should be to send a Commission of Inquiry to Ethiopia and Eritrea with two aims, under the auspices of the United Nations High Commission for Refugees (UNHCR).

The first task is to ensure that no harm must befall the abducted refugees by Isaias and his odious security machine, which is notorious for acts prohibited by International law of Human Rights. Eritrea is a prison nation, with hundreds of thousands locked up in crowded containers and suffering the cold night and the sweltering heat of day, with most of the prisoners suffering from serious illnesses.

The second task of such a Commission of Inquiry is to probe deeply into the circumstances including collecting evidence involving Isaias and his government in the act of abduction, provided the story of such abduction is confirmed. Again, subject to the confirmation of the said abduction, the Commission should spend time both in Eritrea and Ethiopia with demands made that all persons suspected of being involved in the act of abduction should be investigated. And the report of such inquiry must be made available to the United Nations and the African Union, as well as to the internatipnal community at large, including journalists and researchers. But it is the more reason to be clear on some crucial points. Let it be clearly understood and let the world know:

First, Eritrea is not for sale, despite Isaias Afwerki's imperial yearnings and machinations. Eritrea's sovereignty, attained with the precious blood of martyrs will not be bartered away by a power-hungry adventurer and his Ethiopian partner in crime.

Second, the other Eritrean liberation fighters, including the Eritrean intellectuals involved in this book project, are determined to critically and systematically expose the lies and overt and covert schemes in which Isaias and Abiy have been engaged, and will continue the struggle against their imperial machinations. The timely theme and title of the book project, "The Pillars of Eritrea's Sovereign Nation-Statehood," is one reflection of this ongoing effort.

Third, All Eritreans, especially the new generation of youth some of whom have been subjected to servitude and weaponized by Isaias to advance his secret deal, will resist to the last breath, as expressed in the old mantra of the Eritrean revolution—*akhr nas akhr Telga!*

Fourth, There is a new awakening in which the Eritrean masses both at home and in the Diaspora, are making new commitment to see to it that Isaias and his exterminator regime is removed and replaced by a democratically elected assembly.

"The Pillars of Eritrea's Sovereign Statehood" Book Project

This book project reflects a new dedication to add an intellectual version of the ongoing fight for Eritrea's liberation from the exterminator regime. Its aim is also expressed in the title of the book: "Eritrea: Nationhood and Sovereognty."

In what follows, the reader will find the nature and objective of the project and a list of its participants, which appears at the end of the book. A cursory look at the Introductory chapter will give a sense of the reason why the project was conceived. A summary of each chapter is also found at the Concluding chapter.

The effort involved in this book project is a reflection of the depth of our patriotic fervor and our determination to preserve, protect and promote our country's sovereignty, a sovereignty that was obtained with incalculable sacrifice. The imperial yearnings and machinations of Isaias, far from discouraging Eritrean patriots, adds grit to our determination. This land of heroes and martyrs is not, and shall never be, for sale. The sovereignty obtained with inestimable sacrifice must and will be defended by all patriotic Eritreans with all the resources at their disposal.

The Clear and Present danger (as one of our chapters has called it) posed by the unelected adventurer with his criminal intent of smothering our sovereignty, must be seen for what it is: High Treason for which the accused would face appropriate legal sanction prescribed by the law. It has now become clear that Eritreans must decide to realize this clear and present danger and do everything (and anything) to put an end to it once and for all. Failing to do that will mean losing our treasured sovereignty. We must gird our loins for the final fight, the fight of our lives. We must use every available means to put an end to Isaias Afwerki's criminal intent.

The Crisis and Its Challenges

The Chinese define crisis as the coincidence of danger and opportunity. We are now at the crossroads facing the challenge of our life time. With the war in Tigray, we face a challenge presenting us an opportunity of Do or Die, an opportunity to put an end to the despotic regime of Isaias Afwerki. How we do it is not a contested issue. We cannot be distracted by any fancy moralizing about the end not justifying the means. The end of putting an end to the exterminator regime of Isaias prescribes the means. The end of saving a nation and its people, who fought for thirty years for their self-determination and achieved national independence, justifies the means that helps in their survival. Imagine a creature that is cornered and threatened with death with his trembling body put against the wall. What does such an endangered creature do? The answer is simple—the endangered creature does not hesitate. His/her (Its) instinctive act is to charge at the *source* of the danger. Survival is the first law of nature, which we humans share with other fellow creatures. So, we are at a historical moment of DO OR DIE!

Clear and Present Danger—Whither Eritrea?

The writing of the participants of this project is the intellectual equivalent of guerrilla warfare, the warfare which after thirty years of effort of blood, sweat, and tears eventually secured our independent statehood. The various chapters contained in this volume explore the various pillars that support the idea of our sovereignty. It is a national imperative of which every Eritrean must be constantly reminded that there are essential pillars that support the sovereignty of their nation.

The words "Clear and Present Danger..."and "Whither Eritrea..." are titles of two chapters of this volume—words that sum up the challenges our nation-state faces and also raise critical questions that must find answers if we are to have a democratic and optimally developed Eritrea holding her proud place in the family of nations. It is the cautious but firm optimism about Eritrea's possibilities with its hard working, resilient, fervently patriotic, and selfless people not only to survive the present danger, but will thrive and confirm the idealism and patriotism with which its freedom fighters paid huge sacrifice. The common faith uniting the participants of this book is testimony to the hope that sustained us in our long struggle for our independence and sovereignty.

Finally, in as much as we are jealous about of our own sovereignty, we must respect the sovereignty of other nation states, including our neighbors. We must, therefore, make it clear to all concerned that we do not believe in the involvement in the affairs of other nations, including the on-going war in Tigray. This, despite our sincerely felt sadness to see our neighborly Tigrayan brothers and sisters getting embroiled in a devastating war--a war that involves murder, rape and mass displacement, which demand international sanctions against the culprits, including indictments for War Crimes and Crimes Against Humanity.

PILLARS OF ERITREA'S SOVEREIGN STATEHOOD: A BOOK WRITING PROJECT

Bereket H. Selassie

Introduction

This project is academic in form, but profoundly political in substance. Not that its academic aspect in any way diminishes its value; on the contrary, it enhances its value lending it clarity and coherence. Indeed, it is hoped that it will invest it with gravity and rigor in terms of its conception and execution.

The Meaning and Significance of Sovereignty

Sovereignty is a juridical and political concept. Its simple dictionary definition states it as "supreme authority, especially over a state;" and: "Independence—freedom from outside interference and the right to self-government."

It is a defining characteristic of a free state. In its evolution, the term was originally embodied in the person of a monarch, but with the dawn of the democratic era, as political power shifted from the monarch to representative institutions, sovereignty as an abstract concept evolved as separate from the person heading the state hierarchy, shifting to representative political institutions like Parliament. For example, in British constitutional law and practice, the concept of the supremacy of Parliament, signifies the shift of power from the monarch to a representative institution. In other words, it is no longer the

Queen that is supreme (or sovereign) but Parliament. Thus parliamentary supremacy (or sovereignty), together with the Rule of Law and Separation of Powers became the central principles of the (British) constitutional system.

In other constitutional systems (in the majority), in this Democratic Epoch, sovereignty is ordained to belong to the people; and the people exercise it indirectly through their elected representatives. We find this stated in most democratic constitutions. Incidentally, this is the reason why Dictators pay lip service to democracy and the Rule of Law. We Eritreans do not need any other example of a dictator pretending to want democracy. It was how our Supreme Pretender, a certified Confidence Trickster (Con-man), agreed with the passing of solemn Resolutions in two EPLF Congresses (one in 1987, another in 1994) proclaiming that an independent Eritrea would be governed by a multi-party democracy under the Rule of Law. And in accordance with these Resolutions, he presided over the making of a constitution, which was ratified by the National Assembly that he chaired, in 1997, as well as by a Constituent Assembly. How our great pretender and Con-Man tricked us pretending to want a constitution and presiding over a two and half- years of constitution making experience became a matter of great embarrassment when he laughingly announced that the ratified constitution was dead! It is hoped that this topic will be taken up by participants in one of the appropriate chapters, including in part under the chapter titled, "What Is to be Done."

Sovereignty Under the Constitution of Eritrea
The State of Eritrea and its Territory
Eritrea is a sovereign and independent State founded on the principles of democracy, social justice and the Rule of Law. The nation State of Eritrea consists of all its territories, including islands, territorial waters and airspace, delineated by recognized boundaries. In the State of Eritrea, sovereign power is vested in the people, and shall be exercised pursuant to the provisions of

this Constitution. The government of Eritrea shall be established through democratic procedures to represent people's sovereignty and shall have strong institutions, accommodating popular participation and serving as foundation of a viable democratic political order. Eritrea is a unitary State divided into units of local government. The powers and duties of these units shall be determined by law. [The Constitution, Article1 (sub-articles 1-5)].

Supremacy of the Constitution
This Constitution is the legal expression of the sovereignty of the Eritrean people. This Constitution enunciates the principles on which the state of Eritrea is based and by which it shall be guided and determines the organization and operation of government. It is the source of government legitimacy and the basis for the protection of the rights, freedoms and dignity of citizens and of just administration. The Constitution is the supreme law of the country and the source of all laws of the State, and all laws, orders and acts contrary to its letter and spirit shall be null and void. All organs of the State, all public and private associations and institutions and all citizens shall be bound by and remain loyal to the Constitution and shall ensure its observance. The Constitution shall serve as a basis for instilling constitutional culture and for enlightening citizens to respect fundamental human rights and duties. [Article 2 (sub-articles 1-5)]

Eritrean Sovereignty and the Postcolonial State System
The boundaries of African States were established by European colonizers, and the question what to do with the colonially inherited boundaries in a postcolonial Africa was one of the crucial questions facing African governments and peoples. The question was posed but not dealt with at the Founding Meeting of the Organization of African Unity (OAU) in May 1963; It was postponed to the next meeting of the Heads of State and Governments, which was held in Cairo a year later. At the

Cairo meeting, the OAU passed a historic Resolution accepting the colonially fixed boundaries to define postcolonial Africa's legal order and sovereign statehood. At the Cairo meeting, as at the May 1963 Founding Conference of the OAU, Ghana's President, Kwame Nkrumah had become a lone voice demanding a Pan-Africanist answer to Africa's "border problem." The other leaders accepted the *fait accompli* of a postcolonial reality leaving the noble Pan-Africanist objectives that had been passionately advocated by Nkrumah to be dealt with by future generations. For the present leaders, that had become ensconced in the postcolonial power structure, the preeminent consideration was the reality of power and maintaining it.

For Eritreans, the Cairo Resolution was seen as a two-edged sword. On one side, it bodes well for a nation that is itself the outcome of a European colonial experience, inheriting a colonial boundary fixed by agreement between Italy as a colonial power and Ethiopia. On the other side, the Ethiopian dissolution of the UN-granted federation, under which Eritrea's national identity was recognized, had been dissolved by Emperor Haile Selassie. The Eritrean armed struggle that followed the dissolution, or rather had been started one year earlier, in anticipation of Ethiopia's plans, was aimed at reviving the colonial reality under which Eritrea was created as a separate entity, like the other new states of Africa.

Nonetheless, some African writers lament the continued existence of Africa's postcolonial borders. One such writer has wondered when what he calls "The Shackles of Africa's Bondage of Boundaries" will be "loosened."[1] Mazrui's sentiment is a reflection of his quasi Pan-Africanist position, though he does not embrace Nkruma's vision of a United States of Africa. In the above-cited article, Mazrui points out that African governments "have tended to be possessive about colonial borders and have discouraged challenging them."

---

1   See *Ali A. Mazrui. Journal of Horn of Africa, Volume XXIV 2006*

Eritrea in the Context of Regionalism and Pan-Africanism

1. Eritrea and Regional Politics

As the current situation in Eritrea and Ethiopia illustrates, Eritrea continues to be affected by the politics in the Horn of Africa sub-region in one way or another. In terms of recent history, Imperial Ethiopia under Haile Selassie (followed by Mengistu's regime), sought to reorder history by incorporating Eritrea into the empire, citing historical and cultural ties as well as strategic and economic interests. The UN-granted federation that sought to accommodate Ethiopia's interests, was not enough to satisfy the imperial enterprise. Principally due to Haile Selassie's personal ambition to reverse the historical work of Menelik in signing off what later became known as Eritrea (See the Treaty of Wuchale), he unilaterally and illegally abolished the UN-arranged federation thereby provoking "the sleeping lions" to go to the bush to reclaim what their fathers had failed to obtain through diplomacy.[2]

The sleeping lions were indeed awakened as signaled by the firing of the first shots by the ELF in September 1961.[3] Thirty years later, Eritrea became independent having defeated the Ethiopian army of occupation; and two years later, following the internationally supervised referendum, a new nation unfurled its flag at the UN Headquarters in New York, as a new member of the family of Nations.

Things seemed to move smoothly along a peaceful and forward-looking and optimistic line until the end of 1997. A

---

2 The term "sleeping lions" is from my remark addressed to the Emperor when he asked me what would happen if he abolished the federation. See *The Crown and the Pen. Red Sea Press. 2007, pp.154-155.*

3 Hamid Idris Awate, who led the ELF forces of liberation, had become a powerful symbol of Eritrean national identity and fighting spirit. His statue should be erected in Asmara, not out there in a remote place.

new constitution had been ratified and a promising national development plan toward a democratic and progressive future was loudly proclaimed. Relation with Ethiopia seemed to be peaceful and amicable. The leaders of the two countries, Isaias Afwerki of Eritrea and Meles Zenawi of Ethiopia, seemed to be working as comrades and leaders of two brotherly (or sisterly) countries. They were touted by commentators as part of a new breed of leaders of Africa, Musoveni and South Africa's Mbeki among them. This writer interviewed Isaias and then Meles a few months before the "Badme War." Referring to the rumors of differences between the two governments, Isaias was devious in his answers to my question concerning friendly relations between Ethiopia and Eritrea. Meles said that there was "a kind of hiccup," which will be fixed soon. "That's all," he said emphatically.

Then the war clouds had become a storm.

From Peace to War and Uncertainty

Suddenly in the Spring of 1998, war broke out between Eritrea and Ethiopia, a war initiated by the initiative of Isaias who ordered a regiment commanded by his favorite General (Wuchu) to invade Parts of Western Tigray. The war was termed the Badme War, because it followed a shooting incident in which a team of Eritrean troops was killed by elements of the Tigray army. Meles tried to deal with the situation peacefully, making desperate attempts to contact Isaais who had traveled to Saudi Arabia, having given the order. In desperation Meles asked the Ethiopian Parliament to authorize him to declare a defense war aimed at liberating the occupied territories. The war lasted two years after failed attempts at ceasefire and reconciliation. In the Spring of 2000, the Ethiopian army pushed Eritrean troops out of Tigray and penetrated deep into Eritrean territory including Badme. This presented Isaias with a fait accompli that forced him to accept a ceasefire with Ethiopian troops occupying a chunk of Eritrean land, a matter that represents huge humiliation of a once proud and fearful EPLF army. Isaias has not recovered from the humiliation of the defeat and may take adventurous steps, in collaboration with Abiy, provoking war with the TPLF. Such a step would lead to horrific damage to life and property and achieve nothing except further humiliation.[4]

The humiliation of defeat of a once invincible EPLF army has left psychological scars on Isaias whose adventurous action was defeated. Meles described Isais's ambition as reflecting a Bonapartist (i.e., Napoleonic) complex of becoming the arbiter of regional affairs, if not (yet) the leader of the Horn of Africa. That designation is key to explaining the bizarre behavior of Isaias including his readiness to hand over power to Abiy thus compromising Eritrean sovereignty, which would be eliminated and absorbed in a neo-imperial Ethiopia. No sooner had Isaias made such a declaration than *"Abichu"* (the new name by which Abiy is being called somewhat contemptuously) proclaimed the formation of a new Unitary Party called Prosperity. Abiy also promised to change the federal system of government. This declaration aroused Oromo and other people's objection, including the TPLF of Tigray. When the situation seemed to produce more strife and division, Isaias declared that he will not stand by folding his arms but would intervene in Ethiopian affairs. Meles must be turning in his grave!

A Honeymoon of Convenience?

Isaias and Abiy have become new allies and the TPLF is their "common enemy." Clearly the military prowess of the TPLF is such that it cannot be defeated by either Isaias or Abiy alone. Whether a combined assault is conceivable militarily is an open question. One thing is certain, if war breaks out between the TPLF and the combined forces of Abiy and Isaias, the devastation and loss of life will be inestimable. The loss will be all round and catastrophic. The result of such a war reminds me of the Tigrigna saying, *Kilte GoraHAtsi sinqom amukhushti*. (Two

---

4 This was written just before the outbreak of the war between the TPLF army and the Federal Ethiopian Defense Forces

wily partners will have ashes for their reward). That apt saying applies to our two "honeymooning" partners each one of whom is trying to use the other for his own ends. I don't know about Abiy, but the trajectory of Isaias Afwerki's alliance is littered with the mortal remains of many an unsuspecting partners, or those wasting away in remote and inaccessible dungeons, like the heroic freedom fighters Haile Dru'E, Petros Solomon and Mahmud Sherifo, to name a few.

If such a catastrophic war should happen, the men and women of Norway who awarded Abiy the Nobel Peace Prize may regret their act to the days they die, if they are not regretting already. Within Ethiopia, the general feeling of insecurity and instability, particularly in the Oromo areas does not bode well for the country's future. Abiy's threat of dire consequences aimed at the TPLF and the people of Tigray, if not reversed and replaced with reconciliation between the central government and the regional government of Tigray, the state of insecurity and lawlessness will continue. The same is true between Abiy and his group and the Oromo leaders. The arrest and detention of Jawar Mohammed and Bekele Gerba will have to be handled carefully and an amicable solution found to their division and mutual recrimination. There is no indication that this will happen. Add to this the Isaias factor, which is a destabilizing one. The politics of sociopathy by which his conduct is characterized, will not induce any reasonable solution to the outstanding divisions and mutual accusations among the various forces making up present day Ethiopian politics.

And the honeymoon of convenience cannot endure in such circumstances. The economy of Ethiopia, which had been a promising one, is now in free fall. Unemployment is rising and young Ethiopians are voting with their feet, seeking employment abroad including in the Arabian Peninsula and the Gulf Region.

The continuing dispute between Egypt and Ethiopia over the Grand Ethiopian Renaissance Dam (GERD) is an issue over which Isaias had a different position that seemed to be sympathetic to Egypt's position. This was during Meles Zenawi's time of leadership and our great pretender has no qualms about changing position to suit his interest. His visit to Egypt recently and meeting with Egypt's leader, was probably a mission of on behalf of his new ally, Abiy, who has been beating war drums, aimed at Egypt as well as at Tigray.

2. Eritrea in the Context of Pan-Africanist Objectives

A well known Pan-Africanist activist and noted scholar once asked me the following question during an interview:

"Is it true that you were one of the young lawyers who drafted the OAU Charter, when you were Ethiopia's Attorney General?" When I answered his question in the positive, he smiled broadly and, adjusting his specs and looking me straight in the eye, said:

"How can you help draft a Charter that made postcolonial borders sacrosanct, and now act as an Eritrean freedom fighter, seeking to break away from Ethiopia?"

"A Good Question," I answered him calmly and left the answer to sink in while I thought of the answer. I then went on to explain that Eritrea's fight for self-determination does not contradict Pan-Africanist principles. On the contrary, the right of colonized people to determine their political future by all means, including (as a last resort) through armed struggle, is recognized under international law. It is a sad misunderstanding of Pan-Africanism that it accepts the oppression of any people within a nation, in the name of Pan-African unity.

Years later, on the occasion of the "Distinguished Mwalimu Nyerere Lecture" that I delivered in May 2011, the same Pan-Africanist activist, my interviewer, Professor Issa Shivji, acted as my host at the University of Tanzania, Dr-es-Salaam. By that time, Issa Shivji had become a well-informed supporter of the Eritrean struggle for independence. In introducing me to the distinguished audience of scholars and practitioners, Shivji said that I had been the Attorney General of His Imperial Majesty

9

Emperor Haile Selassie of Ethiopia, the Lion of Judah. He added wickedly that I had "the dubious distinction of being ruled by a lion.".…

"But," he said," Bereket refused it. "In 1964, Bereekt Selassie did the undouable by a king's subject—he resigned. "(For) ...*meanwhile he had engaged in an underground movement against the Emperor and had contacts with the liberation movement in Eritrea. By resigning he formally dissociated himself from the Crown and took to the Pen, if I may paraphrase the title of his memoirs, The Crown and the Pen...So Professor Selassie not only used his pen to teach and write but also to propagate the cause of freedom, justice and liberation of the continent.*"[5]

This reference to my own confrontation with fellow Africans on the question of Eritrea's right to self-determination and independence and that this right is in accord with Pan-Africanist principles and objectives, is to drive the point home that our cause is firmly grounded in law and justice. Emperor Haile Selassie used his prestige as a well-regarded leader to close off all of our access to potential supporters in Africa, the only exception being Somalia. In view of that stark diplomatic fact, ours was an uphill fight in terms of diplomacy and propaganda. As the story mentioned above illustrates, even well-informed and highly educated Africans had a wrong view about our right to independence. Our fight was long and hard, and the reward in terms of final victory was all the sweeter.

The Need for Clarity and Persistence

In the context of the current confused situation in Ethiopia, and the Horn sub-region, it behooves us to be clear about one thing. This thing we call sovereignty is a valuable but easily perishable property that we must constantly watch over and fight for. I don't have to go far: just remember what Isais said in Addis Ababa, beating his chest and smiling and embracing Abiy as his partner in a new Ethiopia-Eritrea "Partnership." What he did is a crime of Treason punishable with death, if

---

5 See. *Reimagining Pan-Africanism. Distinguished Mwalimu Lecture Series 2009-2013. Mkuki Na Nyota, Dar-es-Salaam, 2015. Pages116-117.*

10

and, when he is caught and brought to court, hand-cuffed, charged with treason.

Read the Eritrean Constitution carefully and ask anyone of the many fine Eritrean lawyers about the provision of the Penal Code of Eritrea, copied from the Penal Code of Ethiopia, itself modeled on the Swiss Penal Code. Keep this in mind, all of you, cherished colleagues and compatriots, when you draft your respective chapters, including, in particular, the segment *considering the question as to what is to be done.*

THE HISTORICAL BASIS OF ERITREA'S SOVEREIGN STATEHOOD

Awet T. Weldemichael & Samuel Emaha Tsegai

A rapidly growing number of Eritreans are perturbed about the pervasive state of uncertainty surrounding their country under a tyrannical government. The regime's opaque and dangerous foreign dealings and adventures have exacerbated their worries about the fate of their country's hard-won independence. The discursive onslaughts of the very sources of threat to independent Eritrea are gaslighting their legitimate concerns. These are the regime in Asmara and its unlikely Ethiopian partners and their longing for the yesteryears of imperial past and perennial quest for access to the sea through Eritrea.

This chapter traces Eritrea's origins, like the rest of African countries, to the late 19ᵗʰ century and 20ᵗʰ century European colonialism in the continent. The history of that colonial experience as well as the development of African and international legal principles and norms are essential frameworks within and across which the Eritrean armed struggle successfully wrestled independence for the country. That is because the legacy of colonialism defined the geographical referents of the independent African countries, including those not colonized by Europe, and subsequent developments in the international system legalized them. The chapter will specifically document the consolidation of the former Italian colony of Eritrea and the history of its being passed on from one foreign rule to the next against the backdrop of novel African and international norms on accession to sovereign statehood.

Pre-Italian Bedlam and Italian Colonial Rule

In the decades immediately preceding the late 19th century European scramble for Africa, the territory of present-day Eritrea had been a fighting ground for marauding Tigrayan (northern Ethiopian) warlords and successive Funj incursions, Turco-Egyptian expansion and later Mahdyya invasions from Nilotic Sudan. From 1844 onwards, for example, northern Ethiopian, Egyptian and Sudanese Mahdist forces took turns to regularly invade and plunder the Bogos region. Desperate, the war-weary inhabitants even appealed to France and Great Britain for protection, which they did not get.[1] Further west, in the Beni Amer-inhabited areas and the areas surrounding the Gash river similarly faced Egyptian direct conquest and plundering in mid 19th century. From their bases in the western lowlands, Egyptian forces attacked and forcibly converted to Islam the Maria, the Beit Bidel and the Tawke groups in the Anseba region. Meanwhile, the Turks had long been ruling Massawa and parts of Semhar through their Naib agents.[2]

The conditions in the Eritrean highlands were not significantly different. Rivalries between the ruling houses of Hazega and Tseazega; raids and forced taxations by Abyssinian war lords, such *Degiyat* Wubie, *Ras* Alula, created constant insecurity and economic devastation. Egyptian forces, who secured a strong foothold in the Gash area and controlled the Bogos (Anseba region) by 1872, twice tried to control the Eritrean highlands but failed. Having fought the Egyptians alongside Emperor Yohannes's army at Gundet (1875) and Gura (1876), *Ras* Woldemichael Solomon of Hazega rebelled against emperor Yohannes. In 1878, Yohannes dispatched a

---

1 Bairu Tafla and Eva Schmidt, *Discovering Eritrea's Past: Select Documents from the Works of the Pioneers*, (Dettelbach: Dr. Joseph Röll, 2016), p. 31.
2 *Ibid.*, 66-77.

punitive force under the command of *Ras* Bayru Ghebretsadik (Aba Gala). *Ras* Woldemichael routed that force near what is today Asmara and killed *Ras* Bayru.

Italy entered the scene of what was soon to become Eritrea in this context of constant warfare and turmoil across its vast swathes. But the advent of Italy first took the form of business interest. The Rubattino shipping company signed an agreement with local chiefs (Sultan Ibrahim Ben Ahmad and his brother, Hassan Ben Ahmed) in November 1869, leasing an eighteen square kilometer land in today's Eritrean port of Asseb. At the behest of the Italian government, the company started to entrench itself and expanded its territory beyond the agreed upon lease. Hostility of rival powers did not deter Italian ambition of converting Asseb into a coaling depot and a hub for trade with Abyssinia, mainly Shoa, Tigray and Gojjam. In pursuit of an Asseb-Shoa corridor (through Aussa), Italy initiated negotiations with the aspiring south-central Abyssinian ruler, Menelik II of Shoa.[3]

In 1882, the Italian government formally took over the private Rubattino Company's concessionary land grant around Asseb. Less than a decade later, it expanded its colonial presence along the coastal stretch from Asseb to Beylul and Massawa, and into the hinterlands. Whereas some inhabitants had had a shared ancestry due to the waves of migrations, others had started to cultivate a sense of bonding, seeking and/or offering refuge with each other during the long drawn physical and political insecurity, economic and ecological stress, and collective experience under the mercy of foreign invaders. But none were able to offer an effective resistance against rapid Italian takeover. This was due to several factors in Eritrea and further south in Abyssinia.

In Abyssinia, Rome's secret treaty with Menelik II of Shoa helped facilitate the colonial expansion at breakneck speed. By

---

3 Yemane Mesghenna, *Italian colonialsim: A Case Study of Eritrea, 1869-1934, Motive, Praxis and Result* (Lund: 1988), pp. 68–80.

the Treaty of Wichale (of May 1889), not only did the ambitious Shoan king welcome Italy's forcible expansion northward along the Red Sea and its immediate hinterlands (while his suzerain Yohannes IV was fighting against it), but Menelik II also ceded the rest of what later became Eritrea to Italy, over which he had neither effective control nor nominal title. At the zenith of his influence immediately after the Battle of Adwa, Menelik II signed the Treaty of Addis Ababa in October 1896 that confirmed Wichale as far as Italian colonial dominion over Eritrea was concerned.

In Eritrea, not only were the fledgling affinities among the various Eritrean groups inadequate to mount unified and sustained resistance, but several war-weary communities welcomed the advent of Italy while a few individual warriors actively collaborated in establishing its early colonial presence.[4] The devastation of the 1889-1892 "Great Famine" also contributed to ease the colonial expansion and consolidation. But disparate, if short-lived and ultimately unsuccessful, resistance initiatives mushroomed including among those who had earlier on facilitated colonial expansion.

The 1894 peasant rebellion in southern Eritrean highlands under *Dejezmach* Bahta Hagos was the most notable of such resistance to Italian colonial rule when the latter sought to expropriate close to half a million hectares of arable land for use by Italian settlers.[5] Bahta Hagos sent messages to notable traditional leaders in highland and lowland Eritrea and to the peasantry calling on them to join the rebellion against Italians

---

4 Alemseged Tesfai, "Diversity, Identity and Unity in Eritrea. A View from Inside," (an unpublished paper presented at the "Identity and Conflict in Africa" conference, African Studies Unit, University of Leeds, September 1997); Michael Gabir, *The History of the Bilen* (Bagdad, 1992).

5 Mesghenna, *Italian colonialism*, p. 101; Tekeste Negash, *Italian Colonialism in Eritrea, 1882-1941: Policies, Praxis and Impact* (Uppsala: Universitatis Upsaliensis, 1987), pp 122-125.

"who have come to take our lands away."[6] Although many heeded Bahta's call and he went to battle commanding an army of 2,000 men, not only was the resistance put down but Bahta also fell in battle during the 18 December 1894 encounter between the two armies.[7] Writing about this rebellion, Yohannes Okbazghi argues that despite its quick suppression "...the December [1894] revolt was crucial insofar as it marked the beginning of Eritrean nationalism, which had to be reckoned with."[8] Not only was the Bahta Hagos rebellion one of several that followed, but also several developments under colonial rule contributed to the manifestation of a fully-fledged Eritrean nationalism.

There were several smaller-scale manifestations of resistance prior to and after Bahta Hagos's. In 1892 in the central highlands, *Degezmati* Aberra Hailu clashed with a contingent of a colonial army sent to detain him. He fled to Ethiopia, where he received an audience with Emperor Menelik II[9] and joined Menelik's army at the battle of Adwa in 1896, in which he fought with valor. Other notable Eritrean rebels include Zemat Wed Ukud from the Beni Amer in the western lowlands, Ali Nuri from the Assaorta in the southern highlands, *Kentiba* Haiyelom Aradom from Dembelas.[10] The outbreak of resistance to Italian colonialism was so frequent that the first colonial governor, Ferdinando Martini, called it in his diary in 1900 as "*il menu quotidiano*" ("a daily menu").[11] Italian colonialist prevailed not only by military might, but they also relied on age-old divide-and-rule tactics, co-opting some traditional leaders

---

6 Negash, *Italian Colonialism in Eritrea*, p. 124.

7 *Ibid.*, p. 125

8 Okbazgi Yohannes, *Eritrea, a Pawn in World Politics* (Gainesville: University of Florida Press, 1991), p. 9.

9 Negash, *Italian Colonialism in Eritrea*, p. 123

10 Mesghenna, *Italian colonialism*, p. 128

11 *Ibid.*, p. 128

into their administrative and military apparatuses while putting down the resistance of others.[12]

Early Beginnings of Modern Eritrean Nation and Nationalism

Once Italy finished carving up its colony of Eritrea around 1890, Eritreans shared the curses and unintended blessings of colonial rule. On the one hand, the brunt of Italian exploitation and racist policies and practices were felt across the country. On the other hand, the prolonged years of peace along with the newly introduced capitalist economy offered many of the colony's inhabitants employment opportunities that required them to leave their traditional abodes and live alongside others who had come under the same jurisdiction. Under the administration of first civilian governor, Ferdinando Martini, Italian colonial aims for Eritrea itself shifted to reaping commercial benefits by turning the newly formed colony into a source of raw materials and agricultural products. To that effect, Italy carried out infrastructural, administrative, legal and educational programs. The colonial administration initiated a thorough mapping of Eritrean demographic and social landscapes, gathering ethnographic and linguistic information. It systematically collected and codified preexisting indigenous legal systems.[13] Although all these were done in order to help consolidate colonial administration, enforce colonial law and restructure traditional land tenure systems, they had unintended integrative effects on the Eritrean society, a phenomenon that was accelerated by the expansion of infrastructure.

In 1902, Italian colonial authorities commenced the construction of the Massawa-Asmara railway as part of their large-scale infrastructural programs to connect the vast

---

12 Uoldelul Chelati Dirar, "Colonialism and the Construction of National Identities: The Case of Eritrea," *Journal of Eastern African Studies* 1, No. 2 , (2007), p. 258.

13 Mesghenna, *Italian Colonialism,* p. 126; Dirar, "Colonialism and the Construction of National Identities," p. 260

hinterland (within Italian control and beyond) to the port. The project employed 3,000 Eritreans and 300 Italian workers.[14] The ultimate goal of the railway project was to connect Massawa with Ethiopian and Sudanese borders. Upon the completion of that line in 1911, it stretched another 349 kilometers and reached the western Eritrean border town of Tessenei over the following 18 years. The construction of roads also progressed in tandem. Towns like Asmara, Mendefera, Keren, and Segeneiti were connected with Massawa by roads whose constructions employed some 800 native colonial soldiers.[15] A total of 1,130-kilometer-long roads were constructed in the first 23 years (between 1889 and 1922) and another 2,466 kilometers in the subsequent decade.[16]

The capacity of these network of roads and railways to move people and freight from one place to the next progressively increased over the years. Between 1905 and 1931, they ferried goods in the hundreds of thousands of tons and transported an even larger number of people within the territory.[17] This transportation infrastructure, combined with singular political economy (standardized financial and taxation system, and colonial administrative and justice apparatus) constituted the modern materialist cornerstones of the Eritrean nation by turning the newly bounded territory into a homogenized national space in the making.

To facilitate the development of the commercial colony of Eritrea, Italian authorities expanded educational opportunities for Eritreans. They opened vocational schools in Keren (1911), Segeneyti (1914) and Mendefera (1914), training the sons of Eritrean notables and colonial soldiers as administrative clerks, delivery men, telegraph messengers, interpreters, typewriters, and assistant telegraph operators, shop tellers, carpenters, tanners, and loyal colonial soldiers. A 1914 text book titled

---

14 Mesghenna, *Italian Colonialism*, p. 152).
15 *Ibid.*
16 Mesghenna, Italian Colonialism, p. 86.
17 *Ibid.*, p.185.

Industrie, Arti, Mestieri: Manuale Ad Uso Degli Indigeni Nelle Due Lingue Italiano e Tigrigna, or, ናይ ፕሮፌሽን ስራሕን ንግድን መጽሓፍ፦ ንተቐማጢ፦ ሰብ አዛ ሃገር፦ በክልተ ቋንቋ፦ ኢጣልያንን፦ ትግርኛን in Tigrinya explained the educational objectives as equipping young Eritreans with "European/ferenji skills," and "work ethic which would make our country great in arts, skills, knowledge, books and innovations." School instructions combined both technical and military components. Instructions were given in Italian; Tigrinya (to Christian students) and Arabic (to Muslim students) were offered as language courses as was Amharic although it was later classified a "foreign language."[18] This language policy strengthened local linguistic identities and enabled a systematic recruitment of Eritrean teachers into the colonial educational system.[19]

An important integrative aspect of Italian colonial rule in Eritrea was its aggressive recruitment of a large number of able-bodied Eritreans into the Italian colonial army as *Ascari*.[20] Recruitment started in earnest after the Italian occupation of Massawa in 1885[21] and the first batch of conscripted *Ascari* constituted a sizeable fighting force at the Battle of Adwa in 1896, in which they sustained heavy causalities of more than 2,000 captured, injured and killed.[22] Eritrean soldiers also fought Italian colonial wars in Libya, Somalia, and Ethiopia (during the 1935-1941 invasion and occupation). Although the exact figure of Eritrean *Ascari* has not been conclusively established, an estimated 130, 000 Eritreans are believed to

---

18 Dirar, "Colonialism and the Construction of National Identities," pp. 266-267
19 *Ibid.*
20 Negash, *Italian Colonialism in Eritrea.*
21 Uoldelul Chelati Dirar, "From Warriors to Urban Dwellers: Askari and the Military factor in Urban Development of Colonial Eritrea," *Cahiers d'Etudes Africaines*, XLIV (3), No. 175 (2004), p. 550.
22 Mesghenna, *Italian Colonialism*, p.115.

have served in the Italian colonial army between 1890 and 1935.[23]

For a population that was no more than 600,000 in 1935, the number of Eritreans enlisted in the Italian colonial army was significant with equal implications on the socio-economic and political landscapes. A notable impact of this "*Ascari* phenomenon" was on urbanization in Eritrea. Beginning in 1908, Eritrean *Ascari* could bring along their families, and house them in designated family quarters within the limits of burgeoning urban centers, contributing to urban expansion.[24] Another implication of such large number of Eritreans going through similar *Ascari* experience was the sense of communion it nurtured among them. The mobility, settlement, ordeals they endured together nurtured a sense of belonging to a common political community. The Italian colonial administration employed retired Eritrean *Ascaris* as administrative clerks, interpreters, and technical operators, cementing their position to influence political dynamics in their society. The financial, social, administrative and technical capital that the *Ascari* accumulated under colonial rule prepared them to play a crucial role in the emergence and elucidation of Eritrean nationalism. As Uoldelul Chelati Dirar put it, the "urbanised ascaris" played an important role in moulding, renegotiating and redefining ethnic, linguistic, and religious identities; in "smoothing…consolidated localism and ethnic-based antagonisms"; and in paving "the way for the development of a germinal Eritrean nationalist feeling."[25]

Finally, one of the lasting consequences of the Italian colonial economic, administrative, educational and military policies was the creation of a new social class of relatively privileged local actors, such as lower civil servants, teachers, colonial soldiers and their families, entrepreneurs, and farm

---

23 Negash, *Italian Colonialism in Eritrea*, p. 51; Dirar, "From Warriors to Urban Dwellers," p. 549.
24 Dirar, "From Warriors to Urban Dwellers," p. p. 551).
25 *Ibid.*, pp. 559-560.

concessionaries. Acting as intermediaries between the colonial state and the indigenous population, these new social actors reaped educational, administrative and other social benefits and amassed economic and political capital that marked them as an important force behind a collective Eritrean identity. They – and their affiliates – partook in the discursive construction of Eritrean nationalism during the post-Italian decade of British military rule of the 1940s.

The Advent of the British and Further Articulation of Eritrean Identity and Nationalism

In 1940, fascist Italian regime in Rome entered World War II on the side of Germany, which sealed its fate at home and even sooner in its colonies. As the Allies took on Italy's dispersed forces in its colonies one by one, British Commonwealth forces attacked Eritrea to dislodge the Italians. British war strategy involved promising the Eritrean people the realization of their "national aspirations" but first asked for their help to defeat Italian forces.[26] According to Alemseged Tesfai, Eritreans had preserved their traditional socio-cultural, administrative and legal fabrics, which also enabled them to endure the oppression and go a long way to explain the sources of Eritrean nationalism, and when the British offered them the opportunity to do away with Italian rule, they took it. The *Ascaris* massively deserted the colonial army, facilitating a swift British victory, which the Eritrean population celebrated.

Nonetheless, the British failed to deliver on their promise, frustrating Eritreans' hopes and leading to their political organizing to advocate for their rights. A British Military Administration (BMA) held onto Eritrea for a little over a decade while the fate of the territory was being debated among the victors of WWII and later at the United Nations. While immediate post-war pressures threatened to plunge the territory

---

26 Alemseged Tesfai, *Aynefelale. Eritrea, 1941-1950* (Asmara: Hidri Publishers, 2001), p. 5.

into chaos, the BMA sought to maintain the pre-war social order by, among other things, retaining the erstwhile Italian civil service and the status of the Italian civil servants while Eritrean government employees went unpaid and the people's needs unattended. Feeling betrayed, Eritreans organized *Mahber Fiqri Hagher* (Association of Love of Country) in early May 1941 to advocate for the civil rights of the Eritrea people. Despite its apolitical origins, this association was a prototype nationalist organization out of which Eritrea's first political parties emerged to demand an immediate break with European rule.[27]

The entire period of British Military Administration in Eritrea between 1941 and 1952 proved consequential for serious articulation of shared sense of Eritrean identity and nationalism. A crop of urbanite actors who had accumulated certain level of economic, social and educational capital during the Italian colonial period carried the burden of articulating Eritrean nationalism. A fortuitous connection between this group of urban social actors and a radical plebeian Tigre-speaking agro-pastoralists in the Eritrean lowlands against their *Shimaglle* overlords gave Eritrean nationalism its broader popular base.[28]

The publication of vernacular newspapers, like the famed *Eritrean Weekly News* (*EWN*, in Tigrigna and Arabic languages), facilitated the consolidation and dissemination of Eritrean nationalism as well as questions of decolonization, modernization, and democratic governance. Italian colonialism furnished the territorial, administrative and economic spaces in which *EWN* (and, after 1946, other newspapers) performed the pedagogical task of instructing the nation through culturally

---

27 *Ibid.*, pp. 22-36; Lloyd Schettle Ellingson, "Eritrea: Separatism and Irredentism, 1941-1985" (PhD Dissertation, MSU, 1986), pp. 15, 24-25.

28 Fouad Makki, "Subaltern Agency and Nationalist Commitment: The Dialectic of Social and National Emancipation in Colonial Eritrea," *Africa Today* , Vol. 58, No. 1 (Fall 2011), p. 29.

familiar idioms. Its comprehensive news coverage of developments across the country; its routine publication of national commodity prices; its serious engagement with the ethical formation of Eritrean citizens; its constant engagement with questions of national projects of modernity and modernization, *EWN* proved to be instrumental for Eritrean nationalism. The growing sense of being part of a single political community was evident in the routine reference to Eritreans as 'our people' and Eritrea as 'our country' that writers and contributors resorted to in their writings and with which the readers can plausibly be expected to identify.

Meanwhile, following Ethiopia's liberation from Italian occupation and the restoration of Emperor Haile Selassie I to the throne in 1941, access to the sea became a top priority in the country's foreign policy. While Haile Selassie was vigorously working on securing Eritrea, the UN General Assembly took over the disposal of the former Italian colonies. In anticipation of the arrival of the UN Inquiry Commission, the BMA opened the political space in Eritrea, which allowed for contending visions and aspirations for the country to flourish. Between 1946 and 1947, political parties espousing different political options emerged out of the Association of Love of Country.

Whereas those Eritreans who sought independence were diverse and, earlier on, lacked the capacity to constructively manage their diversity, there was a group of cohesive and well-resourced advocates of union with Ethiopia. The Ethiopian Emperor found enough maneuvering room to exploit Eritrean political inexperience and curb the pro-independence tendencies in the territory through deceit, corruption and intimidation. He fully financed and armed the Unionists and enlisted for them the backing of the Orthodox Church in Eritrea.[29] On the other hand, the Liberal Progressive Party

---

29 Even the staunch proponent of independence, Weldeab Weldemariam, does not hold any bad feelings against the Eritrean advocates of union with Ethiopia because he claims that

(LPP, also called Eritrea for Eritreans Association) and the Muslim League (ML) opted for independence. Ethiopia-sanctioned violent actions seem to have pushed the ML, LPP and the formerly pro-Italy parties into a loose pro-independence coalition, called the Independence Bloc.[30] This coalition lacked adequate understanding of the dynamics of Cold War alignments; they hoped that in a liberal democratic order, the people's right to self-determination would win regardless.

Cold War Interests of Superpowers and Origins of Defiant Nationalism

In the context of Cold War rivalry, Eritrea had come to assume an unparalleled geopolitical significance in its region. Located on the African coast of the Red Sea, Eritrea controlled a long swathe of coastline along the shortest route between the Mediterranean Sea and the Indian Ocean, and it faced the oil-rich Middle East where the US had started to have major strategic interests. Ethiopia brilliantly used Secretary of State John Foster Dulles's concept of the Northern Tier, one of America's cordons around the Soviet Union, to propose a Southern Tier as a backup in the Horn of Africa and the Middle East.[31] The US's reluctant acceptance of that idea meant that if

---

Eritreans' fear/hatred of Europe and Europeans threw them into the arms of Ethiopia; Tesfai, *Aynefelale*, pp. 127-128.

30 Tesfai, *Aynefelale*, pp. 278 ff. details how after the arrival in March 1946 of Colonel Negga Haile Selassie as Ethiopia's Liaison Officer in Eritrea, organized political violence against individuals and groups opposed to union with Ethiopia intensified across Eritrea. Also see G. K. N. Trevaskis, *Eritrea: A Colony in Transition* (Westport, CT: Greenwood Press, Publishers, 1975), p. 96ff.

31 John H. Spencer, *Ethiopia at Bay. A Personal Account of the Haile Selassie Years Second Edition* (Hollywood, CA: Tsehai Publishers 2006), p. 267.

Eritrea were not secured, it would risk being a major hole in the US chain of defense.[32]

Eritrea's capital, Asmara, offered a basic radio communication facility and an ideal location to become the most decisive factor by far for American wartime and post-war strategic thinking. Its unique location is able, for unknown reasons, to receive and transmit radio signals to and from most part of the globe, which no other locality around the world can offer. Cognizant of this fact, the Italians had built the Radio Marina communication facility, which fell to the Allies upon the defeat of Italian colonial army in 1941. The Americans discovered this advantage and immediately started using and developing what was a basic radio communication facility into a state-of-the-art intelligence-gathering base, intercepting radio signals from around the world. During the war years, radio traffic between the Axis powers was monitored regularly with instant, priceless payback.[33]

Meanwhile in its quest for access to the sea, Ethiopia persistently endeavored to get American support on the question of Eritrea. In January 1945, Emperor Haile Selassie flew to Suez to meet President Roosevelt to solicit "US support for the return of Eritrea [to Ethiopia] to provide a solution" to what John Spencer said was "the necessity of access to the sea."[34] President Roosevelt was noncommittal in his response.[35]

---

32 Testifying before the 1974 Ethiopian commission that was set up to investigate the government of Emperor Haile Selassie, former Ethiopian Foreign Minister Aklilu Habtewold "boastfully claimed that Haile Selassie's diplomacy exploited the Cold War by openly staking the future and fortune of Ethiopia on the side of the Western powers...in return for a "deal" on Eritrea." Bereket Habte Selassie, *Eritrea and the United Nations and other Essays* (Trenton, NJ: The Red Sea Press, Inc, 1989), p. 35.

33 John R. Rasmuson, *A History of Kagnew Station and American Forces in Eritrea* (Asmara: Il Poligrafico, 1973), pp. 39ff.

34 Spencer, *Ethiopia at Bay*, p. 159.

Nonetheless, as late as September 1945, the US turned down Ethiopia's overtures and rejected its claims on the grounds that the UN Charter provided for the former Italian colonies to exercise their right to self-determination and independence.[36] In the words of US Secretary of State James F. Byrnes, "...trusteeship should be established solely to assist the inhabitants of the colonies to develop the capacity for self-government so that the people might be granted independence [and]...give assurance that the Italian colonies will not be developed...for the military advantage of anyone."[37]

Disagreements and indecision of the victors of WWII on the fate of Eritrea worsened the division-ridden political developments in Eritrea, diminishing any prospect that an independent Eritrea would guarantee American interests. As Trevaskis observed, "[b]y their failure to reach any decision after three and a half years the Four Powers had already caused Eritrea serious injury."[38] Eritrean socio-religious and regional cleavages deepened and became politicized during this time. By far the most devastating blow involved Ethiopia and the violence it unleashed. The Ethiopian Empire took advantage of the superpowers' indecision to deprive the Eritrean politicians the space to cultivate the needed unity of purpose that can sustain independence and to portray an exaggerated picture of this weakness to the superpower with vested interest in Eritrea. Politically, Anglo-Ethiopian propaganda wreaked havoc within the pro-independence political parties that formed the Independence Bloc. With active British and Ethiopian

---

35 Spencer, *Ethiopia at Bay*, p. 201. Later Ethiopia's request evolved to a *quid pro quo* deal with the US whereby the US would back Ethiopia in its claim to Eritrea, and Ethiopia would in turn allow the US to keep the Radio Marina base in Asmara and provide other facilities that served American strategic interests in the region.

36 Yohannes, *Eritrea a Pawn in World Politics*, p. 80.

37 Quoted in Yohannes, *Eritrea a Pawn in World Politics*, p. 79.

38 Trevaskis, *Eritrea*, p. 92.

encouragement, the bulk of Muslim and Christian proponents of independence broke away from the Muslim League and the Liberal Progressive Party, respectively.[39]

At the height of such fragmentation of the Eritrean political landscape, the American Joint Chiefs of Staff (JCS) decided in mid-1948 to bar any rival force from setting foot in the Middle East region whose oil resources should only be exploited by the US and its allies. The JCS planned to secure the region through the delivery of military and economic aid to the countries of the region. Preparing for any eventuality, the JCS recommended securing rights beforehand for the US to expand and build facilities from which American forces can be deployed quickly when necessary.[40] That decision only strengthened the pre-existing vitality of Radio Marina spy station in Asmara to the US's long-term interests. Accordingly, the JCS identified Eritrea as a territory of indispensable strategic value. Admiral William Leahy wrote in 1948 to the Secretary of Defense: "[t]he Joint Chiefs of Staff would state categorically that the benefits now resulting from operation of our telecommunication center in Asmara...can be obtained from no other location in the entire Middle East-Mediterranean area.... Therefore, United States rights in Eritrea should not be compromised."[41]

Meanwhile, the Cold War escalated into a nuclear arms race, the uncertainty of Eritrean politics continued unabated and Ethiopian overtures to become an American ally/client increased significantly, culminating in Ethiopia's dispatch of two of its elite Imperial Bodyguard battalions to Korea alongside American forces. In November 1948, Ethiopian Foreign Minister Aklilu Habte Wold expressed to his American

---

39 *Ibid.*, pp. 97-98; Tesfai, *Aynefelale*, pp. 422-435 best illustrates British collusion in weakening Eritrea's case for independence by dividing the pro-independence politicians.

40 Tesfai, *Aynefelale*, p. 323.

41 Harold G. Marcus, *The Politics of Empire: Ethiopia, Great Britain, and the United States, 1941–1974* (Berkeley: University of California Press, 1983), p. 84.

counterpart, George C. Marshall, that Ethiopia would grant the US the right to continue using the Radio Marina Station should the US support Ethiopia's claim to Eritrea. In a swift and blatant dismissal of the US's stated stand in favor of a people's right to self-determination, Secretary Marshal promised unreserved American support that was to be formalized after Eritrea's fate was decided at the UN.[42]

The US worked relentlessly behind the scenes and, with the British, facilitated the UN General Assembly vote that granted *imperial* Ethiopia administrative responsibility for *autonomous* Eritrea in 1952.[43] Secretary of State Dulles explained the logic behind the American-engineered decision at the UN: "From the point of view of justice, the opinions of the Eritrean people must receive consideration. Nevertheless, the strategic interests of the United States in the Red Sea basin and considerations of security and world peace make it necessary that the country has to be linked with our ally, Ethiopia."[44] This mindset was to shape American policy and that of their Western allies toward the Eritrean liberation movements until the end of the Cold War.

---

42 Tesfai, *Aynefelale*, pp. 322-323. Sure enough, in 1953, the US and Ethiopia concluded an agreement granting the US the right to use and expand the Radio Marina Station - newly renamed Kagnew Station after one of the Imperial Bodyguard Battalions dispatched by Emperor Haile Selassie to Korea - and other facilities in the Eritrean port of Massawa. A concurrent agreement granted Ethiopia economic and military assistance, which the US saw as payment for Kagnew.

43 UN General Assembly - Fifth Session, Resolution 390 (V). "Eritrea: Report of the United Nations Commission for Eritrea; Report of the Interim Committee of the General Assembly on the Report of the United Nations Commission to Eritrea," December 2, 1950. Also see Spencer, *Ethiopia at Bay*, p. 238.

44 Quoted in Bereket Habte Selassie, *Conflict and Intervention in the Horn of Africa* (New York and London: Monthly Review Press, 1980), p. 58.

After the inauguration of the federation of Eritrea with Ethiopia in 1952, Eritrean politicians from the spectrum of political views and convictions assumed a conciliatory posture toward each other in order to preserve what had been salvaged from the turbulent decade, i.e. internal autonomy, and expressed their commitment to respect the terms of the federal arrangement. Nevertheless, the Ethiopian government explicitly expressed from the onset of the federation that it did not recognize any distinction in status between Eritrea and any of the Ethiopian provinces. Accordingly, Ethiopia proceeded unilaterally to dismantle the federal arrangement while unleashing a reign of terror and intimidation to muffle Eritrean opposition.

Since nineteen days after the federal act went into effect, Imperial Ethiopia went on committing one violation of the Federal Act after another. The Eritrean Constitution stipulated that the Supreme Court of Eritrea was the land's final court of appeal. Proclamation 130 of September 30, 1952 made the Ethiopian Supreme Court as the Federal Court, giving it the final say on Eritrea's legal matters.[45] As one of several Eritrean columnists of the time who voiced their concern with the bad precedent pointed out, "because of this [Proclamation] what is called internal autonomy...is rendered powerless, dead word.... What was the purpose of debating the powers of the Imperial Representative [if] the major task accomplished by the representative of the United Nations and delegates of the

---

45 Alemseged Tesfai, *Federation Ertra ms Ityopiya: Kab Matienzo kesab Tedla, 1951-1955* (Asmara: Hidri Publishers, 2005), pp. 274-179. While Alemseged's book is the first comprehensive coverage to have been written in Tigrinya entirely based on the perspectives and experiences of the Eritrean participants in the early years of the troubled and troublesome federation, Selassie, *Conflict and Intervention...*, pp. 59-60; Ruth Iyob, *The Eritrean Struggle for Independence,* p. 88 and Osman Saleh Denden, *Ma'erakat Irytriyah. Al-Juzu Al-Awal* (1996), pp. 11-17, offer succinct accounts of Ethiopian violations of the Eritrean autonomy.

Eritrean people becomes meaningless simply because the Ethiopian Government does not like it..."[46] Ethiopian blatant derision toward Eritrean autonomy was manifest in the Imperial Representative's daily interaction with the Eritrean Government, culminating in the closure of the Eritrean free press, the change of Eritrea's official languages from Tigrinya and Arabic to Amharic, the lowering of the Eritrean flag and hoisting that of Ethiopia alone, the renaming of the Government as the Administration and eventually the disbanding of the Eritrean Assembly.

Eritreans appealed to the UN to guarantee Ethiopian respect for the federal arrangement. The international community turned its back on the very plan it had devised and failed even to speak up against the violations, in spite of the fact that it was supposed to remain "seized of the matter" as stipulated in the December 1952 UN *Final Report*.[47] Ethiopian repression continued unabated and targeted prominent Eritrean politicians like Weldeab Weldemariam, who survived more than a few attempts on his life.[48]

While veteran Eritrean politicians (both pro-independence and unionists) became intensely frustrated with the corroding federal arrangement, and their electorate became increasingly mistrustful of them, a new breed of Eritrean nationalists living in Sudan established the *Hareket al-Tahrir al-Eritriyya* (Eritrean Liberation Movement, ELM) in Port Sudan in 1958. The founders of the ELM sought to separate themselves from the old politics of patronage and the ethno-religious alignments

---

46 A column in independent newspaper *Dehai Ertra*, 1st year No. 10, November 22, 1952 quoted in Tesfai, *Federation Ertra ms Ityopiya...*, pp. 278-279.

47 Spencer, *Ethiopia at Bay*, p. 236.

48 Research and Information Center of Eritrea (RICE) Interview with Weldeab Weldemariam, 1982. See also Ruth, *The Eritrean Struggle for Independence*, pp. 73 ff. for Ethiopian and Ethiopia-sponsored terrorism against pro-independence Eritreans and Italians as early as the late 1940s.

that the old politics engendered. Instead, the ELM envisioned a secular, all-inclusive clandestine movement for independence. The movement quickly sprung up throughout the major Eritrean and Ethiopian towns and villages. The reception it received among the Eritrean people in general and the excitement it generated among its members in particular were ready indications of the people's dissatisfaction with the federation and their resentment of Ethiopia. Further indication was the fact that despite an unwieldy chain of communication between the leadership in exile and the cells in Eritrea and Ethiopia, the ELM managed to operate inside Eritrea until its hostility with an emerging rival organization, the Eritrean Liberation Front (ELF), exposed it to brutal police suppression.[49]

Rearticulation of an Existing International Legal Precept and a Novel African Law

Domestic disunity among Eritreans, Emperor Haile Selassie's expansionist desires and United States' geopolitical interests derailed Eritrea's sovereignty following the end of Italian colonialism. Nevertheless, resolutions of the United Nations General Assembly and, subsequently, of the Organization of African Unity laid the legal and normative frameworks that lent legitimacy to Eritrean claims to independence. Following 30 years of arduous and destructive war, the Eritrean people created a reality on the ground that matched what international law ruled on paper was right, legitimate, and fair. This is the

---

49 Interviews: Mohammed Seid Nawud (April 23-25, 2005, Asmara Eritrea, conducted by Nerayo Bahre under PFDJ's History Project). One of the forerunners of ELM cells in highland Eritrea and Ethiopia, Mohammed-Berhan Hassan, recalls the ease of convincing Eritreans to set up clandestine cells and how the leadership had to cautiously handle the excitement and desire for action of its new recruits from bursting out. Interview: Mohammed-Berhan Hassan (September 13, 2005, Asmara, Eritrea, conducted by Awet T. Weldemichael).

fundamental principle of people's right to self-determination that, in his various works as scholar and practitioner, Bereket Habte Selassie best articulated in the Eritrean setting.

The United Nations Charter enunciated the principle of the right to self-determination in the post-WWII international order. Articles 1, 55, 56 and 73 of the UN Charter, and the Universal Declaration for Human Rights gave fuller expression to earlier conceptions of human rights and rights of non-self-governing peoples to decide their political future. International legal prohibitions against lateral expansion are of the same stock as against European colonialism. As growing number of newly independent countries from the Global South joined the United Nations, they pushed through a succession of resolutions at the General Assembly regarding peoples' right to self-determination.

In 1960, the United Nations General Assembly "Declaration on the Granting of Independence to Colonial Countries and Peoples" equated the denial of non-self-governing territories the right to decide their future with the violation of their fundamental human rights.[50] The next day, Resolution 1541 spelled out how non-self-governing territories could end their dependent status through an inclusive, transparent process and their free and informed decision.[51] Short of a 'freely expressed desire on the part of non-self-governing peoples and through an informed democratic procedure verifiable by the world body,'[52] the acquisition or annexation of territory was regarded as colonialism then and it would not be seen differently now. With none of the conditions

---

50 UN General Assembly Resolution I514 (XV): "Declaration on the Granting of Independence to Colonial Countries and Peoples," December 1960.
51 UN General Assembly Resolution 1541 (XV): "Principles which Should Guide Members in Determining whether or not an Obligation Exists to Transmit the Information Called for Under Article 73 e of the Charter," December 1960.
52 *Ibid.*

of Resolution 1541 met, Ethiopian rule over Eritrea was no less colonial than Italy's prior to it nor would it be different in the future. As far as Eritrea was concerned, however, developments in the African continent did not aid these international legal stipulations.

In 1964, the OAU consecrated inherited colonial boundaries as sacrosanct borders of African countries.[53] It also sanctified the non-intervention of members in internal affairs of others. As far as the African legal system was concerned, Eritrea had long constituted an integral part of Ethiopia when the OAU – an embodiment of continental laws – was formed. Inscribed in high-stakes pan-African politics, Eritrea was lumped together with separatist African movements in Biafra (Nigeria) and Katanga (former Zaire), seeking to establish new states from pre-existing ones against fundamental basis of the continental international system. As the OAU steered clear from the Eritrean issue for fear of opening a Pandora's box, repeated Eritrean appeals failed even to elicit acknowledgements of receipt of the missives much less support from the OAU.

Eritrean nationalists' diplomatic initiatives to impress upon African countries that Ethiopia's incorporation of Eritrea violated a pillar of the OUA – that Eritrea inherited colonial borders – went unheeded.[54] The veracity of Eritrean claims that their predicament was unique had no place in a continental legal system founded to preserve its members' territorial status

---

53 OAU, "Cairo Declaration on Border Disputes among African States; Legitimising National Borders Inherited from Colonial Times," 1964.

54 Idris Mohammed Adem to the Prime Minister of the Republic of Somalia, Dr. Abdul Rashid Ali, 20 December 1960; Tedla Bairu to President of the United Arab Republic Gamal Abdel Nasser, April 5, 1967. [Both of these documents are held at Eritrea's Asmara-based Research and Documentation Center, a copy of which is available with Awet T. Weldemichael].

quo. Moreover, most OAU member states dismissed Eritreans' quest for self-determination as undermining African unity.[55]

Ruth Iyob examined the "'Ethiopianism" of early Pan-Africanism' to explain Eritreans' inability to counter Ethiopian hegemony in the OAU. Ethiopia's mythical millennial history and its military victory against Italy in 1896 set it on a pedestal as a symbol of African freedom. For many Pan-Africanists, Ethiopia represented the driving spirit behind the ideals that later crystallized as OAU's pillars. When Eritreans insisted that they were in essence a colony of Ethiopia – a country that Africans regarded as archenemy of colonialism – the independence activists met with disbelief and angry skepticism. Eritrean solicitation for and receipt of aid from Middle Eastern countries played conveniently into the hands of Ethiopia, which portrayed Eritrean independence as an Arab encroachment into African unity. Eritrean military gains reinforced OAU objections as prospects of Eritrean victory brought closer African fears of surging secessionism.[56]

Eritrean nationalists proved unable to challenge Ethiopia's place in the master-narrative of a proud, free Africa. Nor could any Eritrean rival Emperor Haile Selassie's status as a preeminent African statesman and formidable American client in Africa. Ethiopia's housing of the OAU Headquarters and the UN Economic Commission for Africa reflected and reinforced the Ethiopian Emperor's public relations successes. Both gave and continue to give Ethiopia enormous diplomatic and moral leverage over other African countries.

---

55 Christopher Clapham, *Africa and the International System. The Politics of State Survival* (Cambridge: Cambridge University Press, 1996), p. 209.

56 Ruth Iyob, *The Eritrean Struggle for Independence: Domination, Resistance, Nationalism, 1941-1993* (Cambridge: Cambridge University Press, 1995), pp. 50 ff. This is not to mention Ethiopia's aggressive diplomacy – even retaliatory threats – in Africa to forestall target African countries' proven or suspected support for the Eritreans.

Conclusion

This chapter laid out the historical basis of Eritrea's independent statehood. Like its other African counterparts, modern Eritrea originated in late 19th century European colonial parceling of the continent among themselves – and a handful of Africans. Although Ethiopia's expansionism and geopolitical interests of global powers merged to derail its independence, African and international legal and normative developments enshrined the Eritrean people's right to self-determination. Turning the latter into reality required challenging the former and the creation of new reality on the ground, which demanded 30-year armed struggle that is beyond the cope of the current chapter.

The Eritrean government's current alignment with Addis Ababa has become particularly disconcerting to many Eritreans especially given the absence of alternative Eritrean voices and/or cohesive, credible opposition capable of challenging Asmara to change it course or altogether replace it. Neverthless, as in the past, African history, and international norms and law continue to be on the side of the Eritrean people's right to independent statehood that the sacrifices of yesteryears secured for the future. As current and future challenges evolve, we can neither afford to be paralyzed by anxiety over the wayward dictatorship and its dangerous foreign adventures nor can we afford to feel at ease and fall to complacence. Just as the steely will of the Eritrean people had to turn the principle of the right of a people to self-determination into reality three decades ago, so too the preservation of Eritrean independence, sovereignty and territorial integrity rest on the wishes and vigilance of the Eritrean people and not the whims of the current dictatorship or future government at home nor on the insatiable perennial desires of others.

THE LEGAL BASIS OF ERITREA'S SOVEREIGN STATEHOD

Bereket H. Selassie

1. Eritrea in Transition--A "Proto-State."

General and Historical Introduction

Eritrea's experience under Italian colonial rule, like all colonial experiences in the rest of Africa and elsewhere, was one that involved the introduction of alien ideas and methods affecting the lives and livelihood of the populations found within the territory that became known as Eritrea. This process began when the Italian government proclaimed the creation of a new colonial territory that they named Eritrea in January 1890. It is not relevant, for the purpose of this chapter, to mention the "white heat" of violence that accompanied the Italian conquest of a territorial mass of land and sea over which a new system of government was imposed. Such violence is involved in all conquests. The violence also invariably involves disarming of the conquered populations, taking away all weapons. Disarming includes cultural as much as physical (military) domination. For culture is the vital context for upholding and defending the foundational principles of any political community, i.e, their survival as a distinct historically evolved political and social community.

In this connection, it is also worth noting the historical background that led to the creation of a new territorial entity called Eritrea. Ethiopia's Emperor Yohannes had just been killed in a battle fought with the Sudanese Dervishes, in Metemma. Menelik was then king of Shoa, but with an ardent ambition to become Emperor of Ethiopia. No sooner had the news of Yohannes' death reached his ears than Menelik rushed to claim the throne. He was crowned Emperor in Axum and made Taitu, his equally ambitious consort, Empress. All this happened at a time when the Italians were jostling for influence in the Court of Menelik at his temporary capital, Entoto. The Tigrayan Nobleman, Mengesha Yohannes (Emperpr Yohannes' son) had not yet submitted to Menelik and was toying with the idea of collaborating with the Italians who had just declared their recently acquired colonial possession, baptizing it with the name of Eritrea, as already noted.

The border between the new colony and Ethiopia had not been finally settled with the Italians who had insisted that the Mereb river be declared the border. Menelik, who had benefited from the Italians with the acquisition of newly minted arms and considerable quantity of amunition, agreed to grant recognition to the Italians of their new colony; but had kept complaining when they seemed to want to push the border. Menelik is reported to have complained, "...I thought we had settled everything when I put my seal on the treat (Treaty of Wuchale) ceding territory which you asked for; then when I was no longer poor and had become Emperor, you asked for more and I gave you all of Hamasen. Now you still want more."[1]

The chief negotiator representing Italy was Count Antonelli. Ilg, one of Menelik's trusted European advisers, is reported to have told Salimbeni, Italain envoy to Ethiopia, that Antonelli had told him that the Mereb must be the border "and if Menelik did not give it for love, he must be forced..."[2]

The Mereb did become the border. It bears underscoring that Menelik gave in to the Italians, against the advise of people

---

1 See See Chris Prouty, Empress Taytu and Menelik II-Ethiopia, 1883-1910. Red Sea Press. 1986, at page 77.
2 Ibid at page 79.

like his Swiss advisor, Ilg and the Empress Taytu herself. Menelik's startegic rationale was based first and foremost on the security of his throne against Mengesha Yohannes who claimed legitimacy, being Emperor Yohannes' son. That was in addition to the fact that the Italians had given him enormous quantities of arms and ammunition. The border issue was thus settled and a colony was born leading to events and new social forces and a political economy masterminded by Italian capital and a government serving it.

A New Political Economy and Consequent New Identity

Among the new things that the Italians introduced to Eritrea, their new colony were: the market economy, building of industrial and commercial enterprises, new towns as well as infrastructure in or around the towns and the commercial or industrial enterprises. These were critical factors in shaping the nature and character of the colonial *protostate* thus gradually altering the lives of the populations, which became co-citizens known as Eritreans.

Within the first twenty-five years after the colony was created in 1890, new towns like Asmara, Keren, Decamere, Mendefera, Agordat and Tessenei were established that became magnets for the influx of populations from the surrounding countryside, as manual workers principally to fill the need for labor in the emerging industrial and commercial businesses. The towns also accommodated the arrival of Italian professionals and artisans as well as managers of rapidly emerging businesses. Along side the industrial and commercial enterprises, private companies also emerged, requiring the employment of managers and people with related skills. To those ends, a modern commercial law was adopted to cater to the emerging business class of merchants and owners of industry and agriculture, including plantations like those developed in Ali Ghidir, Ila Ber'Id and elsewhere.

The immigrant Italians needed appropriate housing commensurate with their class aspirations in what became an area for Europeans only. It was thus that a constellation of "shantytowns"like "Aba Shawl," "Idaga Arbi," and "Geza Banda Habesha" were born, serving the modest housing needs of the "native" Eritrean populations situated outside the "modern" segment of the cities, especially the capital city, Asmara. Asmara is a beautiful "Italianate" city designed along Italian architecture parts of which resemble cities like parts of Bologna. It thus eventually became a segregated city until Italy was defeated in World War II in 1941.[3]

The Colonial "Melting Pot" and the Rise of Nationalist Sentiment

The new towns had also become centers for employment of local or "native" populations. The creation of the infrastructures, and commercial and industrial enterprises brought together, for the first time, Eritreans of different ethnic and religious backgrounds. In time, therefore, a new social formation had emerged creating a new social and national consciousness with a new sense of belonging of people that had hitherto lived separate lives practically unconnected to one another.

It is also important to mention that, in addition to the economic enterprises that drew thousands of the local populations to work in the factories, plantations, in the building of roads and railways, there was another group of Eritreans that had become an important part of the urban population living in the shantytowns. These Eritreans were former soldiers that had

---

3 My generation of Eritreans and those of my parents experienced the "apartheid-like" segregation under which the "indigeni" (natives) were forced to create their own residential areas or shantytowns. The Street separating the two domains—one European, the other indigeni—became known by the local inhabitants as the 38th parallel, after the line that separated the two Koreas.

fought wars along or with the Italian army. The earliest of such soldier (also calle *Askari*) was in Libya, or Trubli in the 1920's against the Libyan freedom fighter Omar MuKhtar. Eritreans had also been forcibly enlisted to fight on Italy's side in the battle of Adwa in 1896, and then again, with Mussolini's war in the 1935-1936.[4]

Eventually, by the end of Italy's colonial rule, just before the beginning of the Second World War (1939), thousands of industrial workers were employed and lived in towns creating a new social milieu and heightened sense of consciousness as members of a common country that also became eventually an important factor for the creation of a sense of common nationhood.

Nation-State and Nationalism

There are three powerful forces driving modern politics— nationalism, religion, and the demands of constituent parts of a state in national politics, such demands being based on shared values of democracy and justice. This truism applies to Eritrea. The combined forces of nation and nationalism has been the primal driving force of Eritrea's quest for self-determination and independence. To start with the concept of nation, it is important to know that nations are born; they grow and may die. Nonetheless, the idea of nation as a historical phenomenon is an enduring fact of the constitution of human society.

The modern imagination is hard put to think of the idea of a person without a nation. During the Eritrean fight for independence, for example, a popular slogan was, "*Bizei hager kibret yellen* (There is no dignity without nation). I read a story about a Frenchman who lived in Germany as an exile during

---

4 Many, if not most, of those who were forced to fight with Italy in Adwa, suffered the mutilation of their right arm and left leg. The order to do such a horrific punishment was given by Emperor Menelik, punishing people whom he had signed off to the Italians. Cf. The Treaty of Wuchale signed with Italy under which he had given up the territory that became known as Eritrea.

the Napoleonic period. The story was about *a man who lost his shadow*! It is a parable about a man without a nation. There cannot be a shadow without corporeal substance; a man without a nation (an emigre) defies the commonly accepted categories and induces pity at best—and such pity only by the most *"woke"* members of a country. Although having a nation is not an attribute of humanity, yet in our own time, having a nationality is a human right recognized in constitutions and treaties.

A distinction must be made between nation and nationalism. The latter can and has been used in defense of the former; nationalism in fact holds that state and nation are meant for each other. One without the other is incomplete as the unfortunate case of Somaliland illustrates.[5]

Concerning nationalism, it will help to put the idea of nation and state in context. In modern times—roughly in the last one hundred and fifty years—with the demise of large empires, like the Ottoman and Austro-Hungarian empires (and later, the European colonial empires), the nation had become the only international legitimate form. On the debris of disappearing empires, nation states appeared, many basing their sovereignty on ancient identities, like Ghana and Mali. In the case of the former European colonial empires of Africa, the sovereignty was defined in terms of the colonially fixed boundaries enclosing withing them different ethno-linguistic entities. When the League of Nations assembled in Paris in 1919-20, in the aftermath of World War I, they inaugurated an era in which the nation became the legitimate unit of the international legal order. American President, Woodrow Wilson then championed self-determination as the defining idea proclaiming that every nation has the right to determine its political future, thereby providing the philosophical/moral justification for the dissolution of the Austro-Hangarian and

---

5   See also David, D. Laitin and Said S. Samatar. SOMALIA: Nation in Search of a State. Westview Press, Bolder Colorado. 1987.

Ottoman empires and the emergence of several new nations out of the debris of empires, in the Balkan region of Europe and in the Middle East.

In more recent times, in the post-cold war ear, an explosion of new nationalism broke out in Europe. In fact the world seemed to be witnessing two diametrically opposed trends: one involving the creation of larger units out of many nations typified by the European Union; the other witnessing the rise of national movements breaking out of larger, multi-ethnic nations. At the start of the 1990s, Yugoslavia had disintegrated, and the Union of Soviet Socialist Republics (USSR) had divided into independent states.

Nationalism in Eritrea

As pointed out above, Eritrean nationalism is based on the creation of the territory as an Italian colonial state. Like the rest of colonial Africa, its identity as a nation-state was defined by the boundaries created after Italy declared it as a colony in January 1890. This historical fact, reaffirmed by the postcolonial African legal order under the 1964 Cairo Resolution of the OAU, is buttressed by the factors discussed in the preceding paragraphs about the construction of nationalism. To reiterate, Italian industrial investment and the urbanization and consequent mixing of different ethnic groups in factories, plantations and shantytowns created a sense of community among the colonial subjects who were transformed into fellow citizens following the departure of their colonizers. The struggle against a common occupier—first the Italians, then the British, and finally the Ethiopians—eventually culminated in the triumph of national independence.

2. The Legal Basis of Eritrea's Sovereign Statehood

The law is the corner-stone of a constitutional edifice and of all the infinite varieties of individual or institutional relationships. The law is the final arbiter of questions or disputes arising out of such relationships. All institutions have a legal basis on

43

which they are grounded. The same is true with respect to basic ideas like sovereignty. The sovereignty of Eritrea as an independent state has a legal basis. That is a given; the question may be how such legal basis came about. Hence the preceding paragraphs that provided an account of how Eritrea's sovereignty was created.

Transition Toward a Full-fledged Nation State

Italian colonial rule came to an end militarily in the spring of 1941, following the defeat of the Italian colonial army by British and Allied Forces. Diplomatically, Italian rule ended with the signing of the Treaty of Peace with Italy, signed in Paris in July 1946, in which Italy renounced her claims to her former colonial possessions including Eritrea. The Treaty of Paris was signed 57 years after Eritrea became an Italian colony, in 1889, following the signing of the Italo-Ethiopian Treaty of Ucciale, under which the Ethiopian Emperor Menelik, recognized the present border between Ethiopia and Eritrea, as noted above. The British became the principal agents in the demise of Italian colonial rule, and temporarily stepped into Italian shoes.

Britain occupied Eritrea from 1941 to 1952. During that transitional period several attempts were made to partition Eritrea with the aim of joining western and norther parts to the then British-ruled Sudan, and joining the southern and eastern coastal regions, including the ports of Massawa and Assab to Emperor Haile Selassie's Ethiopia. The Emperor was prepared to compromise, abandoning his demand for having all of Eritrea in favor of having access to the sea and the acquisition of Eritrea's mineral wealth and comparatively more advanced industrial and skilled manpower resources.

The partition idea, which was known as the Bevin-Sforza Agreement, was defeated by the combined political forces, both Christian and Muslim, one of the few actions on which there was national unity by the emerging independence forces led by Sheikh Ibrahim Sultan Ali (a Muslim leader) and Woldeab

Woldemariam (a Christian leader). These two leaders were responsible for the Christian-Muslim unity, demanding Eritrean independence in opposition to the Unionist Party favoring union with Ethiopia.[6]

After the end of World War II, the question of the future of the former Italian colonies was first formally discussed during the Paris Peace Conference. Article 23 of the Treaty of Paris stipulated that the final disposal of the former Italian colonies be determined by agreement among the Four Powers—The USA, the USSR, Great Britain and France. In the event of failure of agreement among the Four Powers within a year, the matter would be submitted to the General Assembly of the United Nations for disposition. The Four Powers failed to agree by the deadline set (September 15, 1947). In November 1947, a Four Power Commission of investigation was established to visit the three former Italian colonies (Libya, Eritrea and Italian Somaliland) and to report on the political situation. The Commission submitted a report in May 1948, but there was no basis on which the Four Powers could agree.

One basis on which they could find common ground would have been to give the Eritrean people the right to determine their future through a referendum. Ethiopia was opposed to this idea because it was believed that the majority of the Eritrean people wanted independence.

---

6   A personal note of interest is that my father of blessed memory was a Unionist, whereas I was a disciple of my mentor, Woldeab Woldemaraim, and a supporter of Eritrean independence. I was a student in England when my father passed away at the age of 56, an untimely death caused by pneumonia, because there was no anti-biotic available in Eritrea at the time. Upon my return from my studies in London, I asked my mother what his last words were. She simply said he died a sadly disappointed man because of the politics of the time in which innocent people had been assassinated by terrorist groups financed by Ethiopian representative, one Colonel Nega Haile Selassie.

Britain was also opposed to referendum for two reason: first Britain had not given up on the idea of partition and lopping off parts of Eritrea to join with the Sudan, secondly because of the implication that it might arouse Africans ruled by Britain to demand the exercise their right to self determination though referendum.

The whole matter was then submitted to the third Session of the UN General Assembly in April 1949. The Third Session of the UN General Assembly debated the matter of the disposal of the three former Italian colonies, but could not come to an agreed solution. So, the matter was postponed to the Fourth Session. The Fourth Session of the UN General Assembly determined that Libya should be granted independence by January 1952, and Italian Somaliland be under ten-year Italian trusteeship after which it would accede to independence. The General Assembly failed to reach agreement on Eritrea, and decided to send a second commission of enquiry composed of five members, representing Burma, Guatemala, Norway, Pakistan and South Africa. The commission was charged with the duty of ascertaining "the wishes of the Eritrean people and the means of promoting their future welfare.

The Report of the UN Commission of Inquiry and Resolution 390 A(V)

The UN Commission of Inquiry presented it report on June 28, 1949. The three members of the Commission (Burma Norway and South Africa) recommended a close association of Eritrea and Ethiopia under Ethiopian sovereignty, while Norway recommended unconditional union with Ethiopia. The minority report—Guatemala and Pakistan recommended a UN trusteeship over Eritrea for ten years after which Eritrea should become independent. Both majority and minority reports opposed partition, thus reflecting Eritrean people's sentiments.

The Legal Effects of Resolution 39 A(V)

The UN Resolution provided for an autonomous Eritrean government with legislative, executive and judicial powers over domestic affairs, with matters of defense, foreign affairs, currency and finance, foreign and inter-state trade and communications falling under "federal' (i.e., Ethiopian) jurisdiction. In the interim period between December 1950 and September 1952, a UN commission was appointed to prepare a draft constitution for Eritrea and submit it to an Eritrean constituent assembly convened by the British "administering authority."

In terms of what rights and obligations the Resolution conferred on whom, clearly, the grant of autonomy on Eritrea, short of independence, meant that Eritreans had been denied the right to self-determination, contrary to what eventually had become a fundamental aspect of international law, fourteen years of Eritrea's denial of decolonization.[7]

No sooner had the Federal Act, the legal basis of the Ethiopia-Eritrea Federation, been put into effect, and the Eritrean regional government established accordingly, than Emperor Haile Selassie began intervening in Eritrean "domestic" affairs, through the agency of his representative, Andargachew Messai, who also happened to be his son-in- law. A struggle thus ensued involving the head of the Eritrean

---

7 Cf. The International Covenant of Civil and Political Rights. December 16, 1966, 99U.N.T.S/171, UN Documents. See also the companion Covenant—The International Covenant on Economic, Social ND Cultural Rights. December 16, 1966. Note Article 1 of each of the Covenants providing: "All people have the right to self-determination. By virtue of that right, they freely determine their political status and freely pursue their economic, social and cultural development." See also Bereket Habte Selassie, Self Determination: The Adventures of an Idea and Its Impact on National and International Politics. In "Words That Govern and Other Essays on Law and Politics. Red Sea Press, 2018. Chapter 6

government, Chief Executive, Tedla Bairu, and Andargachew. Of the three branches of the Eritrean government, the Hagerawi Baito (Legislative Branch) contained former members of the Unionist Party some of whom worked in tandem with Andargachew. The Baito was dominated by a powerful Orthodox Cleric by the name of Dimetros, who had access to Andargachew's "Palace," and enabled the Emperor's Representative to exercise huge influence in Eritrean affairs, including matters covering economic and political issues. Andargachew and his wife, Princess Tenagnework, acquired economic interests and spread their influence in Eritrean affairs using their control of access to levers of power.

This, sooner or later, led to confrontation with the Chief Executive of Eritrea's government, who insisted on strict separation between federal and domestic matters, thereby giving notice to all concerned to keep the separation in mind. In this respect, it should be noted that Tedla Bairu had been the head of the Unionist Party and therefore one would assume that he had the trust of the Emperor's representative. Tedla was also a well educated (with a teacher's diploma from Italy) and also a self-respecting nationalist with appropriate Eritrean pride. However, the "Unionist forces" circling around the "Palace" and their allies in the Assembly, headed by Dimetros, constantly put pressure to bear on Tedla, who became increasingly isolated. Meanwhile those in the Palace, had prepared a replacement for Tedla, who was eventually kicked upstairs and eventually sent abroad as Ethiopian ambassador.

His replacement was a man known fro his cunning and infectious charm who had been one of the interpreters of the Italian governor of the Gonder province , during Italy's brief occupation of Ethiopia (1936-1941). His name is Asfaha Woldemichael, a product of Catholic education and a penchant for quiet intrigue. It is reported by those who knew Asfaha that he was with the Italian governor of Gonder, when the latter was taken prisoner with the defeat of Italy in 1941. The Italian governor, an aristocrat, pleaded with the Emperor's elder son,

Prince Asfa Wosen that Asfaha was a competent and loyal servant and that he would serve the Prince well if he should take him and put him under his wing. Prince Asfa Wosen accepted the Italian's plea and made Asfaha one of his loyal aides. It was the beginning of Asfaha's career, ending in his "election" as Chief Executive" of Eritrea in 1955. He was later elevated to the post of Imperial Minister of Justice and awarded the titel of "*Bitweded*" (a beloved imperial servant).

Before the dissolution of the federation, Asfaha helped lay the ground work for its dissolution by convincing a number of the members of the Eritrean Assembly to vote for complete union between Eritrea and Ethiopia, which was the effect of the dissolution of the federation. The Palace forces made certain that the vote in the Assembly would be secured one way or the other. They made sure that even as the Assembly was debating the proposal for dissolution a company of the Ethiopian armed forces was ordered to parade in front of the Assembly shouting "*Imbi yalewn sew, Tiyyit Agrusew*" (Feed bullets to those who refuse).

Thus ended the short-lived Ethiopian-Eritrean Federation with the Eritrea's supposed autonomy having been practically abolished. The Assembly's vote acted as the *coup de grace* of imperial power disposing of a federation that Ethiopia had not wanted in the first place.

Armed Struggle

As already noted, the "sleeping lions" had gone to the bush. The first shots fired at Mount Adal in Western Eritrea heralded the beginning of a new struggle in which Eritreans sought to reclaim, by force of arms, what the generation of their fathers could not obtain through diplomacy. Indeed, they sought to redeem a betrayed trust in the principle of the people's right to determine their right themselves. The fact that the power that betrayed our people's trust is a nation that had suffered a similar betrayal no so long ago. But that, we were told, is the nature of politics—Realpolitik! So, our young vowed to redress the wrong.

The details of the armed struggle in both its first and final phase, is the subject of other chapters. Here, I will just note the salient features, connecting the armed struggle with the central theme of this book, the pillars of Eritrea's Sovereign Statehood.

The first point to note is that international law, in the form of Treaties, Covenants and Solemn Resolutions has ordained the right of all peoples to self determination. [*See Note 3 above*].

And even though, the lopesided federation and its weakening by the Emperor's loyal elements in Eritrea, Eritreans as a people had tasted the value of a modicum of freedom. Eritrean youth and labor unions also agitated in favor of preserving that modicum of freedom, using it to demonstrate in the streets and other places of Asmara and other towns. And the news of Idris Awate's exploits was received with great excitement, and the news of his exploits was disseminated.

When the federation was unilaterally abolished and Eritrea was annexed and declared a simple province of Ethiopia, "the sleeping lions" had begun to join the Eritrean Liberation Front (ELF) first in the western region, then in other parts of Eritrea. News of exploits by the small army of rebels began to be heard and spread throughout the length and breath of the Eritrean highlands as well as among Eritreans living in Ethiopia. Underground movements sprung up again, involving Eritreans in Ethiopia. The movement was born among Eritreans living in the Sudan, and was called *Harakat-litahrir al Eritrya*, or simply Haraka. It spread in the Western lowlands, and in the highlands, the movement was named *Mahber Shew'Ate* (Unit of seven) because that was the maximum of number of its members in each unit. Secrecy was critical and only the chairman of the unit could create contacts with other units. Alas! The Police sooner or later were able to discover some of the units leading to arrests of several prominent young Eritreans, including well-known teachers. The fight thus continued in the law courts when prominent members were prosecuted. Prominent lawyers and patriots, like Ato Tsegai Iassu, to mention one among many, played a commendable role in defending prisoners and thereby helping spread the cause.

The Need for Clarity About the Basic Issues

It is worth reiterating that the civilian underground movement in the urban areas had been critically influenced by the start of the armed struggle. But the political and legal basis of Eritrea's claim to self-determination and independence was amply and coherently articulated by the writings of civilian patriots inside as well as outside Eritrea. And the urban civilian movement began to insist that their fight is to reclaim the sovereignty of Eritrea that had been abolished illegally by the imperial regime of Haile Selassie. In other words, all thoughtful and informed Eritreans were of one mind when it comes to the real issue, namely that Eritreans had been denied their fundamental right of determining their future of attaining sovereign statehood.

It took over thirty years to realize this fundamental objective, and it involved the sacrifice of thousands of people. To cut a long story short, in the maturity of time and huge sacrifice, Eritreans finally achieved their final objective, i.e., national independence. On May 24, 1991, thirty years after the first shots were fire at Mount Adal by Idris Awate, Eritreans defeated a much stronger Ethiopian armed forces and attained independence.

A New Nation State and Its Government

The EPLF became the government of the new sovereign nation of Eritrea, or to be more formal, the new State of Eritrea. The government was based on the victorious EPLF and its central leadership established a Provisional Government formalized under Proclamation Number 37 of 1993. The Provisional government, in pursuit of the governing policy prescriptions laid down in three meetings of the Party solemn resolutions, proceeded to move along the steps of democratization. Accordingly the government passed

Proclamation Number 55/94 under which a Constitutional Commission was established with a mandate to conduct wide-ranging public consultations in lectures and seminars. The Constitutional Commission of Eritrea (CCE) began its work in March 1994 and, after almost three years of public consultations and expert input, submitted its final draft constitution to the National Assembly.

As a central feature of lending legitimacy to the constitution making process, the final ratifying body was the Constituent Assembly to which the draft constitution was submitted. To that end, the Constituent Assembly was established under Proclamation number 92/96. The law establishing the Constituent Assembly sums up the preceding process of constitution making process thus:

> *"**WHEREAS** a Draft Constitution has been prepared following the establishment of a Constitutional Commission under Proclamation No. 55/94 and, pursuant thereto, wide-ranging public and professional participation was organized involving public meetings, seminars, consultations, and civic education activities:*

> ***WHEREAS** the said Draft Constitution was widely distributed throughout Eritrea and among Eritreans residing abroad, and comments were made and opinions received therein from members of the public; and*

> ***WHEREAS** in order to finalize this process, it is imperative that a Constituent Assembly be established to ratify the Draft Constitution on behalf of the people of Eritrea;*

> *Now **THEREFORE**: this Proclamation is issued in virtue of Article 4(4) of Proclamation No. 55/1994.*

> *Asmara, the 27th Day of December, 1996. Government of Eritrea*

ERITREA: POOR PEOPLE IN A WEALTHY COUNTRY

Assefaw Tekeste

Introduction

I am writing this paper shortly after an interview I did with ERISAT on November 28th because Dr. Bereket Habte-Selassie, a friend, a writer and a passionate Eritrean patriot, motivated me to caption a condensed version of the interview in an article. The aim of the interview was to rebut the current floating theory by our ragged dictator regarding Eritrea's abject poverty despite his relentless effort to grow the economy of the country, hence the inevitable dependency on Ethiopia to guarantee the national survival of the Eritrean State - an unsubstantiated bogus claim that has disappointed all Eritreans.[1] Therefore, this is an attempt to offer readers a glimpse on the past, the present and the future economic realities of Eritrea based on personal account rather than facts or research, with the hope of arousing a debate among young Eritrean economists to dig deeper and bring to surface the hidden wealth of Eritrea and the bright future of our people, once they are free from the fetters of this dysfunctional dictatorship.

---

1 The author is referring here to Isaias Afwerki's statement declaring Eritrea as a poor country that cannot sustain itself.

The Dawn of the Second Eritrean State - 1991

- Soon after the independence of Eritrea and formation of the Provisional Government of Eritrea I was appointed to serve as the Secretary of Social Affairs in 1992.

- Although the EPLF was a State within a State and had Social Affairs department with more than 2,000 staff members during the armed struggle, the structure and content of the Department was tailored to fit the Fronts military organizational edifice constructed to serve the war effort. Hence, the readjustment of the department that fits the State structure in times of peace was essential. It was not an easy adjustment.

- At the onset I started by forming a committee that drafts the National Social Affairs policy of Eritrea. During the process it dawned upon me that this Provisional Government of Eritrea is the second Eritrean government. Four decades ago, there was the first Eritrean government federated with Ethiopia that had undergone similar challenges – creating a State from the scratch.

- There was an event that left an indelible memory in my mind when I was in the 2nd grade in 1952. Ato Tedla Bairu, the new leader of the Eritrean government, visited Serejeqa, a neighboring village to my own village of Weki, as hundreds of villagers gathered to see their first leader and I presented him welcome flowers. It was unforgettable childhood moment I vividly remember today. For it was this government, despite all its historical challenges, that planted the seed of the first Eritrean State deep into the psyche of Eritrean youth. It implanted the original concept and the very being of an 'Eritrean State' that gave birth to Eritrean patriotism that eventually led to the Eritrea of today. It was the first experiment that survived and thrived at least for the first 5years of the Federal period, despite the hostile internal and external forces that worked against the success of the Eritrean State. And my generation was proud of it.

    So, I decide to see Tewelde Kahsai, who was the Secretary of Social Affairs during the first Federal government of Eritrea that was led by Executive

Secretary Tedla Bairu and (Prime Minister) and President Sheik Ali Mohammed Mussa Redaay. To the young reader who might wonder the origin of our State here the following brief introduction may be helpful.

After a prolonged political struggle among Eritrean political parties, it was the UN proposition that Eritrea be joined with Ethiopia with autonomy with its own constitution and elected government in a lopsided federation under the Imperial Crown. Elections to a new Eritrean Assembly in 1952 gave the Unionist Party the largest number of seats but not a majority; the party thus formed a government in coalition with a 'Rabita Islamia' party. The Eritrean constitution was adopted by the Eritrean Assembly on July 10, 1952, and the British authorities officially relinquished control on September 15, 1952 to the newly elected first Eritrean government. Thus, a new State was born.

- The purpose of my meeting with Ato Tewelde was to listen to his story and perhaps draw lessons form the commonalities and particularities that bridges the 4 decades (1952-1992) gap or omission of the two States of Eritrea. His narrative was rich with interesting details, although memories of some events tend to lack some details as times goes by, the events he remembered were retained with remarkable fidelity.

- The difference in the challenges both governments had was stark clear. Secretary Tewelde's memory of the first Eritrean government in 1952 had a steeper learning curve because they were forming the first African quasi-democratic elected government with a modern constitution with its checks and balance through the three branches (legislative, executive, and judicial) of government. They were far ahead of their times at a time when Africa was under European colonialism, except for the following three countries:

  • In 1952 there were 3 independent countries in Africa – Apartheid South Africa, Americo-Liberian regime in Liberia, quasi-independent Egypt under King Farouk although it became fully independent in 1956 after the liberation of Suez Canal from the British under Gamal Abdel Nassar. None of them had an elected participatory constitutional government.

- Then, there was, of course, Ethiopia under absolute monarchy in which the king is above the law. Therefore, the federation of Eritrea with an imperial regime under a federal agreement constituted by the UN was an unnatural marriage and mismatch of two incompatible political systems – a travesty of supremacy of international law.

- In 1992, when I met Ato Tewelde, almost all African States were independent and had passed through tumultuous political journey of coups de eta and legal and illegal constitutional changes. Unlike the first Eritrean government, we had a wealth of experience to learn from, especially on what not to do. We had an advantage.

- In 1952 there were only 3 university graduates in the government (Tedla Bairu, Isaac Teweldemedhin) and the Eritrean Mufti, an Al-Azhar university of Cairo graduate.

- In 1991 Eritrea had university graduates in the thousands all over the world, but more clustered in the West (EU and USA) and the Middle East. Even during the armed liberation struggle, although the exact figure is not known, it is estimated to be over 300 university graduates with first, second and third degrees and over 1000 university students in the EPLF only. It is not comparable to any liberation movement. In the medical services alone there were over 60 university graduates, physicians, nurses and pharmacists.

Conversation with Ato Tewelde

- When I told Ato Tewelde, I came to learn from his experience he laughed loud and said, in a humble self-depreciating way "we had nothing, not even proper office, my file was a regular student exercise book". I delved into the subject matter and asked him about the daily routine of the Executive Body of the new government and he said:

- Tedla walked on foot from his home to the office daily, alone (no bodyguards) and arrived in his office at 8:45 am precisely – a practice inherited from the British etiquette on punctuality. He dressed Italian style three-piece handmade suit that made him distinctly elegant with a glow of confidence. But he had no automobile at the beginning, and people who want to get a glimpse of their new leader walked through the same route as if they are taking casual stroll. He knew and did not mind the curiosity.

- In the Office he spent the first 15 minutes calling all the secretaries to say good morning – although his intention was to check whether the secretaries were in their offices in time. If no one picked up the call, he would call back after few minutes. He was a strict taskmaster.

- When the cars for the Executive office arrived, he assigned one automobile for every Department. He then gave an instruction to all Department heads to spend half of our time in Asmara and half in the provinces to follow the progress in the countryside. We followed his instructions to the letter because he was a strict leader.

- But he respected us because we were his peers. Once during one of his site tours he visited Hibret School in Asmara with Memhir Isaac Tewelde Medhin, Secretary of the Education Department and other officials. During the inspection Ato Tedla almost fell down the stairs when one of the defective wooden slabs gave in. Tedla annoyed chastised Memhir Isaac Tewldemedhin, aying:"the State has provided enough budget to maintain our schools, where is the money going?" Memhir Isaac did not know what to say. The behavior of Tedla disappointed all of us and we later told him such behavior is not tolerable specially to Memhir Isaac who was a respected elder and the oldest among the Secretaries. The next day Tedla went to Memhir Isaac's office and apologized, and he was forgiven. Memhir Isaac said he was sincere. Tedla had a mix of dictatorial tendency as well as unreserved humility. He was a complex man.

- When I asked whether he expected Tedla Bairu to join the ELF, Ato Tewelde emphatically said, "definitely, after all ELF was founded by Idris Mohammed Adem, the President of Eritrea. They were close freinds, especially at the end." Ato Tedla joined the ELF in 1967.

- Regarding the Department of Social Affairs, Ato Tewelde reiterated, the entire department was composed of 8 staff members and that includes the driver. Ato Tewelde spent two weeks of every month touring rural Eritrea and visited all 8 provinces twice a year. He contacted village elders and opinion leaders of the communities to assess the needs of the people. We were remarkably close to our community, he said. We knew almost every Chiqua (village leader) by name and we responded to their needs as much as we can.

- One of the State's practice he was proud of was the display of the annual national revenue and expenditure of the State in detailed tables and graphs and posted at the wall of the Municipality Building corridor so that every citizens can have access to the full information regarding where their tax monies go. Citizen were encouraged to study the tables and ask any question regarding budget allocation as well as the content detail of any table or graph. And citizens did that.

- The Eritrean population owned that State, and he gave me an example. Once a driver left a government car running while he went to a shop to buy cigarette. A private citizen who counted the idling time, probably for few minutes, filed a complaint to the police accusing the driver of wasting tax payers gas and technically shortening the life span of the engine to buy cigarette. The incident attracted the attention of the media and was covered in the newspapers. Civic duty was taken seriously.

- When asked about the shortage of skilled manpower, he told me a remarkable anecdote: Under the British administration Eritrean CID (Criminal Investigation Department) had 'dermatoglyphics' fingerprint investigation section run by British experts that identified suspected criminals. when the British left they closed the department because there was no Eritrean expert who can use the technique. But there was an Eritrean janitor, a custodian who worked in the department. He was appointed to take over the department and to the surprise of the new Eritrean officials he had already mastered the technique by simply observing from the side and was able to run the department from day one efficiently. We were all aware about the contemptuous underestimation of Eritreans by the British, the Ethiopian and the Unionists and we were all prepared to prove them wrong, and we did.

The Economic Challenges of the New Eritrean State at its Inception

- Those who opposed the independence of Eritrea based their argument on the fact that Eritrea is too poor to be a viable independent State. The outgoing British administration, the Ethiopians and the Eritrean unionists firmly believed the Eritrean State cannot survive and will be a temporary experiment that awaits a dismal failure. Isaias's déjà vu mixed with an epiphany, comes to mind.[2]

- The British administration left one penny in the treasury of the newly born quasi-independent State of Eritrea. The secretary of finance Ato Teklehaimanot Bokru, a highly respected person of integrity, started with one penny, and he was unable to pay the salary of the government workers. The Executive Secretary Ato Tedla Bairu borrowed money from Signor Melloti, a wealthy Italian beer brewery and various liquor brands owner and SEDAO, an electric power company, and paid the salary of all government workers at the end of the month, just on time.

- Soon the State introduced an efficient tax collection system, free of corruption and raised enough revenue to run the

---

2 The British Administration of Eritrea in the 1940's and early fifties supported the Ethiopian government claim, and that of the Unionist Party, that Eritrea was not economically capable to becoem an independent country.

government efficiently. When Tedla Bairu left the government, the annual national expenditure of Eritrea was 12 million Birr and he left 12 million Birr in reserve. It was a remarkable economic growth in a country that started with One Penny amid a population of one million. The economic miracle was the result of effective governance with accountable political system and inclusive institutions conducive to private sector development. The protection of fundamental rights, freedom of speech, movement and protection of property was an important component of the progress.

- The system was business friendly and the absence of corruption and well developed independent judicial system paved the way for a new political culture and for rapid growth of market.

- After Eritrea became part of Ethiopia in 1962, according to the State Bank of Ethiopian, 50% of the Ethiopian export was coming from Eritrea until 1974. Eritrea carried the major economic burden of Ethiopia as a result of sound high-quality State revenue system, efficient administration inherited from the State of Eritrea and consequent industrial and agricultural development.

The first State of Eritrea was a kind of a government that is impossible to recognize using today's political lens. It is unreal, out of the world for Eritreans. It is a demonstration of the Eritrean human capital and its capacity to deliver when they rise up for the occasion.

Eritrea Today and the Potential for Economic Growth

The core enabler of all the economic success of the first Eritrean State in 1952 was 'good governance'. Below is a list of the economic sectors that would have created a vibrant economy propelling Eritrea to a middle-income country in the last 29 years of independence had we had a responsive political system that paves the way for citizens to operate the economy under the rule of law.

It is worth underscoring that Eritrea has a highly productive population of 5-6 million and a market of 200+ million people in the neighboring countries if we live in peace rather than continuous hostility. Consider the Following:

TOURISM

-   Eritrea's pristine Red Sea coastline 1,151 km and over 1,083 kms islands coastline along the Dahlak archipelago and islands across the port of Assab, with over 350 islands – the natural treasure of the three "SSS".

The three "SSS", Sea, Sand, Sun – Eritrea's weather conditions are optimal for tourism – with sunny weather throughout the year (25-40 C); warm salty waters with sea breeze; tranquil relaxing beaches; boat riding to the Dahlak archipelago; low cost; tourist paradise. Added to this are ancient artifacts of historical and cultural interest.

Economists estimate Eritrean, under a normal administration, can attract 1.5 – 2 million tourists visit annual generating 1.5 -2 billion USD revenue.

Eritrea's local tourism has a strong base to start with, the Eritrean diaspora. Before the 1998 war, an estimated 100,000 diaspora Eritreans visited Eritrea annually. Eritrea could easily build up on that number by creating attractive resorts in the Red Sea coast and "Bahri Resorts and Spas". For the purpose of comparison: Egypt has 45 separate resort towns and areas on the Red Sea coast, employing an estimated 200,000 people and Kenya generated 1.69B USD in Tourism income in 2019.

FISHERIES

Red Sea waters are highly productive supporting diverse marine species (over 1000) and corals species (about 220). The virgin marine fisheries that include catching, shellfish farms, processing plants are important economic source.

According to the Eritrea National Fisheries Corporation that operates under the Eritrea ministry of Marine resource, the Red Sea Coast is rich in marine resources and can sustainably yield 80,000 to 100,000 tons of fish annually. There is rich investment potential to develop and export these untapped resources in Eritrea

Eritrea has a very underdeveloped fishing industry. For comparison, Egypt harvests from Sea and Aqua farms 1.1 million metric tons (Estimated economic value 2-4B USD) annually, employing 816,000 people. Egypt and Yemen fishing vessels illegally harvest estimated 100-200 thousand metric tons annually from the Eritrean coastline. Eritrea could easily build an industry half the size of Egypt in a decade.

SALT
Eritrea has a long history of salt production. Small and medium salt producers have grown since the Italian occupation. The salt is naturally iodized and has high demand globally. In 2013 Eritrea underproduced 290,000 metric ton per year i.e., 60 million USD.

OIL
Major oil deposit are believed to lie under the Red Sea. Oil refinery in Assab had crude oil refining capacity of 18,000 barrels per day. Since 1997 it is closed

In its National Progress Report 2016, the Eritrean government confirmed there are commercial quantity of oil and gas reserve in the country. The Statement read:

"Recently, commercial quantity of oil and gas reserve has been confirmed. Even though the country's full potential has not been exploited fully, it is reported that it has a potential of producing to 200,000 barrels of oil per day". According to 2020 average price of crude oil per barrel the annual revenue would be 4.1 billion USD.

Anadarko Eritrea Co., Asmara, Eritrea, has signed a second production-sharing agreement with Eritrea's Ministry of Energy and Mines and started exploratory drilling in 1995. The PSA (production Sharing Agreement) covers the 6.7-million-acre Zula block surrounding the Dahlak archipelago off Eritrea's central coast. The acreage lies near the Red Sea coastlines of Saudi Arabia and Yemen. Anadarko Eritrea Co. expects to spend at least $28.5 million in the next 7 years exploring the block i.e. 1995-2002. It was interrupted in 1978 by the Badme border conflict.

Regionally, most of Eritrea's neighbors, including Sudan, Ethiopia, Kenya, Uganda, and Somalia, have found commercially viable oil or gas deposits and are currently at different stages of exploration or production.

MINERALS:

The mineral potential of the rift valley and the location of Nubian shield an extension of the Arabian- Nubian shield is recognized for precious and industrial minerals, such as gold, silver, copper, zinc, tin, and lead as well as granites, in addition to precious metals such as tantalum used for electronic capacitors. The Shield reserve covers 65% of Eritrea starting from Mersa Fatuma in the east to Karora in the north east and Omhager in the south west. The Arabian-Nubian Shield (ANS) is Earth's largest block of juvenile crust endowed with one of the largest repositories of metallic minerals. The range of deposit types and the value of current metal production are the direct result of the rock type and tectonic Rift Valley evolution of ANS.

Current mining revenue:

- Metals

    i. Operating mines
    - Zara mining Share Company: Primary product - Gold (estimated annual revenue 100-150M USD)
    - Bisha mining Share Company: Primary Products - Copper, Zinc & Gold (estimated annual revenue 250-300M USD)
    ii. Implementation ready mine
        1. Asmara mining Share Company (Planned Start date 2021): Primary Products - Copper,

63

      Zinc & Gold (estimated annual revenue 500M USD)

   iii. Exploration licenses: 12 exploration companies – Most waiting for permit to start mining exploration.

- Potash

   Implementation ready mine

    1. Colluli Mining Share Company (Planned start date 2021); Estimated annual revenue 1B USD when Phase I & II fully operational)Exploration licenses

    2. Exploration licenses: 3 exploration companies

- Construction minerals

  - Quarry rocks - In 1993, there were 160 Quarry operators in Eritrea producing enough gravel and crushed rock to supply all the construction for all development projects in Eritrea.

  - Limestone - Eritrean Limestone mining and production is over a century old. There are several inactive quarries and mines that when operational can generate significant local and export revenues. Limestone is used in the Construction, Pharmaceutical, Mining and food processing industries.

  - Marble - Marble deposits have been identified in all regions of Eritrea. The quality of Eritrean marble is considered very high quality that export was started during the italian colonial occupation. There is currently one PFDJ owned company (MARGRAN) producing and exporting Marble. In a free economy, Marble could generate considerable export revenues as well as cover all the local market needs.

  - Cement - Cement production is the basic building block of economic development. The Eritrean coastline has abundant raw materials necessary for cement production.

- **Agriculture** (*Local grains*)
  - Eritrea is capable of being self-sufficient in food production with locally grown grains (Sorghum, Corn, teff, wheat etc) if farmers are allowed to farm independently. This would eliminate the need for food aid in the future.

  - **Agriculture** (*Export Commodities*)
    Sesame and other oil seeds: Omhajer(Eritrea), Humera(Ethiopia) and Gedarf(Sudan) Triangle is considered the source of the best quality of Sesame seed in the world. Eritrea is capable of annual production of 100-200M USD.
    Gum Arabic and Gum Olibanum: These products are tree saps used for incense and perfume ingredients. Eritrea had a very strong and thriving export industry before 1975. This can be resuscitated quickly and easily.

- **Livestock**
  Eritrea has a large market in the middle east for export of all livestock. If private livestock farms were allowed to operate, Eritrea could easily generate 300-500M USD annual export revenues within the next 5-10 years. Livestock from Sahel was the first Eritrean export in 1991.
  - Fruits and Vegetables
    The temperate regions of Eritrea located on the middle altitude (areas such as, semenawi bahri, Ala, Elabert, Ghinda, Dekemhare, Mendefera) are prime land for growing export quality fruits and

65

vegetables. Again this is an industry that existed pre 1975.

- **Industry**
- There were over 50 medium to large size industries in 1991 in various sectors such as Beverage, construction materials, textiles, food processing, tannery). There has been no growth, since independence, in the industrial sector. In fact, most industries have been shut down due to lack of import permits for raw materials.
- Had the Eritrean economy been free and open, we would have at a minimum a 10 fold increase in industrial output by now.

- **Diaspora Eritreans**
- Diaspora Eritreans contribution to the Eritrean economy is multi-fold
  Direct remittances - The US government estimated the local remittances at 450M USD per year in 2009 as part of an effort to sanction Eritrea. In a free Eritrea, remittance would grow by multiple of the above number to feed a growing economy.
  Local Investment - If the economy and construction sector were open, investment in billions of dollars would annually flow to Eritrea for construction of homes, commercial property, investment projects annually.
- It is important to divide the economic power of Diaspora Eritrean by region to appreciate their economic earning capacity and potential.
  Europe, North America, Middle East and Australia/New Zealand - Eritreans living in these regions have income and education/skill levels that are commensurate with the communities that they live in.

Africa - Eritrean Business sector in Africa has grown to a significant degree in several countries. This sector has developed thousands of experienced entrepreneurs that would return home to help build a solid business and investment class.

According to a notable economist, the total wealth of all Eritreans in the diaspora which includes the sum of natural, human and physical assets is estimated to be over a 1 trillion USD.

The Eritrean population at home is primed for productivity with a minimum upgrade of skills to work in all economic sectors, if freed from the lifetime national service (an estimated 85% of the population does not have a release from the military) to participate in the public and private sector economy. It is worth noting, even under the present wretched circumstances with miserable pay and suffocating political atmosphere the Eritrean workers have placed Eritrea near the top of all African nations in the 8 UN millennium Development goals.

Yet in the global data composite index:

- Eritrea ranked 7 out of 7 (the lowest ranking) in the 2020 Freedom in the World index, as well as in prior years. *Freedom House.*
- *Eritrea is the 9ᵗʰ largest country of origin for refugees, with 10% of its population displaced in 2018. UNHCR*
- Eritrea was ranked the world's most censored country by the Committee to Protect Journalists in 2019. *The Committee to Protect Journalists.*
- Eritrea had the second least free press in the world as of 2018 (following North Korea). In 2019 and 2020 it was the third least free (following Turkmenistan and North Korea), but still the worst in Africa. *Reporters Without Borders.*

- Eritrea ranked 179th out of 189 countries in the 2018 report on the United Nations' Human Development Index (2017 figures). *United Nations Development Program.*
- Eritrea ranked 157th out of 180 countries in the 2018 Corruption Perceptions Index (published 2018). *Transparency International.*
- Eritrea ranked 177th out of 180 countries in the 2019 Index of Economic Freedom. *Heritage Foundation.*

A wealthy country with proud history and hardworking entrepreneurial people and rich untapped resources is ranked at the bottom by global statistical measures because of a vital missing link that connects economic potential and the Eritrean workforce elements – leadership. For the last 3 decades an autocratic regime has stranglehold the nation from economic progress by:

- Stifling the human capital by lifetime National service.
- Blocking all construction permits (from personal to large projects) for over a decade.
- Isolating the country and barring import and export activities in the private sector.
- Installing draconian Monetary policies that deter/block any normal economic activity.
- Draining its workforce by pushing out the Eritrean youth to leave the country.

It is ironic and indeed a mockery to hear this very person complain about Eritrea's poverty and blame the Eritrean population for the current economic misery. The only reason that the Eritrean economy is not growing and operating at its full capacity can only be explained by an incompetent leadership that had chocked the public and private economic life in all sectors of our economy.

Conclusion

In the 50s our fathers started with 'one penny' and built the first Eritrean State with vibrant economy. My generation of the 60s failed to appreciate and draw lessons from their momentous achievement because of ideological political myopia. The young generation of today have the burden of transition from a lone leader accountable to no one, to a State governed by the will of the Eritrean people. That is the only remedy for the poor populace who live in a wealthy country.

A NATION WITH A MUSEUM OF PEOPLES: FROM THE CENTRAL AND NORTHERN HIGHLANDS TO THE WESTERN AND EASTERN LOWLANDS

Mohamed Kheir Omer

Introduction

Reading the precolonial history makes one value and cherish the commonality of this beautiful, diverse mosaic called Eritrea. It includes diverse peoples from the Semitic, Kushetic, and Nilotic groups. People embraced both Christianity and Islam at the earliest times of the spread of these two great religions. Some continued to embrace indigenous traditional beliefs. It has one of the oldest written scripts in Africa, Ge'ez, which is also closely related to the Sabaean language in southern Arabia. Everywhere in Eritrea, we see evidence of the complex and interwoven history of this land and its people: the Tigrait-speaking Muslim tribes of the Habab in the Sahel province, who trace their origins some three hundred years back to the Tigrinya-speaking Christian Tzenaa Degle in Akele Guzai; the highland Christian inhabitants of Deki Itaias in Serae, the Tedrer in Akele Guzai, and the Beit Mekhaa in Asmara, who trace their origins to the Tigrait-speaking Belew tribes of Semhar; the Tigrait-speaking Mensaa and Maria tribes who consider themselves closely related to the Saho-speaking

Toroaa, in Akele Guzai, as well as the people of Dembezan in Hamasien; and the Afar, who are linguistically related to the Saho. We have extensions to the neighbouring countries of Ethiopia, Sudan, and Djibouti, and Yemen across the Red Sea.

Pre-colonial History

There was no entity actually called Eritrea (mainland) before 1 January 1890, when Umberto I, Re d'Italia, declared as an Italian colony the areas in the region the region and gave them the name Eritrea (Guerra 1935, 210-211). The new colony was thus an amalgam of parts and pieces of predominantly four existing or former entities, sultanates, and kingdoms, namely the following:

1) **the Aksumite kingdom,** considered to be the cradle of Ethiopian civilization and including the present central plateau areas of Eritrea (Hamasien, Akele Guzai, and Serae) and Tigray in northern Ethiopia;
2) **the Tigre-Beja belt**[1], which extended from Krora to Zula along the western Red Sea coast and related lowlands and included such cities as Ghenda, Massawa, Keren, Agordat, and Tessenei;
3) **the Afar Sultanates,** which had within their domination part of present-day Eritrea, extending from Rahaita in the south to the Buri Peninsula and the Dahlak Archipelago (Dankalia) in the north;
4) **the Kunama and the Baria** (Nara) Group in the Gash-Setit area, including Barentu and its environs.

The Aksumite Kingdom

The Aksumite kingdom was an ancient kingdom that centred in the highlands of Eritrea and northern Ethiopia (*c.* 50 BCE–650/700 CE) and was the main commercial partner of the Roman and Byzantine empires in the early to mid-first

---

1 The term was coined by A-Shami

millennium CE. It adopted Christianity as the state religion in the fourth century CE (Fattovich 2012, 1-2). As a source of the history of the kingdom, inscriptions were found in three languages, Sabean, Greek and Ge'ez and it is reported that Sabean was once the spoken language of the kingdom (Sellassie 1972, 59). It is reported (Fattovich 2012, 2-3), that the occurrence of nine sites in central Eritrea and eastern and central Tigray, with evidence of monumental buildings and artefacts in a South Arabian style, as well as Sabaic inscriptions in South Arabian script, has suggested two different interpretations. Scholars emphasizing the South Arabian elements claim that a South Arabian tribe migrated to the Tigrean highlands and/or Sabeans colonized the region and imposed their dominion on the indigenous people in the early to mid-first millennium BCE (Ludolf 1682, 7-9, Bent 1893, 134-151, Sellassie 1972, 26-34, Taddesse 1972, 5). Other scholars, highlighting the local component (mainly pottery and lithics), stress an indigenous origin of this polity, suggesting that the local elite used South Arabian elements as symbols of power (Fattovich 2004, 71 - 78, Curtis 2008, 329 - 348).

Fattovich (Fattovich 2012, 1), citing several sources, indicated that the northern Horn of Africa (present-day northern Ethiopia and Eritrea) was the core of the Ethio-Semitic Christian state which progressively dominated most of the Horn of Africa in the first and second millennium CE and laid the foundation for the modern national states of Ethiopia and Eritrea. Tamrat traced the origins of the Ethiopian State to the establishment of Sabean settlements in Northern Ethiopia (Taddesse 1972, 5).

Results of recent archaeological investigations in the Asmara Basin show that there is a great potential for understanding the origins of the settled life in the highlands and the growth of communities that acted as urban precursors in the Horn of Africa (Schmidt 2008, 161). Sedentary people were settled in the Hamasien plateau, near Asmara, in the late 2nd millennium B.C.E. ("Ona Group A," ca. 1500-900/800 B.C.E.) and most likely they were mixed farmers (Fattovich 2000, 10).

Contact with the Aksumite kingdom was not limited to that with Southern Arabia. It also included Greeks, the most prominent example being the Ptolemaic dynasty, which established the commercial port of Adulis, Nubia and the Romans.

The supremacy of the Aksumite kingdom started to decline in the sixth/seventh century and ended in the tenth century because of the raids by the Beja tribes and a host of other factors. The emergence of the Solomonic kingdom in the thirteenth century, including the Turkish occupation of the Port of Massawa (Tigre land) in the middle of the sixteenth century, resulted in an encroachment into the territorial sphere of Tigray's hegemony. The rise of power by Tigray's enemies was represented by the Belew (Balaw) and other Muslim tribes on the Red Sea coast, whose land extended from Massawa to Swakin and further inland along this belt. The subsequent replacement of the Turks by Egyptians during the nineteenth century made the situation more difficult for Tigray, including their viceroys in Hamasien and the rest of the central Eritrean plateau, referred to as *Kebesa*. Nevertheless, the Aksumite kingdom remained intact in its epicentre of Tigray, albeit in a loose and fragile manner, until the Italian occupation of Massawa in 1885.

When Atse Yohannes took over in Tigray, the highlands of Eritrea were autonomous regions ruled by local families. Ras Woldemikael Solomon, ruler of Hamasein (1841 – 1879) from Hazega replaced Ras Hailu Tecle Haimanot of Tsatzega who was appointed by Atse Tedros. Ras Alula raided and pillaged several parts of Eritrea at different times before and after his appointment as Governor of Seraye, Hamassein and Akle Guzai on 9th October, 1876. Yet he never succeeded in having full control of Eritrea. Ras Woldemikael, Bahta Hagos, Kifleyesus and the Tigrian renegade Dabbab with his Assawota fighters resisted his presence (Erlich 1997, 11-16, 25, 32). The

Italians were able to control most parts of Eritrea peacefully as the people were fed up with Alula' incursions.

The Tigre-Beja Belt

Beja-Tigre belt (Omer 2020, 21) comprises of the people who speak To-Bedawi and Tigrait extends along the Red Sea coastline from the southern border of Egypt to the south of environs of Badi (Massawa), to the western part of the Arabian Peninsula. The recorded history pertinent to Beja goes farther back than 1500 BCE and can be traced in the narratives of the conflicts between the Egyptian dynasties and the tribes and nations south of the Egyptian border. According to one researcher, the Beja were "a secondary race of invaders whose first arrival has been dated as early as 4000 BCE and certainly prior to 2500 BCE, when they appear first to have come into the notes of Egyptians of the VI Dynasty" (Paul 1954, 21). In fact, they are mentioned by the Greek historian Eratosthenes (276–194 BCE) in Strabo's *Geography*, as stated by Trimingham, and are one of the most important peoples in the region between the Nile and the Red Sea (Trimingham 1965, 47).

A total of 1,469 sherds and 3,958 lithic artefacts found in four different localities (Kokan, Ntanei, Shabeit, and Dandaneit) within Agordat, in western Eritrea, have provided one of the most extensive collections of prehistoric materials in the Horn of Africa (Beldados 2007, 4). The materials were collected, described, and presented in 1942 to the Sudan National Museum by archaeologist A. J. Arkell and Major J. S. Last, the political governor of Eritrea (Arkell 1954, 33-62). New analysis of the materials shows that they are very varied. However, the main connection appears to be, as Arkell suggests, related to the cultures of the Nile valley dated to around the fourth millennium BCE (Beldados 2007, 4-11). An analysis of reconnaissance and test excavations from the National Eritrean Museum in 1994 in Kokan firmly places Agordat within the mix of regional trading systems from ca. 2300 BCE to the "Pre-Axumite period, ca. 400 BCE where it was a center of the increasing trade between the Nile valley and Eritrean/Ethiopian highlands (Brandt 2008, 46-47). The Greeks called the dwellers of the Tigre-Beja belt, from north of Adulis (present-day Zula) along the Red Sea coast to almost about/beyond the port in the Sudan, both Berbers and calf eaters(Anonymous 1912, 22). The Beja were called "Blemmyers" by old Egyptians and Roman Ptolemaics in Egypt.

The Arabs called them Beja and their language Badawie (now called by themselves "To-Bedawie"). To the Ethiopians and the Aksumites, they were known as Bega. It is to be noted, however, that the names Belo, Bellow, and Belew refer basically, and according to many historians, to the Beja.

Conti Rossini, considered an authority on the history of that part of the world, stated, "There were at least two groups of Bellou, a northern one, the Hadareb of the Atbai and the Sinkat hills, and a southern one, which was the nucleus of the Bellu kingdom which flourished between the latitudes of Suakin and Massawa from how early on is not known (Paul 1954, 65)." At the end of the seventh century, the Beja, from their own valley of Baraka, forayed into the central plateau of the Tigrinya-speaking peoples. Particularly a Beja tribe named Zanfaj overran much of Hamasien and the surrounding areas, displacing many and dispersing them towards the south (Trimingham 1965, 47). According to the author, some Beja did remain on the Abyssinian Plateau, and there are still those who claim Beja origin today, particularly Deki Itaias in Serae, Tedrer in Akele Guzai, and Beit Mekhaa in Hamasien. Still today, several place names maintain Tigrait names in the highlands of Eritrea and in Tigray, Ethiopia. The Beja ruled the highlands from the fall of Axum until the end the 13th century (Bereket 1980, 49).

New research in Eastern Sudan and the Eritrean lowlands suggests that the Eritrean–Sudanese lowlands had contact with the Red Sea coast and the Eastern Desert and may have had direct contact with Lower Nubia via the Eastern Desert,

Arabia, and perhaps Egypt via the Red Sea (Manzo 2012, 75-106).

According to Arab historian al-Magrizi, the Beja land extends from south of Egypt, at a place called Kharbe village, to Badi (present-day Massawa) (Al Magrizi 1895, 194-97). He states that the Beja were atheists and fast runners and that "Beja are darker than Abyssinians and dress as Arabs and feed on meat, and every clan/tribe has its own chief." Between the twelfth and sixteenth centuries CE, peoples of mixed Beja and Arab ancestry known as the Balaw (Belew) appear to have been politically dominant in much of Eritrea (Schmidt, Curtis et al. 2008, 284). Another Arab historian, al-Masoudi (Abu Al Hassen 1988, 29), who died in 346 Hegira, writes, "The land of the Beja is between the Nile river and the Red Sea.

The Arab historian Al-Yagoubi, who is widely quoted by western scholars, (Yagoub 1980, 217-19), state that the Beja had six kingdoms: a) a kingdom extending from Aswan city to the kingdom called Hajr (Arabic); b) Baglin, c) Bazen, d) Jarin, which had a great king whose authority extended over a city called Badi (some refer to present-day Massawa, others state that it was a port between Suakin and present day Massawa), from the coast of the greater sea to the proximity of Barakat (present-day Khor Baraka), and from the Kingdom of Baglin to the location called Hal Addogaj, perhaps Hilet Addojaj, referring to its Tigrinya equivalent, Emba Derho) Qita or **Qaṭ'a** Kingdom, of which al-Yagoubi said: "It is the last Beja kingdom. ... This kingdom is very large, extending from the border of Badi to the locality called Feikun" The fifth, called **Qaṭ'a,** was the last Beja kingdom and extended from the border of *Badi'* to a place called Faykun. They were a brave and powerful people and had a military training school called *dar as sawa* where the young men were trained in arms; f) Negash, whose capital, Kebir, was on the coast near Dahlak and whose inhabitants were merchants and Christians.

The Beni Amer were incorporated into the Funj confederation and the Chief of the tribe, the Diglel, received from the Funj, as a symbol of his authority, the three-horned cap, which he wears to this day (Nadel 1945, 63). It is stated that the first king of the Sultanate of Sennar was Amara or Umeira Dungus which means 'Al Njashi Al Azem' Dej Negus, 'Do' means the great and 'Ngus' means king (Ali 1838, 4). Though the origins of the Funj are disputed (Holt 1963, Hasan 1965), Rossini indicated that local stories in Eritrea narrate that when Asgede came to the Habab around 1500 he met the Funj there (Rossini 1913, 387-388, Crawford 1951, 243-44). Rossini also adds that the Funj later settled in the vally of Agra in Sahel. Blin folk tales also refer to a people called Fuj, probably the Funj who had settled in Anseba (personal communication).

Afar

The Afar are a Hamatic people who occupy a vast area stretching from the Jibuti (Djibouti)–Diredawa Railway in the south to the Buri Peninsula in the north, and from the shores of the Red Sea to the eastern spurs of the Abyssinian Plateau (Trimingham 1965, 171). Geographically the region is known as the Afar Triangle. The Afar region is the site of the oldest human settlements, not only in Eritrea but also in the Horn of Africa. One-million-year-old human remains have been discovered in the Danakil Depression in Eritrea (Abbate, Albianelli et al. 1998, 458-460). It seems the contact of Egyptians with the Afar and the Somali regions through trade in aromatic materials and frankincense go back to 2500 BC and earlier (A-Shami Gamaladdin 1997, 39-55).

Al-Shami, based on an extensive review of very old Greek archives, including that of Strabo, notes that many of the ports and places in the Afar region of the Red Sea that were recorded by the Greeks retained the same names, for example Daraba, Hanfale (Amphile), and Elaea (A-Shami Gamaladdin 1997, 60-70). Some ports mentioned by the Greeks on the Afar coast in the Gulf of Avalites, where they described a strait with a width of 60 stadia (meaning Bab-el-Mandeb), were ports such as such as the Deire port, which faced the old Ocelis port on the

Yemen side. Those ports were older than Adulis by several centuries.

Al-Shami's review (A-Shami Gamaladdin 1997, 86) indicates that the Afar practised hunting, cultivation, and fishing prior to 300 BC. The Greeks identified the Afar region as an Aramatx region from which aromatic Strax (Styrax) products, also used in mythology, could be exported in great quantities. Other exports included tortoiseshell and ivory.

The presence of an Afar kingdom called Dankali can be traced back to the beginning of the ninth century. The ruling class was the Dankali tribe which exists until today in Dahlak, Beilul, Dkaa, Awsa, Tajoura, Awash, Ab-Ala, and elsewhere. The name "Danakil", which refers to the Afar kingdom, is derived from this kingdom.

The Dankali was followed by the Ankala kingdom, and later, at the beginning of the thirteenth century, the Adal kingdom/sultanate took over most of the Afar Triangle. Father Francisco Alvares during his travels in Ethiopia referred to the king of Danakil and the kingdoms of Adea and Adal (Alvares 1881, 345-6). Later, just before the mid-sixteenth century, two Afar kingdoms/sultanates were merged into one, becoming the Sultanate of Adal (Afar).

From 1294 to 1467, the war continued between Afar and the Solomonic dynasty with no clear and lasting victory for either side. The Solomonic dynasty was able at the end of the fourteenth century to wage a devastating war against the Adal (Afar) Sultanate. The Adal (Afar) Sultanate was able to recover and in fact defeat king Baeda Maryam's army during 1473–4 (A-Shami 2018, 190).

The Adal (Afar) Sultanate under Imam Ahmed Ibrahim occupied the whole of what is present day Ethiopia and Eritrea by 1535. He was later defeated by a Portuguese expedition in 1542 (Miguel de Castanhoso 1902). An account of Imam Ahmed's conquest is described in detail in a book dedicated to that event (Ahmed 1894). In October 1542, Imam Ahmed Gran was killed by King Gelawdewos's army at Lugna Dega near Lake Tana (Trimingham 1965, 89). The sultanate gradually became weaker, losing more area to the hegemony of the Turks as in Dahlak, albeit without relinquishing day-to-day rule until the time the Italians started to gain a foothold in Assab (1870s), the French in Obock (1862), and the Turks in Zeila. The Afars' power became extremely diminished by the end of the eighteenth century, and Afar disintegrated into smaller sultanates, chiefdoms, and independent tribes. The independent Afar Sultanates signed 19 agreements with European countries, copies of which are indicated in (A-Shami 2018, 512-663).

The Kunama and Nara

The Kunama have been mentioned by many Arab historians and particularly by al-Magrizi and Al Yagoubi (Al Magrizi 1895, Yagoub 1980) using the name Baza. Pollera has written an extensive note on both the Kunama and Nara (Pollera 1913). Other writers include Nadel (Nadel 1944, 10 - 11) and Naty (Naty 2000). The Kunama are also referred to as Baden/Bazen by the Ethiopians and Tigrinya-speaking people. The various ethnic groups in Eritrea refer to the Kunama by different names. Their neighbours and culturally related Nara call them "Diila"; the Tigre and Hidareb refer to them as "Bazen"; but the Kunama use the name "Kunama" for themselves (Naty 2001, 575).

According to Naty, the term Kunama means "natural". The Kunama people believe in traditional religions, and their conversion to Christianity and Islam started very late. According to some estimates, in 1931, during the Italian colonial period, there were 45.8 per cent Muslims, 33.7 per cent Christians, and 20.5 per cent pagans (Trimingham 1965, 217). At present, the Kunama live in the region between the Gash and Setit rivers (the Kunama refer to the Gash and Setit rivers as "Soona" and "Tiika" respectively).

According to historians, their geographical coverage was far wider numerous centuries ago, but their geographical space shrunk because of raids by the Abyssinians and the Beja tribes(Trimingham 1965, 217). From the Abyssinian side, raids were organized particularly during 1585 and 1692. In 1886, Ras Alula (the army general of King Yohannes IV of Tigray), frustrated by his inability to attack the Mahdists in Kassala, ruthlessly decimated about two-thirds of the Baria and Kunama population of Eritrea, looted their livestock, and enslaved the women (Pollera 1913, 50-2, Erlich 1997,101-106). The raids of Alula are referred to as "*Alula masa*" by the Kunama, and because of these raids, there were no cattle for cultivation (Naty 2001, 577). The Kunama took refuge in caves, and the Abyssinians then set fire at the entrance of the caves to force them to come out. They also sprinkled chilli, known as "berbere" in Tigrinya and Amharic, to drive them out.

According to Naty, the Italians brought relative peace to the Kunama, and thus the Kunama remember the Italians with nostalgia. The Kunama also raided the Abyssinians and other neighbours, and their oral history is full of such stories. The Kunama refer to those raids as *sakada masa* or *baada*, and through those raids they were able to take women from other societies as captives (Naty 2001, 577). In terms of the social structures of the Kunama in the old days, it seems that sovereignty was formerly based in the assembly of village elders. The Kunama are sedentary agricultural people.

They have a matrilineal system. In other words, kinship tracing and descent counting is based on the female line. The Kunama live in Eritrea, Sudan, and Ethiopia—a manifestation of the history when they used to inhabit wider areas in the past.

The Kunama are basically homogenous; however, there are two classifications. The first is based on kinship. The second is based on geographic and other factors:

According to Nadel, the social structure of the Kunama is based on a division into six clans (molata)—Kara, Dula, Sagona, Nataka, Serme, and Argatakra. In the nineteenth century, significant numbers of Kunama converted to Christianity by two missionaries—a Swedish Protestant and an Italian Catholic.

The Baria (Nara) are Nilotic tribes. Still today, 98 per cent are Muslims, and many speak Tigre. There are two subtribes, the Mogoraib in the west and the Higgir in the east, each having its own chief (Mashinge or Omda) and a deputy (Nada or Wakil). Unlike the Kunama, the Baria have a paramount chief called nazir, as in Arabic. The social organization of the Baria, too, seems closely akin to that of the Kunama—which is again based on a division into clans (nara) which are invested with magic powers; descent is counted in the paternal line (Nadel 1944, 12). The Baria used to live in the Sahel and intermarried with the Habab. Local history indicate that the village of Naro in the Sahel was named after them. They also lived in the region where the Blin live at present, according to local stories.

Despite the 'Multiplicity' of Eritrean history, we see evidence of the complex and interwoven history of this land and its people: the Tigrait-speaking Muslim tribes of the Habab in Sahel, who trace their origins some three hundred years back to the Tigrinya-speaking Christian Tzenaa Degle in Akele Guzai; the highland Christian inhabitants of Deki Itaias in Serae, the Tedrer in Akele Guzai, and the Beit Mekhaa in Asmara, who trace their origins to the Tigrait-speaking Belew tribes of Semhar; the Tigrait-speaking Mensaa and Maria tribes who consider themselves closely related to the Saho-speaking Toroaa, in Akele Guzai, as well as the people of Dembezan in Hamasien; and the Afar, who are linguistically related to the Saho. We have extensions to the neighbouring countries of Ethiopia, Sudan, and Djibouti, and Yemen across the Red Sea.

Postcolonial History

Less than a month after the British came to control Eritrea, in April 1941, Eritrean intellectuals started to engage in politics, taking advantage of the political sphere created by the British Administration. It is quite astonishing that Eritreans took up the challenges of multiparty democracy in a short period. According to Jordan Gebre-Medhin (Gebre-Medhin 1989, 78-

81), after the defeat of Italy, Eritrean intellectuals of the time met regularly to discuss the future of the country and in 1941 formed the patriotic society known as Society for the Love of the Country (PLC) (Mahber Feqri Hager Eretra in Tigrinya, or Jemiyat Hub al-Watan in Arabic) in a meeting at Aberra Hagos Hotel, Asmara.

They took an oath by the Koran and the Bible and they ate together chicken slaughtered by a Muslim and a Christian to show unity. The executive leaders of the PLC were Gebre-Meskel Woldu, president; Abdulgadir Kebire, vice president; and Haregot Abbay, the only one from the nobility, general secretary. The central committee members included Woldeab Woldemariam, Ibrahim Sultan, Mesgina Gebre-Egzi, Mohamed Omer Kadi, and Berhanu Ahmedin.

As Makki puts it, the initial cohesion of the patriotic society was achieved more by a common anticolonial rhetoric than by the formulation of shared vision or values, and the limited objectives that held the group together were too fragile to sustain it in the face of political pressure and monetary inducements coming from Ethiopia (Makki 2011, 431). From its inception, the organization's mixed Muslim–Christian composition also featured an equally diverse political membership that included those who called for union between Eritrea and Ethiopia and those who argued Eritrea was an entity distinct from Ethiopia and therefore entitled to its own sovereignty (Venosa 2012, 31).

In 1944, the Ethiopian government mobilized those Eritreans living in Ethiopia and formed the Society for the Unification of Eritrea and Ethiopia (SUEE) (Gebre-Medhin 1989, 81-3). Thus, the Ethiopian state had laid the cornerstone of the Eritrean Unionist Party. According to Ellingson, on 27 February 1944, in Addis Ababa, an organization called both Natsa Hamasen (Free Eritrea) and the Society for the Unification of Ethiopia and Eritrea was established. Among its founders was Woldegiorgis Woldeyohannes, the emperor's minister of the pen (Ellingson 1977, 269). In 1946, Ethiopia sent a security officer, Colonel Nega Haile Selassie, as Ethiopia's liaison officer in Eritrea. Meanwhile, as the interests of Abune Markos were opposed to the PLC, the church made a concerted effort to discredit the organization.

The pro-Ethiopian advance made by SUEE and Abune Markos in Kebesa was challenged in the eastern part of Akele Guzai by an independence movement led by Ras Tesemma Asberom and his son Abraha Tesemma. The SUEE succeeded to split the PLC into two factions: unionist (Gebre-Meskel Woldu and Omer Kadi) and pro-independence (Ibrahim Sultan and Woldeab) (Gebre-Medhin 1989, 84). Thus, Ethiopia succeeded in diving Eritreans into two competing factions and gradually brought the Unionists under its full control. Trevaskis noted that from that day onwards, the Unionist Party leaders were no longer free agents but had become servants of Ethiopia (Trevaskis 1960, 74).

The situation in the western lowlands and the Northern Highlands

The growing movement for emancipation across Tigrait-speaking communities during the early and mid-1940s represented a major watershed in Eritrea's eventual push towards decolonization as activists simultaneously challenged the traditional landlord-serf (Shumagulle-Tigre/Arab) dynamic and the colonial authorities' exploitation of such a system (Venosa 2013, 167). Trevaskis indicates that the serf emancipation struggle led to the rise of political consciousness: "In the Northern Highlands, the *Shumagulle* families were threatened by an uprising of their serfs. The peculiar feudal structure of the Tigre tribes was anachronist, which began to disintegrate in the climate of Italian defeat and British liberalism (Trevaskis 1960, 70). The standard of the revolt was first raised by the Tigre serfs of a small tribe called Ad Taklais (Ad Tekles). The author added that parochial though these questions were, it was through them and their interplay that the Tigre tribes acquired political consciousness and an Eritrean Muslim movement emerged."

The representatives of the Tigre wrote a letter to the FPC that described their plight:

> As a continuous state of slavery; slavery which has been fought against and abolished in every part of the world, except in our country and in Ethiopia.[2]

When the pressure of the serfs increased and reached its highest levels, the British Administration gave in 1948. As a result, 20 wholly new tribes comprising a total population of 147,164 emerged as independent units, 8 former non-aristocratic tribes (total population, 32,899) were refashioned, and the former aristocratic tribes were recast in light of their reduced population (Gewald 2000, 1). Twenty chiefs and 591 subordinate chiefs were elected, mainly by unanimous vote (Gewald 2000, 1). According to the author, it was in this region of Eritrea that the first violent protests against the federation took place, and it was also here that, a few years later, the armed struggle against Ethiopia started.

The Situation in the Central Highlands
According to Gebre-Medhin, the British diminished the role of traditional chiefs in the central highlands and thus altered the rural power arrangement, particularly in Hamasein and Serae, as well as in certain districts of Akele Guzai. In Hamasien, they weakened the power of the Beraki family, who had collaborated with Italy and had taken power from Enda Gebre-Kristos (Gebre-Medhin 1989, 109-11). The British appointed a commoner, Afworki Nemariam, in Karneshim and assigned Dej. Berhane (from the *makelai aliet*) to replace Asseressehgn, of the Beraki family, in Loggo Kebesa Chiwa. Thus, according to the author, Dej. Beyene Beraki and other Hamasien nobility

---

2 FBC Report on Eritrea, Appendix 18, letter of Tigre representatives from Keren dated 25 Nov. 1947.

who lost power became staunch Unionists. Gebre-Medhin, further stated that the traditional ruling families in Serae were weak and there was no strong feudal base as in Hamasien. Ras Kidane-Mariam Gebre-Meskel was very old and feeble when the British took over. In the Tsellima and Safaa districts, the nomination of a possible successor to Dej. Beraki Tesfatzion initiated a blood feud that shaped politics in the two districts for years.

When the British nominated Kahsai Mallou as a possible successor to Dej. Beraki, his son Tesfay felt humiliated and agitated against the BMA. The British retaliated by removing him from the Maraguz office. A relative of his became a *shifta* (bandit) and killed Kahsai Mallou in revenge. When Dej. Mengesha, a member of the Areza family who ruled other Serae districts, died, the British appointed a local official, and in retaliation a shifta killed the BMA-appointed atzmatch Berhe Gebre Kidan.

While, in Akele Guzai, one-third of whose inhabitants were Muslims and which harboured the largest number of converts from the Orthodox Church to Catholicism, was least affected by the BMA's administrative rearrangements. Thus, only highland-based party that championed independence was based in this region. According to Gebre-Medhin, most of the nobility in the highlands championed union with Ethiopia because they had lost power under the BMA. But it is difficult to agree with that view as the Orthodox Church was fully behind the Unionist movement, and most of the nobility had lost power or otherwise supported union with Ethiopia.

Formation of political parties
When the British Administration opened-up the political space in 1946, Eritreans soon took the opportunity to form political parties. The most important and influential of those were the Muslim League (ML), The Eritrean Liberal Progressive Party (ELPP) and the Unionist Party. Those were some of the first political parties in Africa.

Eritrean Muslim League

Mufti Sheikh Ibrahim Al Mukhtar has written in detail about the first party formed, the Muslim League (ML) where the founding conference of the ML was convened on 3 December 1946 in Keren in the presence of representatives of the various ethnolinguistic communities of Eritrea [3]. Mohamed Abu Bakr al-Mirghani, was elected as the Chairman and Ibrahim Sultan as Secretary General Venosa noted that internally, in a space of roughly four years (1946–50), many of the activists within the Eritrean Muslim League contributed to a significant political transformation within the country's incipient nationalist movement, while internationally Muslim League officials increasingly framed their struggle as only part of a wave of nationalism spreading across the world and specifically in the Horn of Africa such as in Somalia (Venosa 2012, 51)."

Venosa discusses the rise of Eritrean nationalism in the context of Muslim intellectual activism during the later period of the British Military Administration, defining the leading members of the pro-independence Muslim intelligentsia as a fluid group of writers, Eritreans within the former Italian colonial civil service, and religious scholars serving within or associated with the Eritrean Muslim League, who contributed to the nationalist movement by taking advantage of the extensive Islamic social capital (Venosa 2012, 29). In 1950, the ML, split into three. The parties that split from it were the Muslim League of the Western Province (MLWP) and the Independent Muslim League of Massawa (IMLM).

Eritrean Liberal Progressive Party

The Eritrean Liberal Progressive Party (ELPP) or in Tigrinya Mahber Natznat'n Limaat'n Ertra, but better known as "Eritreans for Eritrea", was established on 18 February 1947. Ras Tesemma Asberom was elected as the ELPP's president,

---

3   https://hedgait.blogspot.com/2015/01/founding-conference-of-muslim-league.html

and Seium Maasho acted as secretary general up to 1950. The vice president was Maasho Zeweldi, but the ELPP's most active member was Woldeab Woldemariam, the subeditor of the Tigrinya newspaper *The Eritrean Weekly News*, published by the British Information Services (Ellingson 1977, 274). The party was a close ally of the ML advocating for Eritrean Independence. The Party later split into two. After leading a delegation of the LPP to Addis Ababa and meeting with Ethiopian officials, Dejazmatch Abraha Tesemma formed the Liberal Unionist Party, which called for conditional union with Ethiopia. Consequently, Woldeab Woldemariam left the LPP and joined a new group, the Association of Eritrean Intellectuals. According to Ellingson, on 25 October 1947, the party unanimously decided that Eritrea must have absolute independence within its present boundaries under the guidance of an Eritrean committee of 'intellectuals' and the present administration which, under the general supervision of the United Nations, gradually would devolve its power during a period of not more than ten years.

Unionist Party

The Unionist Party was one of the two big parties in Eritrea. It advocated union of Eritrea with Ethiopia. It was closely tied to and heavily funded and directed by the Ethiopian government and the Orthodox Church. The Unionist Party, ironically known by the Amharic name *Andinet*, held its founding conference on 21 March 1947, under the slogan "Ethiopia or Death", which literally meant that Eritrea either united with Ethiopia or its members died struggling for unity with Ethiopia. According to Gebre-Medhin(Gebre-Medhin 1989, 115-19) the congress was opened with the blessing of Abune Markos, representing both Akele Guzai province and the Orthodox Church. Representing Serae was deposed noble Ras Kidane Mariam Gebre-Meskel and his asker (servant) Keshi Demetros, who in the 1950s became the most powerful pro-Ethiopian politician in the Eritrean parliament. Gebre-Medhin added that representing Hamasien was Ras Beyene Beraki, whose family the BMA had stripped of their power, and representing Massawa was Ahmed Kekiya Pasha, who was the only Muslim in an all-Orthodox Christian gathering.

Engagement of the Four Power Commission and the UN
The Eritrean question was internationalized and discussed in the United Nations. It was not only Eritreans failing to reach consensus on the future of their country, but also external actors failed to reach such consensus. It was during this period that a Four Power Commission (FPC) to assess the wishes of the people was set up. At the end of World War II, the fate of the Italian colonies in Eritrea, Somalia, and Libya was discussed by Great Britain, the USA, France, and Russia. The Four Power Commission visited Eritrea from 23 November to 14 December 1947 and, unable to reach a consensus, referred the matter to the UN. According to Trevaskis, the commission's investigation confirmed that with the exception of the Muslim League (ML) and the Unionist Party, no other political organization had a valid following (Trevaskis 1960, 89).

Before the arrival of the FPC, the British Military Administration (BMA) formed a committee in January 1947 headed by Frank Stafford to assess the wishes of the population. Eritreans by that time were divided between those who favoured independence and those who supported union with Ethiopia. The committee, in its confidential report, had the following estimations on the supporters of the independence and those who favoured union with Ethiopia: The Unionist support was concentrated in the provinces of Serae (85 per cent) and Hamasien (75 per cent); the support for independence in the other provinces was estimated in Barka at 98 per cent, in the Red Sea province at 98 per cent, in Senhit and Sahel at 66 per cent, and in Akele Guzai at 80 per cent. In terms of absolute numbers, those who supported independence were estimated to be 538,000, while those who supported union with Ethiopia were estimated at 418,900 (Alemseged 2001, 276-77)[4].

The UN commission, comprising Burma, Guatemala, Norway, Pakistan, and South Africa, visited Eritrea from 24 February to 5 April 1950. Jordan Gebre-Medhin reported that Unionist shifta blew up bridges and cut communication lines to towns that were predominantly against union with Ethiopia so that the UN commission could not meet with their residents (Gebre-Medhin 1989, 145-6). Ellingson (Ellingson 1977, 268) noted, "The summer before the arrival of the commission in November 1947 saw unprecedented political violence as the main parties competed for support. In June and July 1947, several bomb incidents occurred in Asmara, with attempts on the lives of Dejazmatch Hassan Ali Shum, a leader of the Muslim League, and Woldeab Woldemariam, subeditor of the Tigrinya newspaper *The Eritrean Weekly News.*"

Ellingson added that following these incidents, several persons with connections to the Unionist Party were arrested with hand grenades and other types of ammunition found in their possession. By the end of July, violence culminated in the arrest and conviction of three members (who had posed as Muslims) of the Andinet Party, the youth section of the Unionist Party. When the British officials raided the Unionist Party's headquarters, they found various documents suggesting that Colonel Negga Haile Selassie and his chief secretary, Tecola, may have had some connection with the assassination of Abdulgadir Kebire (Ellingson 1977, 268).

The brilliant Eritrean politician, a Muslim League representative, was fatally wounded by Unionist thugs in the main square in Asmara as he was preparing to leave for New York to attend the UN session on the future of Eritrea. He died two days later, on 29 March, at the age of 47. The shifta activities became so serious that the BMA chief administrator D. C. Cummings wrote to the principal secretary of the state

---

4 The Arabic version

affairs of the UK, comparing data of dead persons in Palestine and Eritrea. The data showed that for the period 1946–1950, the total number of people who died as the result of shifta violence in Eritrea was 368, compared to 312 who died due to the terrorist activities of the Zionists in Palestine (Gebre-Medhin 1989, 133). This commission, too, failed to reach consensus on Eritrea. For the details of the engagement of the United Nations in Eritrea, one can refer to (Bereket 1989, 27 - 57).

The Attempts to Partition Eritrea between Sudan and Ethiopia

The partitioning of Eritrea was also formally proposed by the British representatives in London and Paris in 1945 and 1946. The British foreign secretary Ernest Bevin and Italian foreign minister Count Carlo Sforza came up, on 10 May 1949, with a joint package plan for the former Italian colonies; hence the plan is known as the Bevin–Sforza plan after them. Concerning Eritrea, the plan proposed the partition of the country between Sudan and Ethiopia. The western lowlands were to be part of Sudan, and the rest was to be given to Ethiopia. But for the plan to be approved, the whole package for all the colonies had to be approved as one piece. Ethiopia was for the partition plan after some initial reluctance. Eritrean delegations representing parties opposed to unity with Ethiopia were present at the UN corridors to foil the plan. But Eritrean opposition did not have much influence. It was mainly due to other factors that the partition of Eritrea was averted. Following that the LLP, together with the Muslim League, the Pro-Italian Party, and other, smaller parties, formed the Independence Bloc in 1949, which advocated independence.

When the General Assembly voted on the disposal of Italian colonies on 17 May 1949, voting took place first on each territory separately, and then for the whole package of proposals. The proposal to partition Eritrea between Ethiopia and Sudan was approved by thirty-seven votes in favour, fourteen against, and seven abstentions. But the whole proposal failed to gain approval because of disagreements over Libya; thus Eritrea avoided partition (Trevaskis 1960, 93). In a final vote on the package, the Bevin–Sforza plan was, ironically, rejected by thirty-seven votes against, fourteen in favour, and seven abstentions. Thus, the partition of Eritrea was averted by mere luck, and a new proposal had to be presented.

At this juncture, all Eritrean parties opposed to union with Ethiopia formed the Independence Bloc and a new round of proposals were made possible, which ended up in the federation decision.

The Eritrean-Ethiopian Federation

The Eritrean–Ethiopian Federation, which was the first of its kind in Africa, was an internal compromise to the division between those who wanted independence and those who wanted unity with Ethiopia. It was also a compromise between the world powers who favoured independence and those who wanted to unite Eritrea to Ethiopia.

On 24 November 1950, the United Nations Ad Hoc Political Committee adopted, by a vote of thirty-eight to fourteen with eight abstentions, the fourteen-power draft resolution containing the plan to federate Eritrea with Ethiopia. The fourteen sponsors of the resolution were Bolivia, Brazil, Burma, Canada, Denmark, Ecuador, Greece, Liberia, Mexico, Panama, Paraguay, Peru, Turkey, and the United States. The General Assembly approved the plan on 2 December in its Resolution 390 (V) by a vote of forty-six to ten with four abstentions(United Nations. and Boutros-Ghali 1996, 9 - 10).

Following the federal act, Eritrean parties who favoured independence accepted it as a compromise and the Independence bloc was changed to the Democratic Front to safeguard it. The federation was born lame and became easy prey for Ethiopia's expansionist desires due to superpowers' interests and intrigues.

John Spencer explained in detail how he and Aklilu Habte Wold tampered with the federal arrangement between Eritrea and Ethiopia so that, rather than a three-level government (federal, Ethiopia, and Eritrea), it ended up with the Ethiopian government assuming the role of federal government (Spencer 2006, 232-7). He further added, "In attaining this formula, we were greatly aided by Stafford and Noyes and the Mexican Ambassador Nervo. Eventually, we agreed on a formula reflecting these solutions for the legislative and judicial branches of the federal government at the same time avoiding all reference to the basic reality that no separate federal government would be established. The elliptical formula covering these matters appears in the final UN resolution 390 V. "They assured us that an agreement was indeed involved: One exclusively between Ethiopia and the Eritrean Assembly. *That very fact divested (deprived) the United nations of all further jurisdiction in the federation* (emphasis mine). If at some time in the future, the Eritrean Assembly and Ethiopia should agree to terminate that agreement, the federation itself would be automatically dissolved without any possible recourse or objection by the United Nations."

The Dismantling of the Eritrean Federation, 1952–1962
As predicted, Ethiopia started from day one to dismantle Eritrea's autonomy and democratic rights guaranteed by the Federation Act. This process intensified with the election as chief executive of Asfaha Woldemichael, who was the most Ethiopian of all Unionists. When Asfaha Woldemichael became the chief executive in Eritrea on 15 September 1955, his job was to dismantle the Eritrean Federation Act from the outset. Zewde Retta (Retta 2014, 472) recalls in a book he wrote on Eritrea that Asfaha wanted to begin by doing the following:

1. Banning Arabic as an official language and replacing it with Amharic.
2. Replacing the Eritrean flag with the Ethiopian flag.

3. Banning the Eritrean government seal and replacing it with that of Ethiopia.
4. Declaring that the position of chief executive was to rotate between Muslims and Christians with the chief executive being appointed by the emperor, instead of being chosen by the assembly. His suggestions also included that if the chief executive was a Muslim, the assembly chair should be a Christian and his deputy a Muslim, and vice versa.

Within six weeks of his term, Asfaha replaced Blatta Demsas Woldemichael, a vice chair of the assembly, with Keshi Demetros, a Unionist hardliner. Blatta Demsas declined to resign. Asfaha's next move was to replace Idris Mohamed Adem with Hamid Faraj Hamid as chair of the assembly (Retta 2014, 474). On the issue of languages, Zewde Retta recounted that Asfaha formed a committee chaired by Tesfayohannes Berhe which recommended to the Eritrean parliament for Tigrinya and Amharic to be the official languages in Eritrea. They expected Idris Mohamed Adem, who was the chair of the parliament, would follow their recommendation and so informed him about their intention in advance. Idris Mohamed Adem, however, alerted all branches of the Muslim League and, to the disappointment of Asfaha and Berhe, was the first to oppose the motion in parliament, leading to the motion being withdrawn. Later, in 1956, the federal government banned the legal Eritrean languages (Arabic and Tigrinya), and Amharic was made the official language. Freedom of the press, political parties, and trade unions were banned. Increasingly more Ethiopians took over government positions, replacing Eritreans. Journalists and independent politicians were harassed and jailed.

Ethiopia soon banned the Eritrean official seals and the coat of arms and, in 1958, lowered the Eritrean flag. There were large student and worker demonstrations in Asmara and other towns opposing the move. In September 1959, Eritrean laws were replaced by the Ethiopian Penal Code, and in May

1960, the name "Eritrean government" was changed to "Eritrean Administration", and the title "chief executive" to "chief administrator". It was under these circumstances that prominent Eritrean politicians headed into exile. The first to leave was Woldeab Woldemariam, who had earlier survived seven assassination attempts on his life. It is interesting to note that the Ethiopian government (after an appeal by Asfaha Woldemichael) gave him a passport and allowed him to leave the country through Asmara Airport (Retta 2014, 384-388).

Exile of prominent politicians
Woldeab proceeded from Sudan to Egypt and started Radio Free Eritrea, which broadcasted in Tigrinya and promoted the cause of independence. The broadcast was closed in 1956 when Haile Selassie supported Egypt during the Suez invasion. Even though he continued to live in Cairo, Woldeab never joined the Eritrean Liberation Front (ELF), which came into existence there in 1960.

The next prominent politicians to leave for exile were Muslim League secretary general Ibrahim Sultan, and Idris Mohamed Adem, the second chairman of the Eritrean Assembly. Idris was elected to the Eritrean Assembly in 1952, and in 1955 became its chairman, but his determined support for independence led to his removal in 1956 under pressure from the Ethiopian government. In March 1959, he left for Sudan, accompanied by Ibrahim Sultan, at the request of members of the Eritrean Students Association in Cairo and Eritreans in the Sudanese army, who wanted him to lead the independence movement. The travel of the two exiles was carefully planned and executed in secret by Eritrean political activists serving in the Sudanese army.

The struggle of workers and students to defend the Federation
The Eritrean labour union called for a strike and demonstrated on 10 March 1958, with a huge turnout. Skirmishes with the

police continued for 5 days, and according to Tzeggay [5], workers were injured and treated in hospital, 9 were killed, and 13 of the wounded became handicapped. Tzeggay recalled that, from 9 May 1957 to 4 April 1961, he was arrested 38 times, after which he left Asmara on 7 July 1962. The union was later banned. Thus, the first democratically formed Eritrean Workers Union, one of the first in Africa, was brought to an end.

Student activities intensified in Asmara and other towns. Abdella Hassen[6] provides a glimpse into that environment, including the student strike of 1965 in Asmara in which he had participated. He explained that he was recruited along with other students by Woldedawit Temesgen and Sium Ogbamichael, who had then secretly returned to Asmara from the field. Because in Leul Mekonnen Secondary School we had a favourable ground, immediately we formed a student organization in the form of cells. Then we expanded to Haile Selassie I Secondary School and we started some cells. After that we passed on to such towns as Dekemhare and Massawa. Also, in the Western Lowlands, there were some activities for the student organization, and by 1967 almost all the towns had student organizations. And through other channels the organizing activities went as far as Addis Ababa. So by this year the student movement was almost intensive and we had relations to each other. The higher body of Asmara of this student movement was called Central Committee, and there were local committees in the schools. For a short time, I was leading the student movement, and for another short time Gerezgiher Tewelde was leading it, and it kept on functioning. There was a contact to the field, but sometimes it got delayed. It was not developed in a way that it ... functioned smoothly.

---

5   Gunter Schroeder interview with Tzeggay Kahsay in Rome, 28 May 1988.

6   Günter Schroeder interview with Abdella Hassan, Kassala, 13 Feb. 1991

New Forms of struggle for liberation

Having exhausted all peaceful means, including appealing to the United Nations, the Eritrean people began to think about other alternatives to assert their rights. On 14 November 1962, Emperor Haile Selassie dissolved the federation between Eritrea and Ethiopia in violation of UN Resolution 390 A(V) of 2 December 1950. He declared Eritrea as a province of Ethiopia, a decision that cost both Eritrea and Ethiopia tens of thousands of lives and incalculable destruction and suffering.

Trevaskis (Trevaskis 1960, 130) noted in 1960 that the Eritrean Muslim accepted a federal association with Ethiopia reluctantly, and he would be the first to resent undue Ethiopian control over his affairs. He added, "The Muslim leaders in Eritrea came to learn the political value of their Islamic connexions during the latter part of the occupation. If they have reasons for discontent, in the future, they will undoubtedly exploit them. Should they do so, their appeals are likely to command Muslim sympathy, entailing the threat of active subversion and encouragement to revolt, not only among Muslims of Eritrea, but among the very much larger Muslim population of Ethiopia, as well."

Killion noted that institutions created by Italy, and the separate consciousness which they fostered, were perpetuated in modified form through the period of Ethio-Eritrean federation, and their destruction was a key factor in catalysing the Eritrean nationalist movement during the 1950s (Killion 1989, 129).

Eritrean Liberation Movement

The most well-known organization of the time with a national character was the ELM, led by Mohamed Saeed Nawd and established on 2 November 1958 in Port Sudan. It was known as *Harakat al-Tahrir al-Eritriya* in Arabic, or in short *Haraka*, and informally known as *Mahber Shewaate* in Tigrinya, in reference to its organizational structure, mainly in Eritrean towns. The Haraka was based on forming seven-member clandestine cells.

The Eritrean Liberation Front (ELF)

There were two main groups that played a major role in the creation of the ELF: Eritrean students in Cairo and Eritreans who were serving in the Sudanese army in the 1950s. It was in Cairo that the oldest Eritrean student club was established in 1951. It introduced the Eritrean people's struggle to the world. This club later bred the ELF, the leaders of the Eritrean liberation struggle, and the General Union of Eritrean Students (GUES). A booklet prepared on the fiftieth anniversary of the establishment of the club in 2002 narrates the journey of the club with historical documents.[7] The students in Cairo were very much influenced by the Arab and international liberation movements. The revolt by Gamal Abdel Nasser and the Free Officers in 1952, which dismantled the monarchy in Egypt, paved the way for political activism in Cairo. Students were also influenced by the Algerian Revolution and by the independence of Sudan in 1956. One of the versions is that the ELF was formed on 7 July 1960 (Mohamed 2016, 15) in a meeting (following several previous meetings) held in Cairo at Hadiget al-Asmak (Fish Garden) in Zemalek. But, according to Idris Galaidos, the meeting was held on 10 July 1960[8].

The founders of the ELF were as follows:
Idris Mohamed Adem (former chair of the Eritrean Parliament), Taha Mohamed Nur (a law graduate from Padova University, Italy), Seid Hussein Mohamed Hussein (a student at Faculty of Arts, al-Azhar University), Idris Osman Galaidos (law graduate, Cairo University), Seid Ahmed Mohamed Hashim (business graduate, Cairo University), Mohamed Saleh Humed (law graduate, Cairo University), Adem Mohamed Ali Akte (graduate, Cairo University) and students: Suleiman Mohamed Ahmed, and Ibrahim Ahmed (nicknamed Blenay),

---

7 https://hedgait.blogspot.com/2016/02/blog-post_26.html
8 Idris Gelaidos interview with Günter Schröder, 11 July 1988.

Mohamed Seid Antata (student). In the meeting, the founders decided to send a delegation to Eritrea to explain the objectives of the new organization and a second one to countries they regarded friendly. The chairman was entrusted with the task of contacting Hamid Idris Awate to begin the armed struggle.

Some Ethiopian scholars have stated that it was Egypt who was behind the establishment of the ELF in order to undermine the Eritrean revolution that was initiated by foreign powers. This claim, however, is not supported by the facts, as the Eritrean independence movement was well entrenched in the 1940s, long before the Egyptian revolt of 1952 that brought Nasser to power. All political parties in the 1940s, except the Unionist Party, sponsored by Ethiopia, had been campaigning for Eritrea's independence.

Conclusion

Many generations of Eritreans have struggled to fulfil the dream of an independent, free and democratic country. Among them, to mention a few, are Bahta Hagos (Akle Guzai), Mohamed Nuri (Saho), and Zamat Wed Ukud (Beni Amer) whose village Ad Zamat still exists close to Mensura. They resisted Italian colonialism. During the 1940s and 1950s prominent nationalists included Abdulgadir Kebire, Ibrahim Sultan, Idris Mohamed Adem and Ras Asberom Tessema and Woldeab Woldemariam. Hamid Idris Awate played a crucial role in the start of the armed struggle. Since the start of the armed struggle, tens of thousands of Eritreans sacrificed their lives for the independence of Eritrea. Eritrea was freed from the Ethiopian occupation on the 24th of May 1991 and became a member of the world community of nations in 1993, yet the struggle for a democratic country continues, unabated.

References

A-Shami, G. A.-D. a. H. G. (2018). The source in History and Narratives of the Afar (Danakil). Cairo, Al Kotob Khan for Publishing and Distribution.

A-Shami Gamaladdin, H. A.-S. (1997). AL-Manhal Fi Tarikh Wa Akhbar AL Afar (Al-Danakil), (The source on History and Narrative of the Afar (Al-Danakil. Cairo, Kamil Graphics.

Abbate, E., A. Albianelli, A. Azzaroli, M. Benvenuti, B. Tesfamariam, P. Bruni, N. Cipriani, R. J. Clarke, G. Ficcarelli, R. Macchiarelli, G. Napoleone, M. Papini, L. Rook, M. Sagri, T. M. Tecle, D. Torre and I. Villa (1998). "A one-million-year-old Homo cranium from the Danakil (Afar) Depression of Eritrea." Nature **393**(6684): 458-460.

Abu Al Hassen, A. M. (1988). Kitab Murewij al Zahab wa Maadin Al Jewhar. Syda, Lebanon, Dar Neshr Al Mektaba Al Asria.

Ahmed, S. A. D. (1894). Futuh Al Habesha or the Conquest of Abyssinia. London, Edinburgh, Williams and Norgate.

Al Magrizi, A. B. A. (1895). Kitab al ilmam Bi Akbar Men Bi Ard Al Habesha Min Muluk Al Islam, Al Talif Printing Press, Egypt.

Alemseged, T. (2001). 'Aӯnfalāla : 'Éretra¯ 1941-1950. Asmara, Eritrea, HIDRI Publishers.

Ali, A. B. A. H. A. (1838). Makhtutet Katib Al Shuna Fi Trarikh Al Sultana Al Sennaria (مخطوطة كاتب الشونة في تاريخ السلطنة السنارية). Cairo, Egypt, Ministry of Culture and National Guidance.

Alvares, F. (1881). Narrative of the Portuguese embassy to Abyssinia during the years 1520-1527. London, Haklut Society.

Anonymous (1912). The Periplus of the Erythrean Sea: Travel and Trade in the Indian Ocean. New York, Longmans, Green and Co.

Arkell, A. (1954). "Four Occupation sites at Agordat." Kush **2**: 33-62.

Beldados, A. (2007). "New perspectives on the Agordat material, Eritrea: A re-examination of the archaeological material in the National Museum, Khartoum." NYAME AKUMA **68**: 4 - 11.

Bent, J. T. (1893). The sacred city of the Ethiopians: being a record of travel and research in Abyssinia in 1893. London, New York, Loghams Green and Co., Longmans, Green and Company.

Bereket, H. S. (1980). Conflict and intervention in the Horn of Africa. New York, Monthly Review Press.

Bereket, H. S. (1989). Eritrea and the United Nations and other essays. Trenton, N.J., Red Sea Press.

Brandt, S. A. M., A.; Perlingieri, C. (2008). Linking the Highlands and Lowlands: Implications of a Test Excavation at Kokan Rockshelter, Agordat, Eritrea. The Archaeology of Ancient Eritrea. P. R. Schmidt, Curtis, Matthew, Zelalem Teka. Trenton (NJ), Red Sea Press. : 33-47.

Crawford, O. G. S. (1951). The Fung Kingdom of Sennar. Gloucester, John Bellows, Ltd.

Curtis, M. C. (2008). New Perspectives for Examining Change and Complexity in the northern Horn of Africa during the First Millennium BCE,. Archaeology of Ancient Eritrea. P. R. Schmidt, Curtis, Matthew, Zelalem Teka. Trenton (NJ), Red Sea Press: 329-348.

Ellingson, L. (1977). "The Emergence of Political Parties in Eritrea, 1941-1950." The Journal of African History **18**(2): 261-281.

Erlich, H. (1997). Ras Alula and the scramble for Africa -a political biography : Ethiopia and Eritrea 1975-1897. Trenton, N.J., Africa World Press.

Fattovich, R. (2000). Aksum and the Habashat : state and ethnicity in ancient northern Ethiopia and Eritrea. Boston, MA, African Studies Center, Boston University.

Fattovich, R. (2004). The 'pre-Aksumite' state in northern Ethiopia and Eritrea reconsidered. Trade and Travel in the Red Sea Region. A. P. Paul Lunde. Oxford: 71-77.

Fattovich, R. (2012). "The northern Horn of Africa in the first millennium BCE: local traditions and external connections." Rassegna di Studi Etiopici, Nuova Serie **Vol. 4**: 1-60.

Gebre-Medhin, J. (1989). Peasants and nationalism in Eritrea : a critique of Ethiopian studies. Trenton, N.J., The Red Sea Press.

Gewald, J. (2000). "Making tribes: social engineering in the Western Province of British administered Eritrea 1941-52." Journal of Colonialism and Colonial History **1**(2): 23.

Guerra, M. D. (1935). Storia Militare Della Colonia Eritrea, 1869–1894. Rome.

Hasan, Y. F. (1965). "The Umayyad Geneology of the Funj." Sudan Notes and Records **46**: 27-32.

Holt, P. M. (1963). "Funj Origins: A Critique and New Evidence." Journal of African History , **4**(1): 39-55.

Killion, T. (1989). "Reviewed Work(s): Italian Colonialism in Eritrea, 1882-1941: Policies, Praxis and Impact by Tekeste Negash." The International Journal of African Historical Studies, Vol. 22, No. 1 1989) **22**(1): 128-130.

Ludolf, J. (1682). A New History of Ethiopia London.

Makki, F. (2011). "Culture and agency in a colonial public sphere: religion and the anti-colonial imagination in 1940s Eritrea." Social History **36**(4): 418-442.

Manzo, A. (2012). "British Museum Studies in Ancient Egypt and Sudan." 18: 75 - 106.

Miguel de Castanhoso, J. B., Gasper Correa (1902). The Portuguese Expedition to Abyssinia in 1541 - 1543 as narrated by Miguel de Castanhoso, Joao Bermudez, Gasper Correa. London, Haklut Society.

Mohamed, A. I. (2016). Adwaa Ala Tejribet Jebhet Al tahrir al Eritrea, Highlights of the Experience of the Eritrean Liberation Front. Birmingham, UK., Seebawaih Publishing Ltd.

Nadel, S. (1945). "Notes on the Beni Amer Society." Sudan Notes and Records **26**(2): 51 - 94.

Nadel, S. F. (1944). Races and Tribes of Eritrea. Beirut?, s.n.

Naty, A. (2000). Environment, society and the state in Southwestern Eritrea. Bergen, CMI.

Naty, A. (2001). "Memories of the Kunama of Eritrea towards Italian colonialism." Africa **56**(4): pp. 573-589.

Omer, M. K. (2020). The Dynamics of an Unfinished African Dream: Eritrea: Ancient History to 1968. USA, LuLu Publishing Services.

Paul, A. (1954). A History of the Beja Tribes of the Sudan. Cambridge, University Press.

Pollera, A. (1913). I Baria e I Cunama. Roma, Roma, Tipografia dell'Unione.

Retta, Z. (2014). Ye Eretra Guday. Addis Ababa, Ethiopia, Shama Books.

Rossini, C. (1913). "Studi su popolazioni dell'Etiopia." Rivista degli studi orientali **6**(2): 365-426.

Schmidt, P. R., M. C. Curtis and Z. Teka (2008). The archaeology of ancient Eritrea. Trenton, NJ, Red Sea Press.

Schmidt, P. R. C., M. C.; Zelalem Teka (2008). The Ancient Ona Communities of the First Mellenium BCE: Urban Precursors and Independent Development On the Asmara Plateau. The Archeology of Ancient Eritrea. P. R. C. Schmidt, M. C.; Zelalem Teka. Trenton (NJ), Red Sea Press: 109 - 161.

Sellassie, S. H. (1972). Ancient and Medieval Ethiopian History to 1270. Addis Ababa, United Printers.

Spencer, J. H. (2006). Ethiopia at bay: A personal account of the Haile Selassie years. Hollywood, Tsehai Publishers.

Taddesse, T. (1972). Church and State in Ethiopia 1270-1527. Oxford, Oxford University Press.

Trevaskis, G. K. N. (1960). Eritrea : a colony in transition : 1941-52. Westport, Conn., Greenwood.

Trimingham, J. (1965). Islam in Ethiopia. New York, Routledge.

United Nations. and B. Boutros-Ghali (1996). The United Nations and the independence of Eritrea. New York, United Nations, Dept. of Public Information.

Venosa, J. L. (2012). ""Because God Has Given Us the Power of Reasoning": Intellectuals, the Eritrean Muslim League, and Nationalist Activism, 1946-1950." Northeast African Studies **12**(2): 29-62.

Venosa, J. L. (2013). ""Serfs," Civics, and Social Action: Islamic Identity and Grassroots Activism during Eritrea's Tigre Emancipation Movement, 1941-1946." Islamic Africa **4**(2): 165-193.

Yagoub, A. B. A. (1980). Kitab Taarikh Al Yagoubi. Beirut, Lebanon, Dar Beirut Lil Tibaa Wel Neshir.

THE RISE AND FALL OF THE ELF AND FORMATION OF ERITREAN NATIONHOOD

Anghesom Atsbaha & Ghirmai Negash

A major irony in the history of Eritrean nationalism's formation is that the Eritrean Liberation Front (ELF), the organization that sparked an armed revolution against the Ethiopian occupation of Eritrea in 1961, became the target of an armed eviction two decades later. In 1981, the ELF's rival Eritrean organization, the Eritrean People's Liberation Front (EPLF), and its then Ethiopian ally, the Tigray Liberation Front (TPLF), collaboratively drove the ELF across the Sudanese border, effectively sealing its military and political demise.[1] The

---

1 The very final days of the ELF were marked by a series of dramatic events, which culminated in killings and arrests of high-ranking leaders and cadres of the organization, in an area called Rasai, a Sudanese territory bordering Eritrea. The killings occurred on March 25, 1982 and were preplanned by Abdalla Idris, the organization's head of the Military Office. In the incident, Melake Tekle, the organization's head of the Security Office was murdered by the perpetrators, and a few others were wounded, including Tekle Melekin, one of the senior political figures of the organization. For a full description of the event, see Tekle Melekin's first-hand, witness account in the link below. In the YouTube link Tekle Melekin is interviewed by Dr. Mohamed Kheir Omer, author of *The Dynamics of an Unfinished Dream* (2020).

ELF's birthing of the Eritrean struggle for independence had helped intensify Eritrean national consciousness politically. Militarily, as the first armed political movement in Eritrea, the ELF developed the idea of a "protracted war" as a strategy of liberation for the country. This led to the emergence of a highly experienced and, according to many observers, one of the most powerful national liberation armies in Africa. The ELF, in its military context, was the sole organization to wage war effectively against the Ethiopian imperial state under Emperor Haile Selassie, from 1961-1971. Between the mid-1970s and 1980s, the ELF was instrumental in liberating a wide swath of the rural countryside and capturing several important cities, including Agordat, Tesseney, Adi Qula, and Mendefera.

By then, the ELF had restructured its small army units into larger units, comprising battalions, brigades, and divisions equipped with modern weapons. Although the history of the ELF and the EPLF has been rightly interpreted as mainly characterized by animosity and rivalry, the ELF also fought alongside EPLF forces in many battles, when leaders of the two organizations temporarily set aside their differences in order to counter massive Ethiopian military campaigns. This was especially true during the 1980s when the two organizations joined forces to counter a major military campaign by the Ethiopian army, under Colonel Mengistu Haile Mariam's military government. That force was heavily armed and supported by the Soviet Union's military arsenal and special advisors, under the leadership of Leonid Ilyich Brezhnev. As stated, the ELF/EPLF rivalry culminated in the demise of the ELF's active military presence in 1981, with the EPLF support from Ethiopia's TPLF (Tigray Liberation Front). Before its organizational collapse, however, the ELF left behind a profound legacy in the military history of Eritrea.

---

https://www.youtube.com/watch?v=7Wm4dL   XFbU0.
Accessed on December 29, 2020.

The Eritrean Liberation Front (ELF) was, however, much more than an armed nationalist movement that played a critical role in the armed struggle in Eritrea between 1961 and 1981. It was also a major political institution and a social force of transformation. After a difficult start in 1961, followed by several tumultuous years that persisted until 1965, the ELF made significant contributions in adopting and practicing national and democratic programs that were implemented experimentally during the struggle, with the anticipation to be expanded in the post-independence era. The organization's political, social, and economic vision was developed and revised in two important ELF National Congresses, held in 1971 and 1975, in the liberated areas of Eritrea. The programmatic plans reflected the complexity of the movement's challenges amid internal divisions and conflicts, often along ethnic, religious, and regional lines – which all contributed to the ELF's final downfall in the 1980s (as we shall see later). At the same time, however, the programs clearly reflected the organization's determination and strenuous efforts, at least at the level of policy, to resolve the prevailing problems and challenges democratically and through dialogue, by all means at its disposal.

In this contributing chapter we seek to explore the question, *"Considering its historically significant politico-military role in the Eritrean struggle for independence, why then ELF disintegrated with such finality?"* In other words, how does one explain, or rather historically interpret, the organization's decline, given its programmatically declared democratic ideals and objectives for the country's independence and post-independence future, as enshrined in its various documents? This is not the first time that such questions have been raised about the ELF's history. Several important works have attempted to tackle the issue, focusing on various aspects of the question. These works also use diverse sources and methods, which necessarily drive the historical interpretations and conclusions of the various authors. A short list of these works, which readers of ELF history likely are familiar with, include: Ibrahim M. Ali (2007); Kidane Mengesteab and Yohannes Okbazghi (2005); Michael W. Tedla (2014); Redie Bereketeab (2007); Tricia R. Hepner (2009); Bereket Habte Selassie (1980, 1989, 2003); Roy Pateman (1990); Drar Mantai et al. (2016); Ruth Iyob (1993); Richard Lobban (1972); Woldeyesus Ammar (2005); John Markakis 1990; and Ibrahim Idris Toteel (unpublished manuscript).

In this chapter, building on the existing scholarship, we seek to add to the accessible information and knowledge about the ELF. The goal is to provide a balanced understanding and assessment of the organization not only as a military entity (which is a common thread in many accessible publications) but also in relation to the immediate and larger political, social, and economic agendas the organization harbored during its active years in Eritrea (1961-1981). To do so, the chapter will highlight the organization's major historical events and look critically at how the ELF sought to respond to its many challenges amid internal and external conditions, both favorable and restrictive, during the movement's active years. As the discussion will show, while replications of policy and practice connected the different historical events of the ELF, a careful look at the discontinuities and ruptures (often emanating from internal weaknesses, mainly group and leadership disagreements, lack of vision, and civil wars) and external pressures (superpower and TPLF interventions) reveal that some of the discontinuities (for example, the introduction of the *Zebene-Kifletat* and its problems) can be interpreted as well-intentioned, corrective changes or measures intended to guarantee the organization's "continuity" during different phases of its history. Methodologically, this project will make extensive use of published and unpublished resource materials in Eritrean languages, mainly Tigrinya and Arabic, in addition to published international resources in English. We believe a systematic use of both resources provides an added value to the scholarship. Considering the significant gap in adequate employment of local-language sources in most research done on Eritrean history, we believe such coalesced use of available texts will help provide a nuanced reconstructed narrative of the ELF's political and social contributions, as well as an understanding of the multi-faceted roles the organization played, especially, in the areas of culture and education. Structurally, the chapter will be organized chronologically focusing on historical events, while integrating overlying elements that stretch across periods.

The Post-Colony of Eritrea, the U.N., and the Emergence of the ELF

Eritrea, like many African nations, came about as a result of European colonization. The territory was under Italian rule for half a century, from 1890-1941. After Italy's defeat and the wholesale surrender of the Italian army to the British in 1941, the Italian post-colony of Eritrea was expected to gain its independence – similar to Libya and Somalia, which were also Italian post-colonies in Africa. Ignoring demands from various Eritrean popular and political constituents, the United Nations decided to federate Eritrea with Ethiopia.

The U.N. decision was resented not only by the Eritreans, it was also widely criticized by various observers from members of the international community. They denounced the U.N. decision for disregarding the nationalist sentiments, wishes, and aspirations of Eritreans to determine their own destiny as an independent national entity. One such international voice who slammed the U.N. handling of the Eritrea situation was Albert Reid. He had served as the administrative finance officer of the U.N. Tribunal on Eritrea. In an interview with a Canadian newspaper in the 1940s, he said, "the tragic loss of life and property (in Eritrea) must be placed at the doorstep of the world organization".[2]

---

2   Albert Reid, a former member of the UN Secretariat wrote an article in a Canadian newspaper, on March 25, 1980.

To be clear, the U.N. decision to join the post-colony of Eritrea with Ethiopia in a federal arrangement was the result of, or was driven by, a complex intersection of internal[3] and

---

3   Lloyd Ellingson, "The Emergence of Political Parties in Eritrea, 1941-1950," *The Journal of African History*, Vol. 18.No.2 (1977), provides an insightful analysis of the complex internal political dynamics of the time. The article shows internal Eritrean divisions about the future of the country and Ethiopia's interventions in support of the unionists. Ellingson writes: "In May 1941, after the Italians' capitulation, the British immediately took over the administration of Eritrea for the duration of the war and until an international body could decide the former colony's future. From 1941 to 1950, the political direction of Eritrea remained uncertain until the U.N. commission reached its compromise solution. Ultimately, the Ethiopian Government contravened the U.N. agreement and unilaterally annexed Eritrea in 1962, which set in motion the present struggle for independence. The British Military Administration, acting as an interim government, attempted with moderate success to create an atmosphere in which all people of Eritrea might have the maximum voice in determining their political future. From the end of the war through the arrival of the U.N. commission in February 1950, there was a flurry of political activity. Although initially five political parties were formed, which in time became splintered and re-emerged as other parties, two main groups could be distinguished along geographical boundaries: the lowlands versus the highlands, separatist Muslims versus irredentist Christians. The historical suspicion and aloofness between Orthodox and Muslims continued to divide Eritrean loyalties. Affiliation, however, with one or another political party was not observed strictly on geographical or religious grounds. A small number of educated Orthodox saw no advantage in Eritrea's incorporation into Ethiopia and thus formed a pocket of Christian separatists who would have undoubtedly obtained greater allegiance had not the Orthodox priesthood threatened excommunication for anyone not espousing the Unionist cause. On the other hand a small nucleus of Muslims, mostly chiefs and landed aristocracy, favored union with the government in Addis Ababa, for their feudalistic hold on the large number of Tigrai serfs (numbering three-fifths of all Muslims in

external factors. However, the United States played a decisive role in the context of evolving global politics, manifested following the end of the Second World War. Emerging as a super-power, the United States, amidst its over-arching Cold War global strategy, wanted to take possession of and repurpose an existing Italian communications base in Eritrea, the "Radio Marina," into a substantial military establishment. In return for its appropriation of the base and the right to use the military installation, that after the American takeover came to be known as the *Kagnew Station*, the United States government actively supported the U.N. sanctioned annexation of Eritrea. The U.S. also provided the Ethiopian state, under the monarchy of Haile Selassie, with a heavy injection of military aid. The *Kagnew Station* and the U.S. aid to Ethiopia began in 1953, and as Robert A. Diamond and David Fouquet Richard revealed in their article "American Military Aid to Ethiopia and Eritrean Insurgency," it was conducted in official and covert ways:

> Both countries were embarrassed by the disclosures in 1970 by a U. S. Senate subcommittee investigating U. S. military bases overseas. The group's detailed findings showed a secretive U. S. commitment which resulted in Ethiopia's receiving more U. S. aid than all African countries combined in recent years. The report questioned whether this generosity was "rent" for the large U. S. communications-intelligence facility in Ethiopia or whether the base might be an executive branch pretext to provide Congress with a rationale for supporting the government of Emperor Haile Selassie.[4]

As Eritreans' discontent with the federalist structure that aligned their country with Ethiopia continued to spread, in

---

Eritrea) would have been retained under Ethiopian rule" ("Extract" from article "Published online by Cambridge University Press: 22 January 2009"). Accessed November 30, 2020.

4   *Africa Today*, Vol. 19, No 1 (Winter, 1972), 1.

1961 the ELF declared an armed struggle against the Ethiopian state, aiming for national independence. It is important to emphasize here that the ELF's armed uprising did not come as an unexpected or spontaneous reaction to Ethiopia's unilateral abolition of the federation agreement in 1962. Rather, for several years the ELF sought to maintain the federal arrangement, or achieve total independence, with a variety of peaceful protests and through diplomacy. Failing in those efforts, in the face of the impending annexationist threat, the ELF started a war as an act of defiance. Backing this view of what happened, historian Akinyote, in his book *Emergent African States*, explains that the armed struggle was a move taken by "some Eritreans [who] formed in 1961 the Eritrean Liberation Front" to "...counter the growing threat of annexation by Ethiopia."[5] And Richard Lobban, who in 1971 visited Eritrea with the ELF in the field established: "In 1961 the underground ELF organization had asked Hamad Idris Awate, a daring liberation fighter, to initiate armed resistance against the Ethiopians, as the only way they could see to possibly restore freedom and dignity to the Eritrean people. Emperor Haile Selassie's response to this move was unilaterally to declare complete annexation of Eritrea on November 14, 1962, and abolishment of the UN resolution".[6]

As a political entity, the ELF was formed in 1960 in Cairo, Egypt. According to Michael W. Tedla, "three groups... played an important role at the initial stage of the Eritrean armed struggle for independence ... [t]hese groups were found among Eritrean students in Cairo, Eritrean members of Sudanese armies, and Eritrean political refugees".[7] The armed struggle

---

5   S. A. Akintoye, *Emergent African States: Topics in20th century African History*. London: Longman Group, 1976.

6   Richard Lobban, 'Eritrean liberation front: A close-up view', *Munger Africana Library Notes*, 1972: 2(13), 10.

7   Michael W. Tedla, *The Eritrean Liberation Front: Social and Political Factors Shaping Its Emergence, Development and Demise 1960-1981* (Master's thesis), 2014.

was led by the aforementioned Hamid Idris Awate. According to a recently published book by Haile Selassie Woldu, ሐምድ ኢድሪስ ዓዋተ: 1915-1962 (2018), Awate formerly served with the Italian colonial army and had some international exposure, including traveling to Italy. According to the same book, by the time he assumed the leadership, Awate had also earned a reputation as a fighter and leader. During the transition years of 1941 to 1961, he fought against both British and Ethiopian presences in Eritrea, interchangeably operating as a "fugitive" and political rebel. On Awate's return from Italy, the Italian administration in Eritrea appointed him as a security officer in the Western lowlands of Eritrea, and later promoted him to the rank of a deputy-governor of the Sudanese city of Kassala in 1940-1941, when it briefly came under Italian rule. Awate grew up in a culturally mixed family, with parents from the Nara and Tigre ethnic groups, and spoke several local languages as well as Arabic and Italian. Although no available research indicates whether that ethnic heritage played a role in the ELF's political leadership in Cairo's decision to elevate his role, it seems in retrospect that, alongside his military and leadership qualities, Awate must have made a perfect candidate when they put him in charge as a leader of the armed struggle for national independence in a country with such diverse ethnicity.

For the first few years, the ELF had a limited military reach into the different regions of Eritrea. Nonetheless, the launching of an armed struggle was a historical milestone. Representing the deepest aspiration of the Eritrean people, it gained their whole-hearted support.[8] As Eritrean author Redie Bereketeab explained, "the making of Eritrea was fundamentally the result of the actions of two groups of collective actors – the colonial powers and the nationalist movements. ELF was the heart and mind of the movement, representing the national sentiment of the Eritrean people, as well as representing the various ethnic

---

8   'Eritreans for Liberation in North America', July, 1978.

and religious groups throughout the country".[9] Similarly, the American author Tricia R. Hepner, who found the ELF's history largely erased from authorized chronicles of Eritrean nationalism, expounded on the enduring influence of the organization, noting that even now, several decades after its disappearance the ELF's memory continue among many while its history stays under-researched.

> Today, many Eritreans, both Christian and Muslim, retain an emotional connection to ELF (if not always a political, programmatic one) but have found little in narratives of nationalism or nationalist history that genuinely values ELF's contribution to the independence struggle and the nation-state. Rather, the ELF remains woefully under examined in the scholarly literature except as a negative foil for the EPLF".[10]

A Decade of Armed Struggle and Political Maturation: ELF (1961-1969)

The early military activities mainly included attacks on selected enemy posts and events, and clearing passageways between major roads connecting towns. While the armies of the ELF and Ethiopia fought many small, guerilla-warfare style battles and skirmishes, some of the ELF's major operations targeted national and international arenas. In 1972, the American writer Richard Lobban provided the following account of the geography, purpose, and impact of the organization's military actions:

> One of the ELF's more significant military actions took place on November 7, 1966, when seventeen Eritrean towns were

---

9   Redie Bereketeab, *Eritrea: The Making of a Nation. 1890-1991.* Trenton, NJ: Red Sea Press, 2007.

10 Tricia R. Hepner, *Soldiers, Martyrs, Traitors, and Exiles. Political Conflict in Eritrea and the Diaspora.* Philadelphia: University of Pennsylvania Press, 2009, p.37-38.

simultaneously attacked at midnight while an OAU summit conference was being held in Addis Ababa. This was designed to focus world attention on the Eritrean struggle. Another action occurred on March 25, 1967, when a notorious official from the Ministry of the Interior was shot and killed. During a large-scale Ethiopian offensive, the ELA [i.e., ELF army] reported 793 Ethiopian soldiers killed, while their own losses were relatively slight. In March 1969 the ELF blew up an Ethiopian Airlines plane at Frankfurt, Germany. In June of the same year another plane was attacked in Frankfurt and one was damaged in Karachi. In September a plane was hijacked to Khartoum and one to Aden. In December another hijack attempt was foiled over southern Europe. These events brought world attention to Eritrea. On May 17 and May 19 of 1969, railway tracks and bridges were destroyed between Djibouti and Ethiopia; an explosion occurred at the Ethiopian Consulate in Djibouti and another bomb exploded at the Central Bank in Addis Ababa.[11]

From a political-strategic point of view, the major military action that marked a turning point in ELF's history was the battle of *Togorba* (March 15, 1964). The battle was remarkable in its magnitude as well as in the composition of the soldiers on both ends of the fighting. On the Eritrean side, this was the first time the combatants had faced the Ethiopian military, instead of the police force they had been engaging before. As Muhammad Ali Idris ("Aburjela"), then commander of the ELF units, explained in an interview, the Ethiopian infantry was composed of soldiers who had returned from the international wars in "Congo and Korea," and were, in stark contrast to the ELF army, outfitted with superior equipment

---

11 Richard Lobban, 'Eritrean liberation front: A close-up view', *Munger Africana Library Notes*, 1972: 2(13), 12.

and international combat experience.[12] It was a particularly bloody war, with casualties suffered during the battle and horrible scenes unfolding in the aftermath. According to Aamer S. Hagos who compiled the document for this website source (March 15, 2019), "in this battle, 84 officers and soldiers from the enemy side were killed, and 22 were seriously wounded who most of them died shortly thereafter. From the brave Eritrean army, 18 fighters were martyred and 3 others were wounded. The defeated and coward Ethiopian army tampered with the corpses of the brave martyrs in public domains until they were rotten and mutilated. The corpses of 6 martyrs were hanged in Aqordat, 6 in Keren, 3 in Barentu and 2 in Haikota".[13]

ELF's military victory at Togorba shifted the balance of political power in its favor. It greatly boosted morale for the combatants and the people, improving Ethiopia's understanding of the magnitude and combat capability of the ELF.[14] Inspired by that success, new recruits from different regions and ethnic groups in Eritrea joined the ELF ranks, substantially increasing the size of its army to about 1000 combatants by 1965. However, the increase in numbers also created new pressures. Political tensions and clashes emerged between the "old" and "new" generation of fighters, often along religious and ethnic lines.

To resolve these emerging conflicts, a meeting with ELF fighters and leaders were held in 1965 in Kassala, Sudan. They agreed to reform the organization's structure with a military organizational model that was attempted in Algeria by the

---

12 http://www.togoruba.org/togoruba1964/mainTogorubamap/mainMap/headingMap/2019/1403AA9-04AE.pdf.　Accessed November 8, 2020.

13 Ibid.

14 'The "Battle of Togoruba" 15 March 1964 Martyr fighter Muhammad Ali Idris (Aburjela)', prepared by Aamer S.Hagos 15 March 2019.　http://www.togoruba.org/togoruba1964/mainTogorubamap/mainMap/headingMap/2019/1403AA9-04AE.pdf. Accessed November 8, 2020.

Algerian Liberation Front, the FLN, during the war of independence against colonial France between 1954 and 1962. Based on the Algerian experience of the "Wilayas" (zonal or regional system), the ELF army was divided into five regional forces, known as the *Zemene Kiflitaat*. According to the thinking, each regional headquarter would stay aligned under the central authority of the organization's top command, called the "Supreme Council." The introduction of the "Zonal System" helped diffuse tensions between groups, at least temporarily, and also enabled each regional headquarter to independently recruit fighters and expand its base of supporters from ethno-linguistic communities faithful to them. However, in the long run the disadvantages outweighed the gains. It became increasingly difficult to sustain coordination between the "Supreme Council" and regional leaders. This problem was compounded by charges of nepotism, uneven distribution of resources, and outright financial corruption. These issues solidified simmering misgivings between and within regional headquarters, and ultimately undermined the authority of the central command structure of the organization. The reformist-oriented "Final Statement" of the *Adobha Conference* (August 25, 1969) of the Eritrean Liberation Front, provides the following reconstruction of the experience:

> In 1965, the revolution entered a new stage when the leaders decided to divide the army into four, and later five, separate military commands meant to widen the military strategy and expand the revolution in all parts of Eritrea. Though the five commands played a role in disseminating the message of armed struggle in all parts of the country, the zonal structure was left unchanged for a long time, and this caused disunity in the army. Such structure also resulted in the isolation and stagnation of political work for more than three years.[15]

---

15 'Final Statement Adobha Conference', August 25, 1969.

The Reformist Movement and Aftermath: The *Adobha and Awate Conferences* (1969-1971)

Several official and covert political attempts were made to correct the mistakes of the *Zemene Kiflitaat* (the region based zonal system), replacing it with democratic improvements to the failing authority of the "Supreme Council". Crucial in the endeavor was organizing by left-leaning reformist elements within the ELF at the *Adobha Conference*, convened between August 10 and August 25 of 1969, in the liberated areas of Eritrea. In her critically acclaimed book, *The Eritrean Struggle for Independence: Domination, Resistance, Nationalism, 1941-1993*, Ruth Iyob, an Eritrean-born American political scientist, asserts that a series of meetings were held (including the Anseba Conference on September 11, 1968, which culminated in unifying three of the five zonal commanders) that led to the launching of the rectification movement aimed at overhauling the entire organizational structure.[16] Iyob adds: "the reform was directed against the dictatorship of the Zone Commanders, the abuse of civilians, and the corruption of the leadership in exile". In ELF oral history, the *Adobha Conference* is remembered as a herculean effort. It was held under immensely challenging conditions, on the one hand, engendered by hardline conservative elements in the Supreme Council who resisted change, and on the other by the emergence of factions that threatened to splinter off and separate from the ELF. A retrospective reading of Eritrean history clearly shows that the *Adobha Conference* did not have sufficient political leverage to reconcile the accumulating contradictions within the movement. Nonetheless, the *Adobha Conference* marked "an end of an era and the beginning of another".[17] It represented an

---

16 Ruth Iyob, *The Eritrean Struggle for Independence: Domination, resistance, nationalism, 1941-93*. Cambridge University Press, 1995, p. 21.

17 http://www.ehrea.org/adob.htm (original source: From the Experiences of the Eritrean Liberation Army (ELA) Part VIII and Final by 'Nharnet Team' (Jan 13, 2005).

undeniable victory that defined the future of the front. The conference, at least in our view, was instrumental – for the first time in the history of the Eritrean liberation movement history – in proposing democratic processes and principles as a fundamental way of resolving conflicts. The conference highlighted the necessity to 1) establish a provisional General Command to replace the Supreme Council; 2) convene a national congress within one year; and 3) create a commission of inquiry to investigate past mistakes; unify the divided army; and restrict the powers of the Supreme Council.

Some critics of the outcome of the conference assigned blame to the reformist groups' inability to curtail the influence of the Supreme Council on the outcome of the conference. They also contend that an acrimonious atmosphere with a high level of mistrust among groups hindered the potential success of the conference. The problem with this kind of hindsight reasoning, however, is that it conveniently disregards a significant historical fact: one of the democratic achievements of the conference was that it was organized without consulting the Supreme Council. This was quite a bold step at this time. As the late Abdelkader Romodan, one-time Chief of Staff of the ELF army, and architects of the *Adobha Conference*, once was heard talking about his experience that Adobha was regarded as the final hope (1976). That's why the "conscious militants" pushed for it to succeed amid the substantial constraints.[18] Michael W. Tedla validates this line of argument in his records of the movement's democratic composition and objectives. He reveals that the conference was a result of an initiative undertaken by a grass-root "Committee of Fighters," which

---

18 In 1976, Abdel Kadir Romodan was in Akelguzay to reorganize the Eritrean Liberation Army and he was asked about his experience of the late 1960s, including his role in Adobha. (From personal recollections of Anghesom Astbaha.)

together with another group commonly known as *Eslah*, devoted themselves to "rectifying the problems". [19]

The democratic achievements of the *Adobha Conference* were nonetheless bound by internal limits on the degree of that success. The conference was attended by 101 strong delegates, exclusively composed of combatants. It also established a new 38-member leadership, the "General Command," mainly referred to by its Arabic name, *Al Qiyadah Al Ama*. In other words, the conference and the newly created leadership did not include civilians. Additionally, the physical and political circumstances of the conference prevented organizers from producing democratically elected members to serve in the new leadership, the General Command. Instead, its members were pre-selected by the fighters in their respective regional zones. Another controversial factor (though understandable considering the precarious political environment) was that the General Command retained the Supreme Council with its powers until the first National Congress could be organized. Equally contentious was the decision that while part of the General Command, three zones were allocated a total of 18 seats, two other zones –namely zones one and two – were allocated 10 seats each. The latter decision was taken as an act of political goodwill toward those two regions to mollify underlying sensitivities.

The *Adobha Conference* was followed by the *Awate Camp Conference*, held two years later, from February 26 to March 25 of 1971. At this conference, participants planned out all of the groundwork for a national congress. The conference's optimistic final statement declared:

> From this spot at which more than 300 fighters representing all sections of the ELA and its various organs congregated; where all questions of the revolution were put forward and

---

19   Michael W. Tedla, *The Eritrean Liberation Front: Social and Political Factors Shaping Its Emergence, Development and Demise 1960-1981* (Master's thesis), 2014, p. 84.

exhaustively discussed in an atmosphere characterized by revolutionary spirit, clarity, frankness and responsibility; this spot at which all problems hitherto unanswered were consciously dealt with and handled with full awareness of the situation; from the Awate Camp, we come out with historic statement which represents a big leap forward and genuine start for building the revolution on correct and scientific basis which lacked throughout the past stages of the struggle. This statement shall constitute a conscious review and practical complement to the tasks whose foundation have been laid down by the resolution of the Adobha Military Conference of August 1969.[20]

The *Awate Camp Conference* is also credited with recognizing the voices and demands of the ELA to find a national forum to unify all Eritrean factions. And in practice, a "Dialogue Committee" was established to contact splinter groups. The highly respected veteran ELF leader Ibrahim Mohamed Ali, in an interview available in Tigrinya, said the following about the committee and its trials:

ጉባኤ ዓዋተ :ምስተን ዝተፈንጨላ ሽነኻት ዝዛተያ ብዙሓት ሽማግለታት አቚሙ ነይሩ'ዩ:: እታ አነ ዝመርሓ ዝነበርኩ ንቐዳማይ ሃገራዊ ጉባኤ እተሰናድእ ሽማግለ ውን አካል ናይ'ዚን ሽማግለኤ ዘተታት እዚአተን ኮይና ተንቀሳቒሳን ኢያን:: እንተኾነ ግን፡ እቶም ተፈንጨልቲ አብ'ቲ ምእንቲ ሓድነት ዝግበር ፈተነታት ክሳተፉ ስለዘይደልዮን፤ ናቶ ውድብ ከምስርቱ ስለዘወሰኑን፤ ዝግበርናዮ ጻዕርታት ኩሉ ክዕወት አይከአለን፡ :[21]

(The Awate Conference had created several committees to negotiate with the faction groups. Also, the preparatory committee for the First National Congress, which I was leading, was an active part of the dialogue committees. However, because the splinter groups did not want

---

20 'Awate Camp Conference Statement', February 26 1971 - March 13, 1971.

21 'Interview with Ibrahim Mohammed Ali', former member of ELF Executive Committee. Interviewed by Mohammed Idris Abdalla in Syria. (Text in Tigrinya translation was obtained from Anghesom Astbaha's private archives.)

to participate in the attempts aimed at unity, and because they wanted to create their own organization(s), all our efforts could not succeed.)

ELF's Prominence Amidst a Bitter Civil War with the EPLF (1971-1974)

Between 1971 and 1974, the ELF's reputation grew significantly, inside and outside of the country. Its popularity was a result of intertwined factors, of which the following arguably can be considered the most salient. First, having successfully convened its First National Congress in 1971, the ELF was able to canvass broad popular support based on the democratic appeal of the "National Democratic Program" that emerged from the Congress. Second, in contrast to earlier years, many Eritreans recognized the leadership elected in the 1971 First National Congress as more diverse and better equipped to lead the revolution's objectives to fruition. Third, in addition to the increased publicity the ELF won by stepping up its military operations against the Ethiopian army in rural areas as well as urban centers, the organization – supported by other African and Arab liberation movements and some sympathetic governments – managed to open semi-official offices in foreign lands and tell the world about Ethiopian atrocities and the legitimacy of the Eritrean people's struggle for self-determination. From a nationalist perspective, the 1970s were also the saddest years for the people of Eritrea. In 1973 and 1974, the ELF and its main rival, the EPLF, fought a bitter civil war. The two-year war was a serious setback to building the nationalist political project, with its long-term goal of nation-formation. This created ample mistrust, despair, and disappointment among the Eritrean people.

The destructive nature of the 1973-1974 civil war with its far-reaching consequences is a theme that recurs in many publications, both in Eritrean and international languages. Reading those publications, one can clearly recognize that the civil war was fought to address historical grievances on both sides, whatever the justifications. In many accounts of the war, one also observes a tendency toward apportioning praise to one side of the conflict and blame to the other. To put it more strongly, during our research, we did not come across much literature that treats the conflict in a comprehensively "non-partisan" fashion. We recognize that historical narratives and studies, including our own, are built on available information and knowledge but also carry along their authorial ideological stances and individual biases. With that being said, in this section of the chapter we want to briefly comment on two aspects of the war. First, neither of the warring sides in this conflict was "more genuinely nationalist," a proposition favored by pro-ELF authors, such as Habtegiorgis Abraha in *Eritrean Pride: Melake Tekle* (2019); or "more progressive and leftist", a point often emphasized by pro-EPLF authors such as Dan Connell. It is difficult for us to believe that the 1973-1974 civil war was driven by any discernable ideological differences, after closely observing the unmistakable streak of political pragmatism and opportunistic shifting of alliances, notably by top leaders such as Isaias Afwerki (the EPLF strong man and current president of Eritrea, who to date continues to practice a dangerous and self-centered politics). Another point, which is not widely known, is that the war was halted toward the end of 1974 primarily due to internal pressure within the ELF ranks to make peace with the EPLF. The pressure came from a dissenting group of ordinary fighters who rejected fighting a "fraternal war". The call of the dissenting group to stop the fratricide also won support from a similarly concerned assembly of civilians, who met frequently in the vicinities of Asmara to help the fronts sort out their disagreements. The intervention of civilian activists, who worried that more bloodshed could endanger the life of the revolution, was crucial. It was essential at this phase of the revolution that they step in and play their role as mediators, which forced both organizations to come together and resolve their conflict through dialogue and peaceful means.

The Good Years of the ELF (1975-1978)

Coming out of the 1973-1974 civil war, the ELF once again rose to prominence, proclaiming unity as its main priority. The ELF's numbers dramatically increased, drawing thousands of students and youth especially from the Christian highlands, but also from refugee camps in Sudan. They arrived en masse to join the Eritrean struggle. The number of women joining the struggle also increased dramatically, which contributed to changes in age, gender, and ethnic demographics of the revolution. Adding to its ranks, in 1975 the ELF succeeded in freeing 1,000 Eritrean political prisoners from Ethiopian jails in Eritrea, through covert military operations. Among the freed political prisoners were not only prominent ELF members, such as Seyuum Ogbamichael (renowned for his dazzling rhetorical skills, and later Chairman of the General Union of Eritrean Peasants) and Woldedawit Temesgen (distinguished for his unbending patriotism, and later Provincial Administrator, and Brigade Commander); but also EPLF fighters such as Haile Diruu Woldetensae, who ended up becoming the Foreign Minister of Eritrea (but later jailed again, this time by Isaias Afwerki for his involvement with the anti-government opposition group G-15 in 2001). The rescue mission of prisoners by the ELF was covered by the *New York Times*, with a cover story that proclaimed, "1,000 Inmates Escape With Guerrillas' Help" (*New York Times* February 15, 1975).

Amidst these new developments, the ELF organized its second National Congress in 1975. The Congress drew combatants and representatives of mass trade unions and community members from across the country and abroad. The Congress adopted a comprehensive and consensual national democratic political program. The national democratic program of 1975 offered the social base of the organization, and Eritreans in general, a strong package complete with a display of democratic and progressive ideals. These included: democratization of landownership, the right of workers to form trade unions, protections for women's rights, and the "removal of all historical prejudices against women", free access to education and medical care to all, and the creation of institutions to take care of war veterans and orphans.[22]

On the ground, one of the major achievements of the ELF was opening the "School of Political Cadres." Between 1975 and 1981, hundreds of fighters and civilians received training in political matters and learned administrative skills. While figures for all of those years are difficult to obtain, in 1978, 118 individuals participated in a 45-day seminar on the role of mass organizations in the revolution. In 1980, a group of 146 political cadres completed a four-month intensive course. After completion, the political cadres were assigned as political commissioners in the army, or to work with the public engaging with organization, dialogue, and dissemination of information and orientation that characterized and sustained the political culture of the organization. The ELF "School of Political Cadres" was started in 1973 but upended its operations to cope with the ever-expanding goals that the ELF needed to accomplish. In the words of then Security Chief Melake Tekle, "raising the political consciousness of the masses to a very high level [was considered] a determining factor to accomplishing the tasks of the national democratic revolution".[23] In the area of information, the ELF also reorganized its capacity and, under the competent direction of the late poet Tesfamariam Woldemariam, who was then the head of the Department of Information, began publishing magazines and bulletins in three languages; Tigrinya, Arabic, and English. The Tigrinya language publications especially are remembered as paramount contributions in the development of local language writing, as well as believed to represent "some of the most powerful

---

22 'Eritrean Liberation Front: Political Programme Approved by the National Congress of the ELF', Liberated Areas, May 22, 1975.
23 *Eritrean Newsletter* Issue #39, April 1980.

African language journals produced by a resistance movement on the continent during the 1970s and 1980s".[24]

Between April and December of 1977, all of the major Eritrean towns were liberated by the ELF and the EPLF. As pointed out in the introduction to this chapter, between 1975 and 1978 the two groups fought in a united front to counter Ethiopian military campaigns in Eritrea. The collaboration was especially strong in 1978 when the Ethiopian military government, under the *Derg*, intensified its operations in Eritrea with the support of the Soviet Union.

The ELF army liberated the towns of Teseney, Mendefera, Agordat, and Adi Quala. After liberation, the fertile agricultural areas of Tekreret and Engerne, near the town of Teseney, were allocated to the poor and landless peasants of the surrounding areas. Although not fully operational, setting up cooperative farms and banks in the liberated villages and towns was also a priority for the ELF. As stated in an editorial in one of several magazines published by the ELF, "revolutionary war is not only a military and political confrontation but also an economic combat. Eritrean Liberation Army fights and produces".[25]

In the areas liberated by the ELF, its educational programs aimed to ameliorate people's lives during the struggle and after. By the end of 1978, 138 schools, with more than 14,000 enrolled students, were set up and run under the supervision of the ELF.[26] In tandem with this, literacy classes, as well as workshops and specialized courses (which included nursing, veterinary, agriculture, auto mechanic, music, and photography), were established, both for the army and the public.

---

24 Ghirmai Negash, "In Memoriam: Eritrea's Tesfamariam Woldemariam, in: http://www.warscapes.com/poetry/ memoriam-eritreas-tesfamariam-woldemariam. Accessed on November 29.

25 *Gedli Hzbi Eritra*, September 1979.

26 *Eritrean Revolution*, Vol. 3 No.2, September 1978.

Similarly, the ELF worked in tandem with refugee and mass organizations to provide resources and organizational support. In addition to the existing unions (Eritrean Students Union, Eritrean General Women's Union, and the General Union of Eritrean Workers) new unions for youth and peasants were formed. Civil organizations drew members across the country, as well as from around the world. Together with official representatives, they acted as ambassadors of the ELF in garnering international diplomatic and public support, along with material resources. They also collected money that the ELF depended on to feed its army and run the various economic, social, and educational programs in the liberated zones described above. At some point in the decade, the ELF also established a semi-independent "Red Cross and Crescent" society as a platform from which to secure humanitarian aid. It was set up with the particular aim to aid refugees in the Sudan and Eritrea to specifically take care of Ethiopians in Prisoner of War (POW) camps. Their numbers had increased considerably during the liberation of the cities, and after the major advances of Soviet-assisted Ethiopia into Eritrea in 1978. The Ethiopians' major victory over the Eritrean fronts (ELF and EPLF) in the summer of 1978 resulted in the recapturing of Eritrean cities and a "*strategic retreat*" of the movement, but also left thousands of captured Ethiopian soldiers in the hands of the ELF, many of them wounded, putting extra burden on the ELF's scant resources.

The "Strategic Retreat", New Cycle of Civil War, and the Last Years of the ELF (1978-1981)

We started this chapter by stating a central aim to seek and explore the question of why the ELF could not prevail, defending itself and its achievements, given the national democratic orientation and the progressive political, economic, and socio-cultural practices emanating from its principles. Put in simpler terms, what factors led to its fall, despite its historical popularity and contributions to the Eritrean struggle for self-determination?

One important cause was the loss of the liberated cities to the *Derg* in 1978. This was a crucial military setback that forced the ELF to declare a *"strategic retreat"* and move its base and forces to far remote locations, alienating it from large populations of the country. The withdrawal left many of the combatants and civilian supporters demoralized, creating discord and disagreements about the capability and wisdom of the leadership in handling various issues, and especially in the area of foreign policy. Prior to the 1978 Ethiopian takeover of the cities, there was a widespread suspicion that some, if not all, of the ELF leaders were particularly keen to resolve the Eritrean question by reaching a negotiated agreement with the *Derg* authorities. Ironically, this was going to happen with the mediation of the former countries of the Soviet Union and East Germany (the GDR), countries that fully backed the *Derg* and were ultimately instrumental in crushing the Eritrean revolution's gains. The actual contents of the alleged agreement (or even if they existed at all) are uncertain,[27] but whatever the case, this did not sit well with rank-and-file fighters, and many important members and political figures stationed in the field and abroad.

Another important factor that contributed to the weakening of the ELF after the "strategic retreat" was its inability to find alternative ways of reinventing itself. For example, the ELF maintained larger organizational structures and units of its army, rather than looking for models that would allow flexibility and efficiency. Although the ELF Executive

---

27 Former ELF Chief of Foreign Office, Mr. Abdella Suleiman, in his keynote speech at the "ELF Reunion Conference," held in Denver, Colorado, in the Summer of 2017, confirmed the contacts made between the *Derg* and the ELF, through the mediation of the former states of the Soviet Union and East Germany (DDR). It is also significant to note that similar contacts between the EPLF and the *Derg* had occurred.

Committee conducted a number of meetings, it became clear that it had no backup plan to deal with the major crisis it found itself in. Instead, leaders fell into quibbling and back-and-forth accusations against one another, often as a prelude to strengthening their own power at the expense of comrades. In the most extreme cases, leadership disunity trickled down to lower echelons, triggering divisions and a sense of general helplessness among fighters and professional personnel. Throughout this time, the overwhelming majority of ELF fighters and leaders fervently wished to renew the organization and continue with the struggle. However, the pervasive dissatisfaction had eroded the moral and resiliency of many of the ELF members and in different ways. Consequently, a good number of combatants and high-level professional elements abandoned the ELF, further diminishing the numbers and capacity of the organization.

The last blow to the ELF, however, came from the EPLF. In 1980, in a new cycle of the civil war, the ELF met its abrupt demise after the EPLF, this time supported by the TPLF, launched an all-out attack against it. As outlined in earlier sections of this chapter, the Eritrean struggle for nationhood had been characterized by the bold faith and resiliency of its people and the defiant tenacity of its fighters, but also had been shaped negatively by a variety of setbacks, prompted both by external invasions and internal infighting. The elimination of the ELF marks one of the major tragic episodes in Eritrean history. Indeed, as Roy Pateman wrote in 1998, the continued hostility and violence had a compelling and long-lasting effect: "Until 1980, the EPLF and ELF waged a bitter civil war, a war which reflected badly on both parties; such fighting also seriously affected the chances of success for the war of national liberation. In the view of some writers the impact was permanent".[28]

---

28 Pateman, *Eritrea: Even the Stones are Burning.* Trenton, NJ: Red Sea Press, 1978, p. 7.

Pateman's reflective comment illuminates the setbacks and prolonged suffering of the Eritrean people that resulted from the recurring and senseless civil war(s) that culminated in the extinction of the ELF. The defeat of the ELF delayed the "success of liberation". It took the EPLF a decade of costly fighting against the Ethiopian state to achieve independence. It also exacerbated the deeper divisions in Eritrean society, along ethnic and religious lines, highlighting the fragility of nation-building in a multi-ethnic and multi-religious society.

At the time of this chapter's writing, November 2020, history is repeating itself – some forty or so years later. Another atrocious civil war is under way between the Ethiopian central state and the TPLF. The observation by Pateman further reveals a repetitive and unsettling trend on the part of the EPLF and its leader, Isaias Afwerki. In this Ethiopian civil war, the EPLF is fighting on the side of the government of Ethiopia's Abiy Ahmed, in a bid to crush the TPLF, its one-time ally, in much the same way that it did in the 1980s when it eliminated the ELF by aligning with its now declared enemy, the TPLF. Among the many articles written to comprehend the dynamics of this seemingly curious shifting of alliances in the Horn of Africa, *Al-Jazeera* reported this explanation:

The mutual animosity between Eritrea's longtime ruler Isaias Afwerki and the TPLF goes back decades – but it was not always like this. From the mid-1970s to the early 1990s, the Eritrean People's Liberation Front (EPLF), which Isaias co-founded, and the TPLF were brothers-in-arms in the long struggle against Ethiopia's military government led by Mengistu Haile Mariam.[29]

However, if any lesson can be drawn from the history of the ELF, it is that, despite the weaknesses within, the ELF's final fall ultimately came from without, from the machinations of the EPLF. In a broader sense, the history also reiterates the

---

29 https://www.aljazeera.com/news/2020/11/8/fears-on-eritreas-secret-role-in-ethiopias-brewing-civil-war. Accessed November 27, 2020.

lesson that the recurring differences and conflicts between and within Eritrea and Ethiopia have seldom been managed or negotiated peacefully by their leaders. To score grievances, they have selfishly and cynically plunged their people into ruinous and bloody wars, by shifting alliances whenever it suits them, with the sole purpose of prolonging their rule and power.

THREE DECADES OF AUTHORITARIANISM: CHALLENGES ON ERITREANISM, NATIONAL IDENTITY AND SOVEREIGNTY

Abdulrazig K. Osman

Introduction

The Ethiopian prime minister, Abiy Ahmed, ordered Ethiopian National Defence Forces to commence a military offensive against Ethiopia's northern region (Tigray), which was controlled by the Tigray People's Liberation Front (TPLF), on 4 November 2020. The order seems to have caught most of the world by surprise[1]. Regardless of the ample indicators of the deteriorating relationship and tension between the federal authorities in Addis Ababa and the regional government in Tigray's capital Mekelle, the surprise is plausible. This plausibility stems from the fact that Abiy Ahmed, just a year ago, was awarded the Nobel Peace Prize for his effort at making peace with his neighbouring country, Eritrea, transcending the enmity that had characterised the relationship between these two countries for almost two decades since the Algiers Agreement was signed in 2000. Indeed, very few people

---

1 The then-deputy army chief of Ethiopia's ENDF stated that Ethiopia 'entered into an unexpected war': https://www.aljazeera.com/news/2020/11/5/ethiopias-conflict-continues-as-pm-vows-further-operations.

expected a war to be declared by a Nobel Peace Prize laureate who, in his acceptance speech stated,

> War is the epitome of hell for all involved. I know, because I have been there and back. I have seen brothers slaughtering brothers on the battlefield. I have seen older men, women, and children trembling in terror under the deadly shower of bullets and artillery shells.[2]

Nevertheless, for Eritreans, particularly those who are striving to bring about democratic change in their country and who have looked sceptically at the rapprochement between Abiy Ahmed and Eritrean President Isaias Afwerki, the ongoing war in Ethiopia was not a surprise. To them, this war was the very underlying aim of the Abiy-Isaias friendship; in other words, it was in the making since the signing of the agreement that qualified the former for the Nobel Peace Prize[3].

Eritreans' anticipation of this war was not mere prophesying or an ill wish stemming from desperation, but an affirmation based on five decades of knowing, working with and for, and observing and studying one of the parties of the agreement. As mentioned in this book's Introduction, Eritreans might not know Abiy Ahmed, but they know Isaias very well. Among the many characteristics Eritreans know their president has, is that he is incapable of living peacefully or making peace with others or for others. Therefore, the moment they saw Abiy Ahmed signing a deal with Isaias without adequate consultation and coordination with the regional governments bordering Eritrea, namely Tigray and Afar, Eritreans suspected that the deal was sinister. In an elite forum that was held in

---

2 Abiy Ahmed's Nobel Peace Prize acceptance speech can be found here:
   https://www.nobelprize.org/prizes/peace/2019/abiy/109716-lecture-english/.

3 Check the introductory chapter that was written before the war broke out, where you will find clear indicators that this war was coming.

Addis Ababa on 25 March 2019, the former Eritrean ambassador, Haile Menkerios, raised the alarm, stating, 'Peace is not the absence of war and it has to be institutionalised, it cannot be personalised, it cannot be directed against their enemies or what they want weakened but toward what they need to build[4]'.

Eritreans fought for thirty years for an independence that cost the country around one hundred thousand martyrs and millions of refugees and internally displaced people, and this was followed by war with Yemen and a deadly war with Ethiopia between 1998 and 2000. Therefore, they have every right to be paranoid about the potential for war in the region. Nonetheless, Eritreans' concern that the peace agreement between Abiy and Isaias might lead to war with TPLF transcends this justified paranoia and goes to the heart of Isaias's long-awaited dream of being the region's kingmaker, if not king. In his endeavour to realise his dream, Isaias is willing not only to kill, jail or exile his perceived adversaries – as he has been doing for the last five decades – but also to compromise Eritrean identity and the country's sovereignty. Isaias's attempts to weaken Eritrean identity and compromise sovereignty is not a notion that suddenly emerged in association with the peace deal between Abiy and Isaias; it is a process that started long before the deal was signed. The peace agreement between Abiy-Isaias served only as a significant moment in Isaias' trajectory towards his dreams. Therefore, although the phrase 'Eritrea is in a critical conjuncture' is a common and overused cliché in the Eritrean political literature, I find myself inclined to reuse it because there was no stage in Eritrea's history where this phrase captured the reality as the present stage. Although the criticality of the present stage is multidimensional, in this chapter, I will address only two pressing and overlapping dimensions: the issues of Eritrean national identity, referred to

---

4 Check Ambassador Menkerios's remarks here: https://www.youtube.com/watch?v=fBJOcBnKGag.

as 'Eritreanism'; and Eritrean sovereignty, which Isaias compromised well before the current war in Ethiopia. This war, however, has affirmed the legitimate concerns of many Eritreans about the fate of their beloved country.

Academic context for used terms

Identity and nationalism are contested concepts and have attracted heated debate. Nonetheless, in this chapter, Eritreanism refers to the accumulation of notions about citizenship's regime and belonging.

The term 'citizenship' can be traced back considerably in history. In each historical period, the term has had a different meaning. Currently, most definitions of citizenship include international and national aspects. For the domestic aspects of citizenship, Marshall's account is widely accepted (particularly in the West, where democratic systems based on civil rights exist). Marshall has linked citizenship to equal access to key rights. This notion has evolved gradually. These rights included civil rights in the 18th century, political rights in the 19th century and social rights in 20th century[5]. Other scholars have dealt with citizenship from two dimensions: descriptive factual and normative philosophical. Whereas the factual dimension focuses on empirical facts, such as legislation, interpretations and practices, the normative one deals with the role of citizenship in solving problems related to inclusion, social cohesion and power relations in multicultural societies: 'Citizenship is the status of a person owing allegiance to and being entitled to protection of government, in other words it is a legal bond linking the individual body to the body of politic'[6].

Deconstructing citizenship reveals five elements: state, person, entitlements and responsibilities, practical aspects and

---

5 T.H. Marshall, *Class, Citizenship, and Social Development: Essays* (Westport: Greenwood Press, 1973, 14).

6 C. Westin, S. Hassanen, and E. Olsson, *People on the Move: Experiences of Forced Migration with Examples from Various Parts of the World* (Trenton: The Red Sea Press, 2014), 192.

emotional attachment. The relations between these elements are complex. The ideal citizenship situation presumes that these elements are optimally balanced. Nevertheless, this ideal situation seldom exists. Hence, several perspectives on citizenship have emerged, such as the liberal perspective, the communitarian perspective and the civic republican perspective. Regardless of the applied perspective, however, the attainment of citizenship privileges that manifest in rights and obligations within the state is more likely to be affected by political, cultural, social and international factors, resulting in different levels of citizenship or multilayered citizenship[7].

Emotional attachment, the fifth element, is the most controversial of citizenship's components. In most cases, it manifests in imprecise concepts such as nationalism, patriotism or belonging. In an ideal situation, where the 'nation' and 'state' can be used interchangeably (i.e., where a nation state exists), citizenship, belonging and nationality may be understood as synonymous. Nevertheless, such a homogenised state rarely exists because of geopolitical and social factors that affect border demarcation as well as migration, which has occurred throughout history for various reasons. This has resulted in multicultural, multiethnic and multi-religious states. In such states, emotional attachment manifests in the everyday practices of inclusion and exclusion and migration to or from the states. In some cases, it serves as a trigger for peace or war within and between nations or states.

Belonging

Belonging is an appealing subject in disciplines such as psychology, anthropology, sociology and political science. Belonging is present and pivotal in almost any study related to individuals' behaviour within groups that are formed based on blood ties or social or political associations. Regardless of this

---

7 N. Yuval-Davis, "Intersectionality, Citizenship and Contemporary Politics of Belonging," *Critical Review of International Social and Political Philosophy* 10, no. 4 (2007): 561-574.

subject's breadth, there seems to be a consensus among scholars concerning the identification of those human needs that are fulfilled by belonging. The needs include gaining an identity, being a part of something (collectivism), acceptance, security, inclusion, connection with those who are similar (affiliation) and solidarity in politics and economics (obligations and loyalty). By contrast, there is an ongoing debate concerning how, when and why belonging manifests; how the boundaries of belonging are drawn; whether belonging is inherited or constructed; and whether it is exclusionary or inclusive. Whereas primordialists suggest that belonging is exclusionary, based on the notion of common culture and ascribed identity[8], constructivists believe that belonging is inclusive and voluntary, that the notion of identity is flexible and compound, and that history has witnessed many tribes or nations merge and fully assimilate to create one identity for various incentives[9].

Yuval-Davis distinguishes between belonging as a neutralised feeling and the politics of belonging, which tend to be affirmative or passive depending on the nature of the threat. Further, Yuval-Davis identifies three layers of belonging: social location, self-identification and an ethical and political value system. These levels are interrelated but not synonymous.

These three layers start with individuals' internal consciousness of belonging and the extent to which their need to belong is fulfilled. Second, there is the impact of this consciousness and the energy that is consequently generated and manifested in affirmative or passive form and, finally, the impacts of these manifestations of these actions on the group's

---

8 R. Bellamy, "The Making of Modern Citizenship in Lineages of European citizenship: Rights, membership and participation in eleven nation states," eds R. Bellamy, D. Castiglione, and E. Santoro (UK: Palgrave, 2010), 1-21.

9 H. E. Hartnell, "Belonging: Citizenship and Migration in the European Union and in Germany," *Berkeley Journal of International Law* 24, no. 1 (2006): 329-400, accessed 5 April 2015, http://scholarship.law.berkeley.edu/bjil/vol24/iss1/7.

behaviour. Indeed, the input of individuals that is generated as a result of belonging varies based on factors such as social ranking, wealth, knowledge and skills.

The delineation and maintenance of boundaries is always associated with belonging. This is a crucial factor in not only determining community actions or reactions but also predicting them. Boundary maintenance may be perceived as promotion by expansion or consolidation by maintenance, which is true in most cases. In a few cases, however, the disadvantaged group, in terms of its number of members or its share of power and wealth, may loosen its boundaries for historical, social, economic, cultural or political reasons. As a consequence, individuals may start to disassociate themselves from the group in a phenomenon known as self-hatred.

The formation of Eritreanism

The formation of a nation is a gradual and ongoing process. This makes it difficult to determine the exact time of the beginning of the formation process. Further, quantitating the socioeconomic and cultural factors that contribute to the process is almost impossible. For the formation of Eritreanism, however, two salient factors can easily be identified: First, the existence of Eritrea as an autonomous colony under Italy and the role of colonialism; and second, the desire to negate Ethiopianism.

Italy, by virtue of its fifty years of occupation, is credited not only for creating the political entity called Eritrea but also for contributing greatly to the formation of Eritreanism. Although Sir Kennedy Trevaskis's claim that there was nothing in common among the people of current Eritrea 'but the accident of their residence in the territory Italy conquered and named Eritrea'[10] is contested, the role of Italy in the formation of Eritreanism is enormous. The centrality of the Italian

---

10 S. G. Trevaskis, *Eritrea: A Colony in Transition: 1941-52* (London: Oxford University Press, 1960), 17.

occupation in the formation of a sense of belonging among Eritreans, regardless of their similarities or differences, can be looked at from two dimensions, affirmative and passive. The affirmative dimension manifested in the active role of Italy in creating a centralised administrative system within the demarcated borders of the colony: 'The very fact that they now shared a common territory, common name and paramount chief – even if white – who imposed his laws and his administration over them all, slowly awakened a sense of unity among these peoples[11]'. Further, the construction of roads and railways linking Eritrea's regions and the development of its cities created an opportunity for economic and cultural exchanges within the realm of a common identity.

The passive dimension, meanwhile, manifested in the anti-colonialism awareness within Eritrean elite Muslims and Christians. Such awareness was due to not only the exploitative nature of Italian occupation but also to its divisive policies that may have negatively affected the potential for Eritreans' coexistence. In 1938, Muslim and Christians elites came together to affirm their national identity and vowed to protect and preserve their people's and country's unity in the face of future challenges by establishing the first Eritrean political entity, *Maber Fiqri Hager*, meaning 'Association of the Love of Nation'. The association considered the chasm between Muslims and Christians the most challenging issue facing Eritrea. Concerned that it could easily be exploited, the association's members decided to form an executive committee of twelve members equally divided between the two religions' affiliates[12]. This nascent Eritreanism and sense of belonging to

---

11 W. Ammar, *Eritrea: Root Causes of War & Refugees*. (Baghdad: Sindbad Printing Co, 1992), 15.

12 H. S. Turki, *Eritrea and the Fateful Challenges* (2nd ed.), (Beirut: Dar Alknooz, 1979, 206). Many historians consider 5 May 1941 as the date of Maber Fiqri Hager's inception, but Turki cites an earlier date, arguing that 5 May was the date of the formal inception of the organisation.

the natural and political entity called Eritrea, formed during the era of Italian colonialism and motivated by anti-colonialism sentiments, managed to thwart the British plan to partition Eritrea between Sudan and Ethiopia along religious lines. In this regard Woldeab Woldemariam stated, 'we were all determined to maintain above everything else the unity of our people and our county. Because of this unity, we were able to defeat British schemes for [the] partition of Eritrea'[13].

Eritreanism: A disputed identity

Although the nascent Eritreanism managed to withstand the divisive approach of the British, it was not strong enough to withstand Ethiopian machinations. The end of the Italian regime in Eritrea ushered in new opportunities and challenges, with new winners and losers. Eritrean elites start to compete for managerial positions within Eritreanism and take control of power. A managerial role within a disputed identity or nascent one, generally asserted through the utilisation of accumulated capital that may consist of race, colour, taste, physical appearance, accent, cultural preference as Professor Ghassan Hage in *White Nation: Fantasies of White Supremacy in a Multicultural Society*, elucidated[14]. For most Eritrean Christians highlanders (*kabasa*), their natural sources of capital were derived from the history of the Axumite civilisation, Christianity associated with the Ethiopian Coptic Church, and cultural and linguistic ties with Ethiopianism. Most important, however, was their attraction to the glories of the Ethiopian Empire and the role of Eritreans in its trajectory, particularly the triumphant return of Emperor Haile Selassie on May 5, 1941. Anti-Ethiopianism, in contrast, grew exponentially

---

13 L. Cliffe and B. Davidson, "The History of the Eritrean Struggle," in The Long Struggle of Eritrea for Independence and Constructive Peace, edited by Cliffe, L; Davidson, B (The Red Sea Press, 1988), 72.

14 G. Hage, *White Nation: Fantasies of White Supremacy in a Multicultural Society* (Annandale: Routledge, 2000), 53.

among Muslim elites from both the lowlanders and *kabasa* in addition to the Christians elite mostly from the Akele Guzai region. They conceptualised Eritreanism as a distinctive identity that negated both Ethiopianism and Western colonialism. The Ethiopian Orthodox church and Emperor Haile Selassie were salient components of Ethiopianism, which had little consideration for non-Orthodox, let alone non-Christians. Dejat Abraha Tesemma, a prominent Eritrean who advocated for anti-Ethiopianism, articulated what Eritrea and Eritreans should be: 'Eritrea or Merab Mellash belongs to Christians and Muslims alike, and does not belong to either one of us. We are children of one mother'[15]. Dejat Abraha Tesmma and his fellows in Akele Guzai were not alone in their assertion of Eritreanism; Tesmma's call was echoed by Azmatch Berhe Gebrekidan, another prominent figure from the Seraie region. Gebrekidan dismissed the notion of associating anti-Ethiopianism with converting to Islam or the Muslim League.

Drawing from the scholarly work of Professor Göran Therborn, *The Ideology of Power and the Power of Ideology*[16], Mesfin Araya attributed the dichotomisation that shaped Eritreanism in this early stage of its formation to the *revival and anticipation of hope* within those who strongly advocated for Ethiopianism as a notion that negated white colonialism, in contrast to *the revival and anticipation of fear* within those who passionately promoted Eritreanism as a distinctive identity negating both white colonialism and Ethiopianism[17]. Indeed, endogenous factors such as religion, culture, regionalism and elite hopes and fears played an important role in this stage of the Eritreanism

---

15 R. Iyob, *The Eritrean Struggle for Independence Domination, Resistance, Nationalism, 1941-1993* (Cambridge: Cambridge University Press,1997), 71.

16 G. Therborn, *The Ideology of Power and the Power of Ideology* (London: New Left Books, 1980).

17 M. Araya, "The Eritrean Question: An Alternative Explanation." *The Journal of Modern African Studies* 28, no. 1(1990): 79-100. https://doi.org/10.1017/s0022278x00054239.

formation process. The divisive factor, however, was the exogenous factor, namely, the role of Emperor Haile Selassie and his use of the Eritrean Orthodox Church in his efforts to undermine Eritreanism as a crucial step forward in his colonial expansion endeavours.

Ironically, there is a consensus among both pro-Ethiopianism and anti-Ethiopianism followers that the exogenous factor of the British military administration in particular shaped Eritrea's fate during this critical stage in the formation of Eritrea's contemporary history. This consensus, however, emerges from opposing perspectives. Whereas pro-Ethiopianism blamed Italy and the United Kingdom (UK) for the formation of Eritreanism and Eritreans' quest for independence, anti-Ethiopianism blamed foreign powers such as the United States and the UK for depriving Eritrea of its rightly deserved independence because of Eritrea's geopolitical significance. In this regard, Eritreans for generations recalled the infamous statement of the then US representative in the United Nations, John F. Dulles:

> From the point of view of justice, the opinions of the Eritrean people must receive consideration. Nevertheless, the strategic interests of the United States in the Red Sea basin and consideration of security and world peace make it necessary that the country has to be linked with our ally, Ethiopia.[18]

Although this stage of Eritreanism's trajectory was characterised by a bitter rivalry between Ethiopianism's advocates and opponents, the divergent point between these two blocs is; their advocacy and rejection of what they perceived as colonialism. For those who conceptualised themselves within Ethiopianism, it was only a matter of time before they discovered Ethiopia was no different from any

---

18 A. W. Giorgis, *Eritrea at a Crossroads: A Narrative of Triumph, Betrayal and Hope* (Houston: Strategic Book Publishing, 2014), 100.

white occupying power, if not worse.

As a result of the acute polarisation due to both endogenous and exogenous factors, as well as the geopolitical interests of the United States, which necessitated the appeasement of Emperor Haile Selassie, Eritrea was forced into a federation with Ethiopia. In this regard, Professor Bereket Habte Selassie wrote,

> U.S. imperialism using the legal cloak of the U.N. deprived the Eritrean people of their right to independence, handed over the colonial authority to the Ethiopian feudalists and turned Eritrea into an imperialist outpost. The change that took place in 1952 was not in the colonial status of Eritrea but in the faces of those wielding the colonial state machinery.[19]

The federation and the revival of Eritreanism

Although there were two proposals calling for Eritrean independence, one sponsored by the Soviet Union and the other by both Iraq and Pakistan, the UN General Assembly adopted the US proposal and that was enshrined in UN General Assembly Resolution 390 A (V) of 2 December 1950, whose main point read as follows: 'Eritrea be constituted an autonomous unit federated with Ethiopia under the sovereignty of the Ethiopian Crown'[20]. Ethiopia fought against the proposal to the bitter end. The debate was particularly furious regarding the term 'autonomous unit', and when the resolution was adopted, Ethiopia's foreign minister Aklilu Habtewold stated that Ethiopia accepted the resolution in 'the spirit of

---

19 B. Davidson, L. Cliffe, and B. H. Selassie, *Behind the War in Eritrea* (UK-Nottingham: Spokesman, 1980).
20 UN General Assembly, "Eritrea: Report of the United Nations Commissioner in Eritrea," last modified 17 December 1952, https://www.refworld.org/docid/3b00f1de54.html.

compromise'[21]. The low likelihood of the federation's success was due to not only Emperor Haile Selassie's premeditated intention to abrogate it but also the notion of injecting a democratic autonomous unit into a theocratic, autocratic and feudalist regime that was unlikely to function: 'The implication of a democratic unit grafted onto a feudal system was like an antibody imposed on a body politics that was not able and willing to receive it'[22].

The federation was not only a compromise deal among the United States, the United Kingdom and Emperor Haile Selassie, but also an attempt to contest and compromise between two identities, each underpinned by underlying incentives and having its own constituencies. Ethiopianism was vigorously advocated for by unionists under the motto 'Ethiopia or death', in contrast to nationalists, who asserted the uniqueness of Eritreans and Eritreanism. The protagonists of 'Great Eritrea', a project calling for a 'Tigray-Tigrinya' identity, started to dwindle because of the shift in power from the nobility of Tigray to the Amhara of the Shoan elite in Ethiopia as well as because of the lack of significant constituencies. This bloc, incentivised by anti-Ethiopianism, shifted towards Eritreanism and adopted the motto 'Eritrea for Eritreans'.

The Ethiopianism movement utilisation of aggression, intimidation and control of power by the emperor and his representative in Eritrea spurred many of Ethiopianism's protagonists to rethink their positions, particularly the educated young generation. There is another crucial factor that contributed to the revival of Eritreanism at this stage: the inclination of the young generation in Ethiopia – including Eritreans – towards the burgeoning ideology of communism, which strove to dismantle the emperor's feudalist regime and advocate for the right of people to self-determination.

---

21 B. H. Selassie, *Eritrea and the United Nations and Other Essays* (US-Trenton: The Red Sea Press, 1989), 41.
22 Selassie, *Eritrea and the United Nations and Other Essays*, 40-41.

The Ethiopian federation, which was meant to address the dichotomy of the *anticipation of hope and anticipation of fear*, as Mesfin Araya conceptualised it, was proving inadequate to the task. With every passing day, those who advocated for Ethiopianism in *anticipation of hope* witnessed the dashing of their hopes. Tigrinya was marginalised, and Amharic was imposed; the economic infrastructure that was built during the Italian occupation was dismantled, resulting in the deterioration of living standards in urban areas; and Eritrean dignitaries were mostly disrespected. On the other hand, those who rejected Ethiopianism and asserted Eritreanism in *anticipation of fear* were vindicated, and leaders such as Idris Mohammed Adam, Ibrahim Sultan Ali and Woldeab Woldemariam were forced into exile.

More Eritrean nationalists who were targeted by Ethiopian for asserting Eritreanism fled the country, and student and labour unions protested regularly. By the late 1950s, inspired/sponsored by the Sudanese communist party, -*Maber Fiqri Hager* alike-, a clandestine organisation named the Eritrean Liberation Movement was established (known as *Haraka* in the Eritrean political literature). *Maber Fiqri Hager* and *Haraka* were similar in that not only did both assert Eritreanism but also their conceptualisation of Eritreanism transcended the fault lines of religion, region and culture.

The emperor forcefully annexed Eritrea in late 1962, which constituted an important milestone in Eritreanism's revival. *Haraka* called for Eritrea's liberation from Ethiopian occupation and a firm stand against Ethiopianism, which gained more ground in and outside Eritrea. The very own son of Tedla Bairu (Herui), the symbol of Ethiopianism, joined the movement's branch in Addis Ababa[23]. In parallel to the expansion of *Haraka* in most Eritrean urban areas in addition to Ethiopia, exiled Eritrean nationalists, in coordination with

---

23 M. S. Nawed, *Eritrean Liberation Movement –The Truth and History* (Eritrea-Asmara: Nawed Books, 1997), 1180.

the founder of the Eritrean Armed struggle, Hamid Idris Awate, established the Eritrean Liberation Front (ELF) in their endeavour to reclaim Eritreanism. It was not long before Tedla Bairu himself joined ELF, putting the last nail in the coffin of Ethiopianism within Eritrean territory. Eritreanism, therefore, negated not only white colonialism but also Ethiopianism and the Ethiopian occupation.

Armed struggle and the competition for a managerial role within Eritreanism

By design, *Maber Fiqri Hager* was established to address the delicate components of Islam and Christianity within Eritreanism. Thus, it opted to have equal representation in its leadership. In contrast, *Haraka*, although its members were overwhelmingly Muslims, because of its horizontal structure composed of cells of seven people, had cells entirely composed of Christians or a Christian majority. This was the case in *Haraka's* cells in *Kabasa* and Ethiopia[24].

ELF's role in the formation and restoration of Eritreanism is highly contested. The loudest contestation is detailed in the manifesto that was allegedly written by Isaias Afwerki entitled *Neh'nan Elamaa'nan* (We and Our Objectives). The manifesto accused ELF of misrepresenting Eritreanism by invoking Pan-Arabism and Islamic discourse. Additionally, the manifesto accused ELF zone leaders of looting Christian villagers' cattle and discriminating against them.

Although it is true that both Islam and Arabism are important components of Eritreanism because of historical factors, cultural diffusion and geographical proximity to the Arab World and migrations throughout history, Eritreanism has an equally important dimension related to Abyssinianism, Africanism, Kushites and so on. Generally, what makes up a national identity is not only the similarities with other identities but also the uniqueness of its factors and formation process.

---

24 Nawed, *Eritrean Liberation Movement – The Truth and History.*

Revesting the ELF literature reveals the organisation's inclination towards Arabism and to a lesser degree to Islamic discourse. Discourse related to the estimation of Eritrean Muslims' population and the danger that it faced because of the nature of the Ethiopian Empire is less likely to be accurate and reflect the reality. Blood ties with Arabs and cultural associations with Pan-Arabism were common themes in ELF-disseminated materials. These facts, however, must be contextualised to be fully understood. ELF was established in Egypt during the era of Gamal Abdel Nasser and his Pan-Arabism doctrine, and later on, ELF heavily relied on the support of Ba'athism in both Iraq and Syria. To some extent, such inclinations towards Arabism should be understood as a necessity.

The scope and aim of this chapter is not to prove or disprove the allegations in *Neh'nan Elamaa'nan*. Whether these allegations are true and can be objectively gauged or merely perceived does not matter much and as its impacts on Eritreanism has the same effect, because perception is reality in politics. According to the Eritrean People Liberation Front's (EPLF) literature, particularly the *Neh'nan Elamaa'nan* document, the organisation was established as a corrective movement that was necessitated by (a) the lack of clear political program given ELF's random establishment; (b) the domination of Islamic discourse; (c) ethnic tension; (d) lack of consistency and discrimination against Christians in assigning the leadership of military zones; (e) religious tensions and (f) abuse, pillage and discrimination against Christians[25]. Ironically, *Neh'nan Elamaa'nan* objectively explained why the overwhelming majority of EPLF founders were 'Christians by birth, tradition and history' and pleaded to Eritreans to understand that although there are Christians, they are not

---

25 S. Weldehaimanot and E. Taylor, "Our Struggle and its Goals: A Controversial Eritrean Manifesto, *Review of African Political Economy* 38, no. 130(2011):565-585, https://doi.org/10.1080/03056244. 2011. 630870.

'missionaries of Christianity'. The document nonetheless, failed to objectively contextualise the incentives of the ELF Islamic discourse or Arabism inclination. One fact, however, remains uncontested: ELF failed to create an appealing environment for the majority of Christians and was less reflective of the Eritreanism that they perceived and therefore less responsive to their sense of belonging. To its credit, however, EPLF achieved tremendous success in creating an organisation that attracted a large number of Eritreans, particularly *kabasa* who joined the armed struggle after the demise of Emperor Haile Selassie or those who felt uncomfortable within ELF. Further, EPLF through organisational discipline and coercive means if necessary managed to not only make the organisation perfectly appear monolithic but also globally to conceptualise Eritrea and Eritreanism within the frame of the EPLF artificially constructed image. This was perfectly illustrated by the Norwegian professor, Kjetil Tronvoll:

> The EPLF's information and propaganda department was extremely competent and professional in the manner in which they received and treated their foreign guests during the liberation war, imbuing them all with the officially sanctioned narrative on Eritrean nationalism with no deviations, ambiguities, or pluralism being allowed to surface. A key mistake made subsequently by the international observers, activists, journalists, and researchers alike was that they had seen utopia in the liberated areas during the struggle and they projected the image of this artificial community onto the whole of Eritrea, both pre-and post-independence.[26]

---

26 M. K. Omer, *The Dynamics of an Unfinished African Dream: Eritrea: Ancient History to 1968* (Kindle Version: Lulu Publishing Services, 2020), 76-78.

It is plausible to conclude that if ELF, because of objective and subjective factors including its random establishment and lack of a clear revolutionary political programme -based on the *Neh'nan Elamaa'nan* analgy- misrepresented Eritreanism, EPLF, whose establishment was presumably well thought out and which had a clear revolutionary political programme, failed to represent Eritreanism too.

> EPLF leaders and total membership were dominantly from the highland and the Massawa regions since the merger of factions in the early 1970s. Even between 1991 and 2015, there has not been a single cabinet minister from the western Barka region from where a high percentage of Muslim Eritreans hail.[27]

EPLF's misrepresentation of Eritreanism, at first glance, was thought to stem from ideological blind spots in its founding document *Neh'nan Elamaa'nan* concerning two of the main components of Eritreanism, namely, religion and language. Although the document bitterly complained about the discrimination against, mistreatment and mistrust of Christians *kabasa* based on their religious affiliations, EPLF, throughout its trajectory, never showed any sensitivity towards Muslims feelings and dismissed any dissatisfaction of Muslims within or outside the organisation. Regarding language, *Neh'nan Elamaa'nan* and, subsequently, EPLF defined Eritrea as a multilingual nation with nine linguistic groups, ascribed the Arabic language to the *Rashaida* and pointed out that Arabic as an official language in Eritrea was introduced by the British Military Administration. Just as the religious argument failed to hold water, EPLF/EPDJ's conceptualisation of language within Eritreanism, which later manifested in the disastrous adoption

---

27 W. Ammar, "Eritrea's Flawed Beginning in 1991: How it Contributed to What it Is Today," last modified 24 May 2017, https://awate.com/eritreas-flawed-beginning-in-1991-how-it-contributed-to-what-it-is-today/

of the policy of mother tongue in schools, proved to be simplistic if not sinister and was repeatedly refuted.[28]

The failure of both ELF and EPLF to adequately represent Eritreanism should not preclude Eritreans from appreciating the tremendous success of the Eritrean armed struggle and the central role of ELF and EPLF in asserting Eritreanism and negating colonialism – including Ethiopianism – all of which resulted in an independent Eritrea. ELF and EPLF endeavoured to assert that Eritreanism was legally endorsed by 99.81% of Eritreans regardless of their ideological, political, cultural or geographical differences. In May 1993, Eritreans voted in the affirmative to the question 'Do you want Eritrea to be an independent and sovereign country?' in an internationally observed referendum; this included 99.85% of Eritreans residing in Ethiopia[29]. For the referendum to be legally binding, the Eritrean interim government in 1992 issued the *Eritrean Nationality Proclamation (No. 21/1992)*, which addressed the legal frame of Eritreanism as follows: 'Any person born to a father or a mother of Eritrean origin in Eritrea or abroad is an Eritrean national by birth'[30]. If the legality of the referendum necessitated adequately addressing the legal frame of Eritreanism through *Proclamation (No. 21/1992)*, the emotional attachment and sense of belonging that Eritreanism could not be completed without, depended on the government's political will. Unfortunately, in the three decades since Eritreans

---

28 For more on this, see S. Johar, "Language and Religion in Eritrean Politics," last modified 30 November 2016, https://awate.com/language-and-religion-in-eritrean-politics-2/ and A. S. Mohammad, "Mother Tongue Versus Arabic: The Post-Independence Eritrean Language Policy Debate," *Journal of Multilingual and Multicultural Development* 37, no. 6 (2016), 523-535, http://dx.doi.org/10.1080/01434632.2015.1080715.

29 Dept. of External Affairs, Government of Eritrea, *Eritrea: Birth of a Nation*, 1993.

30 "Eritrean Nationality Proclamation (No. 21/1992)," *Refworld*, 6 April 1992, https://www.refworld.org/docid/3ae6b4e026.html.

affirmatively asserted Eritreanism, the government has failed spectacularly to make every Eritrean citizen feel the same way towards Eritrea.

Eritreanism post-independence and the process of deliberate erosion

Although it would have been prudent if both ELF and EPLF conceptualised Eritreanism in its inclusive form, it is not unusual for resistance movements to fall short of inclusiveness. Generally, resistance movements start from a certain ideological, cultural, geographical or demographical grievance that might not take inclusiveness into consideration. Inclusiveness for states, however, is the only remedy for sustainable peace. Any form of domination, marginalisation or coercive assimilation is a recipe for future conflict. It is the imperative of the government, therefore, to strive to reach out to all stakeholders in the country and show sympathy towards their grievances even if it is not able to address them. It is also the imperative of the government to make people's sub-identity a component of the national identity to give them a sense of belonging to their country and its affairs.

Taking into account the dichotomy of Muslim/Christian, Arabic/Tigrinya, lowlanders and highlanders and ELF/EPLF that characterised Eritrean political history, not only was it the interim government's imperative to consider this dichotomy in shaping Eritreanism post-independence, but every Eritrean, including most of EPLF, expected the government to consider it. One of the notable indicators that Eritrean people were looking at to test the interim government's intentions regarding inclusiveness was its application of Arabic and Tigrinya to the formal business of the government and its agencies. Mohammed Nur Ahmed, an Eritrean veteran and former Eritrean ambassador in China, who resigned his position as foreign affairs secretary of the ELF-Revolutionary Council (ELF-RC) to answer the national call to nation building post-independence, stated that 'post-independent EPLF cadres from all levels flocked in significant numbers to attend evening Arabic classes in the Arabic school, known as *Al-Jalia* school. They were very enthusiastic and punctual as they were incentivised by their perceived Eritreanism that will accommodate all Eritrean sub-national identities. Alas, it seemed as they received an unwritten directive not to waste their time, all spirit that led to the enthusiasm and punctuality evaporated'[31]. Tigrinya become the de facto language of the state without a formal decree. Gradually, Eritreanism, in the perception of the government, started to shrink by targeting 'others'. Muslims clerks and teachers were arrested in the hundreds; professors at the University of Asmara, who were mostly from the Akulu Gezai region, were fired; and Jehovah's Witnesses and Pentecostals were jailed, all with no due legal process. In the political dimension, Isaias picked the holy day of Martyrs' Remembrance to announce that 'Eritrea will not be an arena for political parties' festivities' or something to that effect. During the armed struggle, Eritreanism's most valuable capital was anti-colonialism/Ethiopianism, post-independence. however, the capital started to shift towards new components. Being a fighter within EPLF was an asset in the Eritreanism hierarchy. The years someone spent in the armed struggle was valuable capital, and if someone joined the armed struggle during the final days before independence, then they were said to be from the *Weghata* (the dawn) generation with all the connotations associated with it. The most valuable capital for Eritreanism during the first decade post-independence, however, was speaking fluent Tigrinya. It was rare to find non-Tigrinya Eritreans in the diaspora who could not relate to the following conversation: 'Someone who relates to you because of your physical features approaches you in a friendly way and asks you in whatever language she/he speaks – English, Dutch or German – "Are you from Eritrea?" The non- Tigrinya

---

31 Conversation with Ustaz Mohammed Nur Ahmed, Melbourne-Australia, March 2009.

Eritrean answers enthusiastically, "Yes, I am". Then, the enquirer starts to speak in Tigrinya. When he/she sees the perplexity in the face of his/her fellow Eritrean, he/she poses the seemingly innocent question, "If you are Eritrean, how come you do not speak Tigrinya"? Professor Mahmood Mamdani conceptualisation of citizenship and belonging although is important but might not be suitable to understand the reconstruction of Eritreanism post-independent. Mamdani, in his well-argued book, *Citizen and Subject: Contemporary Africa and the Legacy of Late Colonialism*, stated that the African post-colonial state has opted to divide the population into two non-racial categorisations, where they are citizens on one side and subjects on the other[32]. What Eritrea and Eritreanism went through, particularly in their first decade post-independence, is better rationalised by understanding the mechanisms of how certain people assume managerial positions in national identity. This is the conceptualisation Professor Hage used to deconstruct the phenomenon of white supremacy in Australia[33].

The test of 'knowing Tigrinya' as a path towards Eritreanism is similar to what is widely known as the 'cricket test'. Noting the large number of people from the Indian subcontinent in the United Kingdom, in 1990, the former chairman of the British Conservative Party, Lord Tebbit, suggested a simple question to determine who belongs to the United Kingdom: 'Do you support England's cricket team over your "heritage" team?' This came to be known as the 'cricket test'. Fifteen years later, with the number of migrants from Eastern Europe growing, Tebbit suggested another test: 'Did your grandfather fought in the right side during the Second

---

32 M. Mamdani, *Citizen and Subject: Contemporary Africa and the Legacy of Late Colonialism* (US- Princeton: Princeton University Press, 2018), https://www-fulcrum-org.ezproxy-f.deakin.edu.au/epubs/qb98mg950?locale=en#/6/10[Copyright01]!/4/2/4/1:0.

33 G. Hage, *White Nation: Fantasies of White Supremacy in a Multicultural Society* (Annandale: Routledge, 2000), 53.

World War? If the answer's yes, Britain will welcome you"[34].

The Eritrean state assigned a managerial role to Tigrinya within the concept of Eritreanism, which led to Tigrinya's supremacy within the country and aboard. The Tigrinysation of Eritrea was combined with many issues that worried non-Tigrinyans: the issue of land; the hesitation in bringing back refugees, particularly those in Sudan; and Isaias' courting of Meles Zenawi and claims of a close relationship that would lead to some sort of confederation or federation even before the referendum.

> EPLF President Isaias Afewerki told journalists in Asmara on 25 April that he would not rule out very close economic ties or even the establishment of a confederation with Ethiopia – although this was not offered as an option to voters in the referendum.[35]

As a result, non-Tigrayans' perception of Eritreanism was shaken to the core, and they turned to sub-nationality and identity politics to fight back. In particular, Muslims mobilised their constituencies on religious grounds, and Islamism grew exponentially. Others who interpreted EPLF policies to be against their ethnicity fought back using the same concepts, and the organisations Afar and Kunama became a part of the Eritrean political arena.

Sovereignty as a focal point of Eritreanism

Eritreanism pre-independence was essentially constructed as a passive form of anti-white colonialism and then anti-Ethiopianism. Post-independence, however, the passive form transformed into the affirmative form, and sovereignty became

---

34 A. Johnson, *Lord Tebbit's Test For Migrants: Who Did Your Grandfather Fight for in the War?* last modified 29 November 2014, *The Guardian*, https://www.theguardian.com/uk-news/2014/nov/28/lord-tebbit-migrants-grandfather-war.

35 https://www.refworld.org/docid/3df4be300.html.

the focal point of Eritreanism. Sovereignty, as elucidated in the introductory chapter of this book, entails a permanent population, defined territory, one government and the capacity to enter into relations with sovereign states.

Most African post-colonial states have territorial integrity issues due to arbitrary borders demarcation during colonial times. The artificial border, in many cases, divided one people into many countries based on colonial forces' interests and bargaining power. As a result, the same people ended up having different citizenships and allegiances to different political entities. Professor Bereket Habte Selassie called this phenomenon 'border ideology' and illustrated how it correlates with sovereignty:

> There is an organic connection between the concept of sovereignty and the border ideology. The ideology is a powerful force animating people's actions, and underlying it is an inherit tension built along the boundaries with far-reaching implications in terms of interstate conflict.[36]

As is the case in many African countries with disputed territories but rarely opted to war to address this issue, the nascent state of Eritrea, which had inherited a legacy of three decades of destructive occupation and war, was in no need to wage new wars to define its territory and assert the hard-won sovereignty. Eritrea's interim government led by Isaias Afewerki, however, compromised its sovereignty by underplaying the issue of territorial integrity at a time when such issues were easily solvable. A prominent example is 'Badme issue' related to the Eritrean-Ethiopian border. Because asserting sovereignty requires a defined territory, Eritrea had a great opportunity to demarcate its border with Ethiopia before conducting the referendum. In fact, there were many

---

36 B. H. Selassie, *Wounded Nation: How a Once Promising Eritrea was Betrayed and its Future Compromised* (New Jersey: Red Sea Press, 2011), 150.

opportunities to do so even after the referendum, during the years of the Isaias-Meles friendship. The former Eritrean ambassador, Haile Menkerios, frequently pointed out the importance of settling the territorial issue with Ethiopia before and after the referendum to Isaias personally and to his close advisors as well. Menkerios' attempts were dismissed by both Isaias and his close advisors. On one occasion, when Menkerios raised again the issue of the border with Ethiopia, he received a dismissive response from Yemane Gebreab: 'You are really obsessed with this border issue, and you have been repeatedly bothering us with it'. Menkerios replied, 'If it is taken as just an obsession of mine, then I will never raise it again; but I know you will be forced to deal with it with much greater difficulty when it leads to wider bloodshed'.[37]

The pattern of underplaying Eritrean sovereignty and territorial integrity eventually led to the Eritrean-Ethiopian war, just as Menkerios had predicted. Similar conflicts also occurred on a smaller scale with Yemen in December 1995 and Djibouti in April 2008.

In both cases, Eritrea had a better chance of diplomatically or legally settling its issues with these neighbouring countries in the earlier stages before or after the referendum – provided there was the will, check-and-balance institutions and a policy-making process in Eritrea. The know-it-all attitude of the president and his macho style of diplomacy, however, led to disastrous outcomes in all these cases. This begs the question of whether Eritrean sovereignty and territorial integrity were the motives behind these cases, or was the 'border ideology' used for other purposes?

The paradox of war and peace with Ethiopia unmasks the true nature of Isaias Afwerki

One of Benjamin Franklin's famous quotes is 'There never was

---

37 A. W. Giorgis, *Eritrea at a Crossroads: A Narrative of Triumph, Betrayal and Hope* (Houston: Strategic Book Publishing, 2014), 501-506.

a good war or a bad peace'. The quote stands true in Eritrea's case. The war of 1998–2000 between Eritrea and Ethiopia was disastrous, unwarranted and entirely avoidable. In contrast, the peace agreement of 2018 signed by Abiy Ahmed and Isaias Afwerki, which supposed to usher in a promising new era between the neighbouring countries, was in principle commendable. However, 'War demands and reveals the best and the worst in leadership'[38]. In the case of Isaias Afwerki, this war was not so much about revealing what was best or worst about his character as it was about unmasking his true character and ambitions. Professor Bereket Habte Selassie sums up Isaias's character and ambitions in the title and subtitle of his book *Desecrators of the Sacred Trust: The Apotheoses of Donald J. Trump and Isaias Afwerki. Two Preening Would Be Kings and Their Dark Agendas*[39]. He further meticulously details Isaias's steps towards achieving his dreams in chapter four, in his book *'Wounded Nation'*, where he uses the phrase 'immaculate deception' to summarise Isaias's tactics[40]. This chapter sheds light on how Isaias Afwerki used and abused Eritreanism and Eritrean sovereignty so that they fit within his 'immaculate deception' on his way to the throne.

Eritreanism and Eritrean sovereignty sacrificed on the altar of Isaias's dreams of the throne

It is said that 'great leaders read deeply in history when they are young, so that they can place themselves in the continuums of the heroes of their countries'[41]. Isaias, by all standards, is a shrewd and very talented figure, but unfortunately, he has a destructive streak in him:

---

38 A. Roberts, *Leadership in War: Essential Lessons from Those Who Made History* (Kindle Version: Penguin, 2019), 5.

39 B. H. Selassie, *Desecrators of the Sacred Trust: The Apotheoses of Donald J. Trump and Isaias Afwerki. Two Preening Would Be Kings and Their Dark Agendas* (Kindle Version: Author House, 2020).

40 Selassie, *Wounded Nation*, 59-74.

41 Roberts, *Leadership in War*, 5.

According to the testimony of some of his close companions, Isaias apparently demonstrated a command of ideas and issues and linguistic talents, that impressed most of those who came in contact with him. The reference to ideas includes a command of the dominant ideology among the freedom fighters at the time, i.e., Marxism. This was apparent for instance in one particular meeting in Port Sudan, held between leading cadres of the EPLF and ELF. Isaias dominated the discussions in the entire meeting, covering matters about which the top ideologues of the ELF, like the late Azen Yassin, were supposed to excel.[42]

Isaias, confident in his leadership skills and in the acceptance, he had found among the constituencies he purposely targeted, realised the potential of the organisation he created, the EPLF. Since then, 'Eritrea [became] too small to him, however his dreams start[ed] from Eritrea'. Professor Bereket Habte Selassie narrated two conversations he had with two cadres of EPLF. One was a highly influential mid-level EPLF cadre named Mahari Debessay:

All of a sudden, Mahari changed the subject and told me that Eritrea is too small for Isaias, that he deserves a much bigger country beyond Eritrea. His statement was almost word for word the same as the words of the other Eritrean who is still living in Asmara.[43]

It was not only his command over ideas and historical knowledge that bolstered Isaias, but also his years spent in ELF, where he learnt the precise strengths and weaknesses of the organisation. He realised that ELF was not the right vehicle for him to pursue his dream of getting the throne. When he established EPLF, he did not just establish an armed struggle organisation that appealed to the Christians *kabasa* but also constructed a form of Eritreanism that enabled the *kabasa* to

---

42 Selassie, *Desecrators of the Sacred Trust.*
43 Selassie, *Desecrators of the Sacred Trust.*

assume a managerial role in negating the ELF paradigm. Most *kabasa* swallowed the bait, and in one decade, EPLF became a formidable and unchallenged power in the Eritrean arena. Isaias, through his indirect and direct leadership of the People Liberation Forces (PLF)/EPLF managed to sabotage any meaningful dialogue with other Eritrean organisations, such as the Khartoum Agreements on 7 September 1975, and 20 October 1977, respectively. Although many reasons have been given for why these agreements failed, it is clear that the main reason was Isaias's unwillingness to negotiate the form of Eritreanism he had constructed to serve as a steppingstone to his dreams of getting the throne. His dispute with and separation from PLF, or what was then known as the Foreign Mission and was led by Osman Saleh Sabbe, was inevitable. Isaias knew that he could not assume an absolute managerial role, and neither he could mould Eritreanism according to his wishes as long as Sabbe was a part of the same organisation.

The EPLF and TPLF alliance led to the defeat and eviction of ELF from Eritrea, and the two organisations' cultural commonalities helped strongly consolidate the Christians *kabasa*'s managerial role within Eritreanism. The pattern of abandoning any meaningful dialogue and compromise with other national organisations continued post-independence, with Isaias defying the EPLF/The People's Front for Democracy and Justice (PFDJ) own charter that was adopted at the organisation's third conference in February 1994 and that clearly stated its intention 'to make the political system a multi-party system in which political parties legally participate and compete among themselves in a peaceful and democratic way'[44]. In the spirit of PFDJ's third conference charter, ELF-RC was invited to Asmara for a dialogue with PFDJ, but while the delegation was at Khartoum airport enroute to Asmara, it was informed that it was not welcome[45].

---

44 http://ecss-online.com/data/pdfs/PFDJ-national-charter.pdf
45 Conversation with the late Ahmed Nasser the Chairman of ELF-RC, Khartoum, 2003.

In the first decade after independence, Isaias managed to convince or confuse most Christians *kabasa* about their managerial role within Eritreanism and the status quo he had created and was leading. Thus, for many people, the differentiation between Eritrea and the Eritrean government vanished to the extent that criticism of the government or Isaias amounted to undermining the country's sovereignty and belying your patriotism.

All a sudden, war erupted with Ethiopia, and the ugly truth of Isaias was exposed. Christians *kabasa* elite started to pose rhetorical questions. If Isaias wanted a managerial role for Christians *kabasa* within Eritreanism, why did he trigger a war with his closest ally that consolidated the very identity he wanted to promote and preserve? Why did Isaias kill, jail or exile the finest of the Christians *kabasa* elite within EPLF/PFDJ? Why did Isaias undermine the status and autonomy of the Eritrean Orthodox Tewahedo Church and dare to put his Holiness Abune Antonios under house arrest? Why did Isaias purposely depopulate Eritrea by targeting its youth and forcing them to flee the country, where they became victims of human trafficking and organ harvesting and the predators of the Sahara and Mediterranean seas[46]? Why did Isaias disrespect the social norms of the *kabasa* by refusing to bury the remains of Eritrean veteran Naizki Kuflu in Eritrea despite many of *kabasa* community pleading to his humanity and asking him to show respect for *kabasa* social norms for more than two months. Concluding that Isaias had given Christians *kabasa* a managerial role within Eritreanism for the sake of his own ambitions, and when they hindered him or became a burden or liability, Isaias showed no hesitation in sacrificing them on the altar of his ambitions[47].

---

46 Among the 360 plus victims of Lampedusa 88% are assumed to be Christians from Kabasa.

47 These rhetorical questions were mostly raised by Christians kabasa in many forums that the author attended since the Eritrean National Dialogue Forum that was held in Addis Ababa in July-

Isaias's dream of going beyond Eritrea started to change from a mere dream to an action plan with the evolution of the EPLF. This change conspicuously manifested in Eritrea's ambiguous relationship with Ethiopia, particularly during final days of Eritrea's independence struggle. The victim of this transformation was the notion of Eritrean sovereignty, which Eritreans had fought hard to achieve. Isaias in the early stage of independence started to float the idea of a federation with Ethiopia. As mentioned by Mesfin Hagos in his interview with the Australian broadcaster SBS, in February 1991, during EPLF's central committee gathering in *Afabet*, Isaias invited a certain group of members of the central committee for a private meeting. In the meeting, he stated that EPLF and the Ethiopian People's Revolutionary Democratic Front led by Meles Zenawi had agreed to form a united joint government for both countries. Hagos believed that Isaias wanted to inform and explore the reactions of the attendees. When no one spoke, Hagos stood up and said, 'What do you mean? This is entirely antithetical to the objectives of our people's long struggle for freedom and sovereignty[48]'. This account was confirmed by Meles Zenawi in his interview with Paul Henze on 5 April 1990.[49] Andargachew Tsige, Dawit Wolde Giorgis, Sebhat Nega and so on also confirmed the account. Thus, Isaias seemed to fully perceive the eagerness of the Eritrea people for a sovereign nation. He understood that if a referendum was held, Eritreans would overwhelmingly vote for independence.

August 2010 onward. Whenever there were accusations that the regime in Eritrea represents the interests of Christians kabasa, such rhetorical questions were posed to help in deconstructing and understanding the nature of the regime in Eritrea.

48 The interview can be accessed here: https://www.eritreatoday.com/radio-sbs-interview-with-mesfin-hagos-in-tigrinya/.

49 The whole interview can be accessed here: https://tassew.wordpress.com/2012/06/17/meles-zenawis-interview-with-paul-henze-1990/.

Therefore, he was keen to delay the referendum, preferring instead a federation with Ethiopia that could lead to what, in the Sudanese political literature published after the comprehensive peace agreement of 2005, is known as an 'attractive unity'[50].

Given the *kabasa's* managerial role with Eritreanism, the sudden eruption of war raised questions about Eritrean sovereignty, namely, how did the relationship with Ethiopia and TPLF suddenly shift from that of potential federation/integration to war, revenge and enmity? Although this is a complicated question, the answer is simple though hard to digest. Eritrea is too small for Isaias, who greatly enjoyed his senior-junior relationship with Mcles in the early days of Eritrea's independence. He developed a plan to establish a kingdom beyond the realm of 'small Eritrea'. Meles was no less ambitious than Isaias and was looking for a way out of the relationship with him. Isaias used economic pressure and a limited military encounter in Badme to try to discipline Meles, but the latter turned the encounter into an all-out war. Meles saw the war as an opportunity to not only escape his junior role in his relationship with Isaias but also assert his Ethiopianism, which many Ethiopians had started to question. Even some TPLF cadres had been accusing him of inclining towards Eritrean interests more than Ethiopian ones.

The 1998–2000 war with Ethiopia revealed not only Isaias's readiness to compromise Eritrean sovereignty to pursue his dream of going 'beyond Eritrea' but also his inability to protect Eritrean sovereignty when it was no longer a valid currency in his endeavours. Isaias failed militarily to protect Eritrean territorial integrity by instigating an unwarranted war, and then failed to defend the country as commander-in-chief. He further failed politically and diplomatically to negotiate a good terms

---

50 Attractive unity, a concept that the late Dr. John Garang De Mabior promoted, was intended to incentivise South Sudanese people to vote for unity. For more on this, read https://sudantribune.com/spip.php?article23060.

agreement, and even when the Eritrea-Ethiopia Boundary Commission (EEBC) ruled in favour of Eritrea, Isaias failed to mobilise adequate international pressure to force Ethiopia to implement the final and binding rule of the EEBC.

How this is relevant to the current developments in Ethiopia

It is said that 'the dream never dies, if it's strong. Some men dream of heaven. And some of the Lord above. Some men dream about pie in the sky'[51]. Isaias's dream to go beyond Eritrea seems strong enough to have survived three decades of turmoil. Isaias never accepts half-measured solutions; he wants either a resounding victory or a complete defeat. When he suffers a defeat, he is less inclined to any manoeuvring tactics. 'It's finished', Isaias helplessly declared during the events of 1978, known as a 'strategic retreat' in the EPLF literature[52]. During the Eritrean-Ethiopian war of 1998–2000, many initiatives with better terms than the Algiers Agreement were proposed, but all of them were rejected by Isaias. Then, the moment Ethiopia retook Badme in February 1999, Isaias announced his acceptance of the African Union Organisation initiative. When most Eritrean defence lines collapsed in May 2000 and Ethiopian troops penetrated Western and Central Eritrea, Isaias started preparing to withdraw to EPLF bases in *Sahel* and ordered the withdrawal of Assab. This order was defied by the heroes on the Assab front. Finally, Isaias was forced to capitulate and sign the humiliating Algiers Agreement. In contrast, when Isaias feels victorious or vindicated, he shows less consideration for others' views or feelings. After Isaias-Abiy signed the peace agreement, Isaias went on a state visit to Ethiopia, where he triumphantly announced, 'Anybody who

---

51 A song for the Cooper Brothers: https://www.youtube.com/watch?v=hDWKFITHLl0
52 R. Reid, *Shallow Graves* (Place of Publication: Hurst, 2020), 105.

says the people of Eritrea and Ethiopia are two peoples is someone who doesn't know the truth'. Disregarding the more than twenty thousand lives that were lost in war, and the war's devastating ramifications, with no sign of remorse, he declared 'Aykessernan. . .' (We did not suffer loss)[53].

Isaias has every right to feel victorious and to revive his dream after a period of hibernation. Over the last two decades, those who tirelessly worked against him are either dead or in prison. in October 2002, three states, namely, Ethiopia, Sudan and Yemen, formed the 'Sana'a Axis', which mainly aimed to tackle the risk that the Eritrean regime posed in the region. Today, the three leaders that incepted the Sana'a Axis are gone. Meles passed away in 2012, Ali Abdullah Saleh of Yemen was brutally killed in December 2017, and Omar Al-Bashir of Sudan was toppled in April 2019 and is facing trial. Isaias might not have been the main causative factor in these leaders' fates, but he still played a role in their end. Isaias tirelessly supported various Ethiopian and Sudanese opposition groups that contributed to the events of Ethiopia and Sudan, and he hosted training camps for the Houthis militia in Yemen that later assassinated Ali Abdullah Saleh.

Post-independence, there were two major obstacles that prevented Isaias from realising his dream of going beyond the 'small Eritrea': Meles's ambition and the system of ethnic federalism that Meles adopted.

Today, Ethiopia under the leadership of Abiy Ahmed, is likely to abolish the system of ethnic federalism and switch to a unitary system. If that happens, then Isaias's major obstacles will be eliminated. While the senior-junior relationship between Meles Zenawi and Isaias is also applicable to Abiy Ahmed, taking into consideration the factors of age and experience. Nevertheless, Isaias at this stage seems contented with playing the role of kingmaker.

---

53 For the whole speech in Tirinya, check, https://www.youtube. com/watch?v=wAvZpSYjy8w&t=618s

I have told Abiy Ahmed repeatedly: in any front, if there is something that needs action, you are our representative. You are the one to lead us. I am not saying this to flatter him or to please him or for the sake of saying it[54].

It is apparent that these new developments in the region have brought Isaias's dream out of hibernation. Isaias now has two trump cards to barraging with: Eritreanism and Eritrean sovereignty. Since the signing of the peace agreement, there have been worrying signs that Isaias may compromise both of them. Isaias has literally given up governing Eritrea. Since the signing of the agreement Isaias and Abiy met 16 times, but Isaias convened only one cabinet meeting. His discourse and actions have become increasingly confusing, from 'we suffer no loss' to 'we are one people', to the propagation of the notion of joint embassies for both countries, to the stationing of the Ethiopian navy on the Eritrean coast, and to the use of one map for both countries.

Conclusion

With the weakening of TPLF militarily due to the war in Tigray, Abiy's inclination towards a unitary system of governance and Isaias's notable influence in Sudan and Somalia, Isaias, more than ever, feels not only vindicated but also tremendously emboldened. International theories, particularly those of realism, define states as 'rational actors'. The above-mentioned developments created an optimal situation for Eritrea to advance its national security and interests and elevate its regional and international status. However, Eritrea, under Isaias's grip, seldom acted rationally because acting rationally entails doctrine, grand strategy and institutions. Establishing institutions, in particular, is antithetical to Isaias's long-awaited dream of going 'beyond Eritrea'. This chapter has illustrated the

---

54 For the whole speech in Tigrinya, see https://www. youtube.com/watch?v=3XJvEQ1ZiJk.

numerous indicators that Isaias may utilise to realise his dream. To Isaias's advantage, currently the vulnerability of Eritrea is alarming. For three decades, Isaias depopulated Eritrea, impoverished its people, messed up its social fabric and weakened its military. In short, Isaias worked hard to make Eritrea an almost unviable state. History tells us that when a country become unviable, it becomes susceptible to any projects antithetical to its existence as a political entity.

It is up to Eritreans from all walks of life, creeds, political affiliations or ideological inclinations to fully grasp the ramifications of the current developments and urgently prepare to meet the challenges to renegotiate and restore Eritreanism and preserve Eritrean sovereignty.

References

Ammar, W. (1992). *Eritrea: Root causes of war & refugees.* Baghdad: Sindbad Printing Co.

Ammar, W. (2017, May 24). *Eritrea's flawed beginning in 1991: How it contributed to what it is today.* Awate.com. https://awate.com/eritreas-flawed-beginning-in-1991-how-it-contributed-to-what-it-is-today/

Araya, M. (1990). The Eritrean Question: An alternative explanation. *The Journal of Modern African Studies, 28*(1), 79-100. https://doi.org/10.1017/s0022278x00054239

Bellamy, R., Castiglione, D., & Shaw, J. (2006). *Making European citizens: Civic inclusion in a transnational context.* Springer.

Cliffe, L., & Davidson, B. (1988). The History of the Eritrean Struggle. In *The long struggle of Eritrea for independence and constructive peace.* The Red Sea Press.

Davidson, B., Cliffe, L., & Selassie, B. H. (1980). *Behind the War in Eritrea.* Spokesman.

Giorgis, A. W. (2014). *Eritrea at A Crossroads: A narrative of Triumph, Betrayal and Hope.* Strategic Book Publishing.

Government of Eritrea, Dept. of External Affairs. (1993). *Eritrea: Birth of a nation.*

Hartnell, H. E. (2006). Belonging: Citizenship and migration in the European Union and in Germany. *Issues in Legal Scholarship*, *6*(2). https://doi.org/10.2202/1539-8323.1087

Iyob, R. (1997). *The Eritrean Struggle for Independence: Domination, Resistance, Nationalism, 1941-1993*. Cambridge University Press.

Johar, S. (2016, November 30). *Language and Religion in Eritrean Politics*. Awate.com. https://awate.com/language-and-religion-in-eritrean-politics-2/

Johnson, A. (2014, November 29). *Lord Tebbit's test for migrants: Who did your grandfather fight for in the war?* the Guardian. https://www.theguardian.com/uk-news/2014/nov/28/lord-tebbit-migrants-grandfather-war

Mamdani, M. (2018). *Citizen and subject: Contemporary Africa and the legacy of late colonialism*. Princeton University Press. https://www-fulcrum-org.ezproxy-f.deakin.edu.au/epubs/qb98mg950?locale=en#/6/10[Copyright01]!/4/2/4/1:0

Marshall, T. H. (1965). *Class, citizenship, and social development: Essays*.

Mohammad, A. S. (2016). Mother Tongue versus Arabic: The Post-Independence Eritrean Language Policy Debate. *JOURNAL OF MULTILINGUAL AND MULTICULTURAL DEVELOPMENT*, *37*(6), 523–535. http://dx.doi.org/10.1080/01434632.2015.1080715

Roberts, A. (2019). *Leadership in War: Essential lessons from those who made history*. Penguin.

Selassie, B. H. (1989). *Eritrea and the United Nations and other Essays*. The Red Sea Press.

Selassie, B. H. (2011). *Wounded nation: How a Once Promising Eritrea was Betrayed and its Future Compromised*. Red Sea Press (NJ).

Selassie, B. H. (2020). *Desecrators of the Sacred Trust: The Apotheoses of Donald J. Trump and Isaias Afwerki. Two Preening would be Kings and their Dark Agendas.* Author House.

Therborn, G. (1980). *The Ideology of Power and the Power of Ideology.* New Left Books.

Trevaskis, S. G. (1960). *Eritrea: A colony in Transition: 1941-52.* Oxford University Press.

Turki, H. S. (1979). *Eritrea and the Fateful Challenges* (2nd ed.). Dar Alknooz, Beirut.

United Nations High Commissioner for Refugees. (2020, December 18). *Ethiopia: Exact wording of question for referendum of April 1993 regarding Eritrean Independence, whether or not the question made reference to a choice between slavery and freedom.* Refworld. https://www.refworld.org/docid/3df4be300.html

Weldehaimanot, S., & Taylor, E. (2011). Our struggle and its Goals: A Controversial Eritrean Manifesto. *Review of African Political Economy, 38*(130), 565-585. https://doi.org/10.1080/03056244.2011.630870

Westin, C., Hassanen, S., & Olsson, E. (2013). *People on the move: Experiences of forced migration: with examples from various parts of the world.* Red Sea Press (NJ).

Yuval-Davis, N. (2007). Intersectionality, citizenship and contemporary politics of belonging. *Critical Review of International Social and Political Philosophy, 10*(4), 561-574. https://doi.org/10.1080/13698230701660220

CLEAR AND PRESENT DANGER TO ERITREA'S SOVEREIGNTY

Daniel Teklai

The chorus of the Eritrean national anthem that is proudly repeated says:

Eritrea, Eritrea,
has taken her rightful place in the world.

The yearning of generations of Eritreans is felt in these simple yet profound words.

Before the song became a national anthem, during the period known as the struggle, the same song was popularized by the EPLF, with a small but important difference in the tense of the last verse. It used to say, "Eritrea, Eritrea, *will take* her rightful place in the world".

So what did it mean to achieve a "rightful place in the world" to the average citizen and the liberation fighters? Among other things, it meant that one day the country will be governed by the will of its own people and not by foreign occupiers. When that vision was achieved after 30 years of a long and arduous journey that culminated with a military triumph and a vote for independence via referendum, an important milestone was crossed. "Eritrea, Eritrea, *will take* her rightful place in the world" became "Eritrea, Eritrea, *has taken* her rightful place in the world". Mission accomplished. Independence achieved. Aspiration became a reality. Gone were the days where the Italians, the British, and finally, the Ethiopians were going to decide the faith of the country.

If a definition of sovereignty includes the notion of having full right over oneself and the right to manage your own affairs without interference from outside forces, then the chorus of the song might as well have said:

Eritrea, Eritrea,
has achieved her sovereignty.

And as a sovereign country, the "rightful place" is to be equal among the nations of the world. With their flag hoisted at United Nations headquarters, the sense of pride Eritreans feel seems to say: We may not be better than others, but darn it, we are as equal as anyone and deserve to be recognized and respected.

The last 3 decades since that achievement have been bittersweet for the people of Eritrea. The symbols of a sovereign state remain but the people hardly enjoy the dividends that were supposed to come with sovereignty. The ramifications of a horrific border war that claimed tens of thousands of lives and displaced even more are still felt to this day. The rebel leader who led the march to independence turned into a ruthless tyrant who governs at his whims, without any constitution or due process. As a result, the country quickly came to be known for its gross human rights violations and for producing one of the largest numbers of refugees in the world. A stagnant economy that largely depends on remittance of those very refugees as they send money home to support their families, lingers teetering at the edge of total collapse – hardly a dream of sovereignty the people had in mind.

As the years go by and Independence Day is formally commemorated on May 24 each year, Eritreans started to debate what the meaning of independence is if it doesn't also include liberty, freedom, and rights. Unable to openly discuss issues of governance at home, Eritreans find themselves politically divided with a lot of mistrust among different sectors. As if to bring solace to the sad situation however, everyone seems to agree that at least they have a sovereign country. Dictatorships may come and go, most people reasoned, but they will be recovering the deferred dreams of peace, justice, progress, and prosperity.

Unfortunately, the only thing that is left to hang on, the very sovereignty is now in danger.

The following discussion will elaborate on where this threat is emanating from and make recommendations on how to mitigate it. Two intertwined phenomena are currently unfolding. The first one is regarding the unchecked authoritarian power of Isaias Afeworki of Eritrea. The other part deals with the rise of expansionism in Ethiopia and the aspirations of its charismatic leader, Prime Minister Abiy Ahmed.

To make matters worse, these two threats are now working in tandem and for all intents and purposes marching toward the same goal. Unless something is done about it, Eritrea's sovereignty is indeed in clear and present danger.

Isaias: From Liberator to Dictator

During the war for independence, by hook or crook, Isaias Afwerki's reputation became synonymous with the resilience of the Eritrean Revolution. And every revolution needs a leader and a hero. In the eyes of the guerrilla fighters, the public, and in the international arena, Isaias undoubtedly lived up to the myth.

Since then, many books have now been written about the shady ways Isaias rose to the top. A lot of knowledge has been shared about his modus operandi, leadership style, psychological make-up, and the mysterious disappearance of potential rivals. In search for the when and why things have gone wrong, some point to the existence of a clandestine Marxist political party, the Eritrean People's Revolutionary

Party, that secretly guided the EPLF without most of the rank and file of the freedom fighters knowing about it.

Others focus on a manifesto that was allegedly written by Isaias and his inner circle in 1971. This document, known by its Tigrigna title *Nhnan Elamanan* ('We and Our Objectives'), is perhaps still the most controversial manifesto in Eritrea's political history.

True as it may, all that sums up to be is just fodder for his detractors. After so many years of disappointment and utter failure, Isaias Afwerki no longer enjoys the popularity he once had. But his contribution to the triumphant political and military success of the EPLF is undeniable. Feared, hated, respected, adorned ... he proved to be an effective operator who would do anything to reach his goals.

To the Eritrean people, the goal that mattered the most was the defeat of the brutal Ethiopian Army and the achievement of independence, which Front and which leader is going to chart the way was beside the point. Throughout the 1970s and 80s, as the movement for independence enjoyed successes and suffered defeats that almost drove it to extinction, the popularity of the EPLF and its charismatic leader Isaias Afwerki became legendary.

This is not to say that the popularity was grounded in fairness, truth, or democratic participation. Far from it.

Like in many liberation movements throughout history, the rise of a legendary leader is the outcome of fantastic stories, coincidences, half-truths shrouded in mystery, and good old-fashioned lies. In the Eritrean arena, it was inevitable that someone was going to be a living legend.

With a backdrop of a society's culture rooted in military hero-worship and noble intentions and a liberation movement in dire need of discipline and focus, Isaias stepped into the vacuum and into history.

His story is not that different from many other historical figures who drove revolutionary movements. From Robespierre of the French Revolution to Cuba's Fidel Castro, to other contemporary African counterparts like Mozambique's Samora Machel, Angola's Agostino Neto, Zimbabwe's Robert Mugabe, and Ethiopia's Mengistu Hailemariam, history is full of examples of ambitious liberators who rose to the top. Fairly or unfairly, the focus shifts from the revolution to the man who is leading the revolution and produces larger than life, almost mythical figures.

Throughout the 1970s, two armed movements dominated the Eritrean political arena, the Eritrean Liberation Front (ELF) which was founded in 1961, and the Eritrean People's Liberation Front (EPLF), a decade later. The founders and leaders of the EPLF were formerly with the ELF. They defected from the ELF organization for ideological and other grievances and quickly gained momentum by attracting recruits and other fighters who shifted allegiances.

It is at that time that Isaias and his team authored the fateful manifesto Nhnan Elamanan ('We and Our Objectives'). It was a rather simple and short hand-written document that articulated why the newly formed organization was needed and why the ELF should be abandoned.

Nothing novel about it, really.

Naturally, that is to be expected by any off-shoot faction; it has to make its reason for existence, its *raison d'etre*, known. It was not widely distributed either. It is safe to say, most of the fighters of the ELF and later the EPLF never read it or heard about it.

To his believers, he embodied the ability to create a vision, to organize and march forward. To his enemies, he represented a poisonous idea based on lies and the quest for power.

But the result was the same; it helped propel Isaias Afwerki's reputation to the next level.

A decade after its formation, the EPLF emerged militarily and politically stronger while the ELF kept waning away. Finally, the civil war that ensued ended with the ELF pushed out of Eritrea for good, in 1981. This in itself was also a major milestone in helping Isaias consolidate his power.

His fate as the liberator of Eritrea was now almost certain.

The next decade, the '80s was yet another long, bloody, devastating period of time in Eritrean history. But it was also a decade where the war for independence was getting the attention of the world. Dubbed as Africa's longest war by then, and viewed through the lens of the cold war between the West and the Soviet Union, it garnered some attention in the region and on the global stage.

At home and in the Diaspora, most Eritreans pinned their hopes on the achievements of the EPLF and its leaders. The challenges were astronomical and the suffering from the war and famine was beyond endurance. Weaken by infighting, and a push by the Ethiopians, the freedom fighters were forced to retreat into the mountains of Sahel.

In 1982, Ethiopia launched a major military offensive known as the *Key Kokeb Zemecha* (Red Star Campaign), which was advertised as an all-out war to vanquish the Eritrean secessionist movement once and for all. The never-kneel-down mantra of the EPLF became the battle cry upon which the hope and prayers rested – more prayers than hopes at this point.

Miraculously, the rebels were able to resist the more than 100,000 strong army that failed to dislodge them from their stronghold. It was a momentous occasion that signaled that Eritreans could not be defeated militarily. It was also a huge setback for the Soviet-backed military junta in Ethiopia that boasted Africa's largest and best-equipped army at the time.

In the subsequent years, many similar campaigns were tried by the Ethiopians but to no avail. The EPLF's invincibility and the popularity of the leaders were growing, especially that of Isaias Afeworki. His reputation preceded him and slowly but surely a cult of personality was growing.

By 1988, the EPLF started to turn things around was able to come out of its defensive position and occupy towns in Northern Eritrea.

The defeat of Ethiopia's Nadow Command in the Battle of Afabet marked another major milestone in the journey towards Asmara, towards independence. The British historian, Basil Davidson who observed the situation from the Eritrean side of the battlefield compared the Battle of Afabet to the Vietnamese victory over the French at Dien Bien Phu.

Two years later, the port town of Massawa was liberated in another major and bloody battle. By that time, the Ethiopian Army was demoralized and dejected, its own situation exacerbated by the impending collapse of its benefactor, the Soviet Union.

By this time, the EPLF was not only succeeding in Eritrea but was effectively collaborating with rebel movements inside Ethiopia, including the Tigray People's Liberation Front (TPLF), which in retuned played a central role in organizing other ethnic-based rebels.

Many ex-leaders of the EPLF and other experts refer to this period where Isaias Afwerki was showing his bigger ambitions for himself that go beyond the liberation of Eritrea, perhaps as a kingmaker or even a leader of Ethiopia.

It's hard to corroborate or substantiate the alleged statements and conversations Isaias had in private but there is plenty of circumstantial evidence from different sources. But one thing was for sure, by the time the triumphant army of the EPLF entered Asmara in May 1991 and the Ethiopian rebels took over the government in Ethiopia, Isaias Afwerki had consolidated his power and political capital.

The early warning signs were there but no one could have predicted what was going to transpire over the next decade. Surely, Isaias was the strongman co-founder and leader of the EPLF. Still, the presumption was that there was a collective leadership that included other strong-willed, battle-hardened leaders as well. If they could trust Isaias, why wouldn't the public at large?

The odds weren't good. All over the third-world, revolutionaries, and armed groups who seized power promising democracy, justice and equality have largely failed to deliver. Instead, many of them ended up acting just like the tyrants they replaced. Could Eritrea be the exception to that gloomy outlook? The conventional wisdom was that, yes, Eritrea will likely be the exception.

Against all odds, independence was achieved; it actually went beyond achievement and went on to cause the downfall of the Ethiopian regime. As the war years were winding down, Isaias and colleagues were publicly talking about how Eritrea will avoid the third-world curse, especially the fates of African nations.

As Eritrea prepared to conduct a referendum to formalize the process toward sovereign nationhood, the voting process gave an aura of public participation.

The UN-supervised referendum was declared free and fair by observers. Soon after, governments formally recognized Eritrea, and it formally joined the United Nations and the African Union.

The transition was going well for the most part and garnered respect from the international community. If there was any fear that a guerilla insurgency was not going to peacefully shift to a civilian administration, that fear was confirmed. If there was any doubt that, Ethiopia was not going to recognize the secession of a former province, that fear was put to rest as well.

In the Horn of Africa region, after toppling its dictator Siad Barre, Somalia was descending into chaos. The Sudanese civil war was still raging on and the new government in Ethiopia was still on shaky ground. Eritrea was a slim glimmer of tranquility, which led the then US Secretary of State, Warren Christopher to proclaim **"Eritrea...A beacon of hope astride the Horn of Africa."**

No one realistically expected the rebel leaders to quickly hand over their power to the public and simply fade away but the road toward democracy was part of the overarching mission of the EPLF; at least, that is what they were professing. The transitional National Assembly elected Isaias to be president and formally, the political transition process started and the groundwork to transform the EPLF to its civilian version called People's Front for Democracy and Justice (PFDJ). A national charter that included lofty goals of social justice, a centrally planned economy, and constitutional governance was laid out. Overall, there was no reason but to be proud and to be hopeful.

So, it seems we are not going to be like the rest of Africa, the people thought...

As a matter of fact, Isaias Afwerki literally said so to a gathering of African leaders in his inaugural speech at the Summit of the Organization of African Unity (OAU) in Cairo, Egypt in June 1993. He said:

"It is unfortunate to witness the Organization of African Union (OAU) becoming an inept organization that utterly failed to fulfill the objectives and pledges vested upon it. Indeed, it did not strive to translate into action the lofty goals it was entrusted with. And as a result, 30 years since the founding of the organization, Africa is still suffering from mounting poverty, backwardness and civil strife. It has become a continent despised by all partners instead of one in which nationals lead a life of dignity. Although it is indisputable that there exists the ugly legacy of colonialism, such a reality should nonetheless not make the African people complacent and a cover for our weaknesses. We cannot achieve a better future as long as we fail to critically scrutinize past errors. The OAU did not succeed at all in ensuring unity and development in the continent, as well as in safeguarding the fundamental rights of the African people. At this juncture, I would like to underscore that Eritrea opted to become member of this organization not because it was impressed with the organization's successes but only out of the spirit of family responsibility..."

It was an impressive speech. It was said that even the journalists and reporters applauded. Could this be the beginning of an African renaissance? Did the world just witness the launching of a new era led by young African leaders who were going to do away with the old and failed ways? Maybe it was because everyone was yearning for such hope to emerge

179

but the magnificent speech helped take Isaias' image to the next level. Popular at home, respected abroad, he was on his way to achieving greatness.

We must ask: But was this all a façade, a carefully veiled show to buy time so that he can unleash his true nature? His arch enemies, with some ties to the defeated ELF, were always voicing concerns that Isaias is only interested in amassing power and he will not abide by any laws. Their voices were simply drowned out by the gleeful cheers from the rest of Eritreans and everyone who was rooting for the young nation to succeed. And those who knew him well, his inner circle, those who should have known better, were mute. Not muted, per se, just mute. Perhaps the limelight shining on their leader was too bright to compete against, perhaps they were waiting for the right time to ring the warning alarms, or they were just cowardly opportunists in for the ride. Whatever it was, it seemed everyone participated in dressing up the emperor and in giving him more unchecked power. It seemed everyone forgot Lord Acton's famous warning: "All power tends to corrupt, and absolute power corrupts absolutely."

Slowly but surely the façade started to crumble and everyone could see that Isaias Afeworki is just another despot; and not the benevolent kind either.

He was not interested in building institutions with any semblance of transparency or accountability. He would hoodwink supporters and skeptics alike into thinking that this time, this year, next year, soon, very soon things will change.

At the same time, arbitrary arrests, disappearances, forced conscription, torture, and the exodus of citizens in masses became the order of the day.

If there was any hope that the Constitution was going to help with reigning in the dictator's unlimited power, he was not going to give it a chance. The three years it took to prepare the document, get public participation, and create awareness was just a period of hoodwinking for Isaias. In fact, by the time the Constitution was ratified by the National Assembly and a

Constituent Assembly in 1997, he had already made his plans so that it would never see the light of day. Yes, even if he had to instigate war, he would.

And that is exactly what he did; notwithstanding the technicality of who actually fired the first shot in the deadly and rather pointless border war with Ethiopia.

Dictators love war. It gives them the excuse to postpone normalcy indefinitely, to create an atmosphere of fervent ultra-nationalism, to grossly violate human rights in the name of state security, and shift focus away from domestic issues. But there is a cost. The burden of war is paid in human suffering, in death and tears, in disruption and displacement. At least 19,000 Eritreans perished in the war of 1998-2000.

As the new millennium begins, it was no longer deniable that the increasingly authoritarian regime of Isaias has turned for the worse and became a one-man totalitarian system. The short-lived publications of the private press were shut down and its writers and editors were placed in gulags, their whereabouts unknown to this day.

Veterans of the military, religious leaders, members of the regime's own government including cabinet ministers were sacked and put in jails. No courts, no lawyers, no nothing. Just make them disappear without a trace as if they were not even there.

Isaias, the freedom fighter, the *tegadalay*, the liberator is now the unabashed dictator.

He no longer even want to pretend otherwise. The world has shunned him and he shunned the world back. Almost two decades went by, just like that. Other than the stomach-churning death of a beautiful dream revealing itself in the cascade of downward spiraling economy, cruelty, injustice, and the desperate attempts to flee the country. The Eritrean dream essentially became the dream to escape Eritrea and seek refuge elsewhere; anywhere.

In the meantime, it seemed that Isaias gave up on Eritrea and became obsessively involved in Ethiopia's internal political

181

affairs. He dedicated the country's meager resources to training and arming a plethora of armed groups who want to bring down the regime in Ethiopia. The TPLF-led coalition government in Ethiopia effectively played its policy of containment and creating a no-war-no-peace situation. But Isaias was not going to be easily contained and kept on over-stretching himself and the capabilities of the country.

After the terrorist attacks of September 11 in the United States, Ethiopia became an eager partner in the War on Terror. The Bush Administration delegated it to deal with any threats that could come from Somalia. In a desperate attempt to create some kind of proxy war with Ethiopia, and sabotage its operations in Somalia, Isaias started coverts and overt operations that eventually landed him on the wrong side of Washington and crippling UN sanctions.

The years went by. The people at home and abroad despised Isaias' stubborn ways as the country continued to bleed its young population. In Europe, America, and Israel, Eritreans became one of the largest groups to seek political asylum. More years went by but the aging dictator was not mellowing down with age; still no wisdom, still no mercy.

Like manna from heaven – at least in the eyes of Isaias – change finally came to Ethiopia via youth-led street revolution. The TPLF who controlled Ethiopia for 26 years were driven out of power.

A young Prime Minster emerged talking the right talk and seemingly walking the walk as well. Dr. Abiy Ahmed, an enigmatic character who immediately extended the olive branch to end the no-war-no-peace situation with Eritrea, became Isaias Afwerki's new best friend. That friendship and the formal signing of a treaty with Eritrea earned Abiy Ahmed the 2019 Nobel Peace Prize, but not to his partner in peace, Isaias. The Nobel Committee had decided he was not worthy of it; nor did anyone nominate him.

Here we go again …

Another glimmer of hope shined through the dark clouds. Abiy Ahmed released thousands of prisoners in Ethiopia and implemented a series of impressive political and economic reforms.

But when it comes to Eritrea, even though it is not his domain, he chose to be silent about the plight of the Eritrean people. He just chose to focus on flattering the ego of the dictator. It appears that he did his homework well. To make matters worse, even though he was talking about peace with Eritrea, he was not discussing the border issue with Isaias. They were signing treaties and vague agreements but no one other than the two signatories knew the details of what they were really up to. Eritreans became increasingly suspicious.

At home, Abiy intends to do away with Ethiopia's ethnic-based federal system and replace it with a "unitary" one. To him, it is not only about reforming the constitutional arrangement, it was also an ideology of sorts he calls Medemer, which literally means Addition in Amharic. The official translation says "the action or process of adding something to something else."

Fine and dandy. But Eritreans were right to be a little suspicious after all. What the heck does it mean if that same term Medemer is used within the context of two neighboring countries, whose recent past relationship was that of occupied territory and a colonizer? Maybe being suspicious was not enough. Maybe we should have been even paranoid.

The 30-year war for independence was not waged so that Eritrea can be added to something as if it were something else. However, reasonable minds may ask if it is possible to reverse that with a stroke of a pen without the will of the people. Good question. Even a one-man-totalitarian tyrant cannot simply do that by a decree. But it *can* be done in a more creative and sinister way.

All it requires is that Isaias cooperate and collude with Abiy Ahmed as the plan is slowly implemented. Needless to say, to cooperate means to betray the country he was purportedly leading and commit treason against her.

That is exactly the topic of the next segment.

Isaias: From Dictator to Traitor

From the get-go, there were tell-tell signs that Isaias Afewerki had other ambitions that go beyond the mission of achieving an independent nation called Eritrea. It is indeed hard to fathom why a young man who set out to join a liberation movement that had an explicit mission of seceding from Ethiopia, would later have a change of heart. Speaking decades after these tell-tell signs, some of his colleagues now recall some things Isaias has mentioned during the struggle years. In conversations and meetings, he talked about the need to think beyond independence and even entertained ideas of confederation with Ethiopia. At the time, those who were close to him recall, that it was dismissed as just talk and nothing more. After all, so long as independence was still the number 1 goal, the idea of having economic ties via confederation with a future, free-Ethiopia did not sound too wild.

There are also others who point out that, because of his heritage, Isaias suffered from a conflict of interest and even an inferiority complex. Family lineage and the geographical location of an ancestral village is a major pillar of personal identity. Even though Isaias was born in Eritrea, it is said that his family hailed from the Tigray region, which is in Ethiopia proper. As a result, it is likely that he has faced some sort of mockery or discrimination because of his origin. This could have happened when he was growing up in Asmara or even when he joined the liberation movement. Perceived or real, this feeling of not fitting in, some analysts say, made him vengeful enough to secretly shift his desire of intertwining Eritrea and Ethiopia.

There is a lot to unwind here. First, it is virtually impossible to know what one's heart harbors and to diagnose the psychological implications of a wounded ego during childhood.

184

Secondly, even if that was indeed true, it does not explain why he chose to eventually risk his life to join a rebel movement that is largely based on Eritrean nationalism. If Tigrayan kinship was important to Isaias, he could easily have opted to join another liberation or revolutionary group based in Tigray.

It is only in recent years that the issue of his ancestors became more widely known, and the related psychoanalysis of his motives entertained even more so. In hindsight, it is hard to say what kind of impact this information could have had if the rank and file members of the EPLF were aware of it. But, even if we give this angle some weight, the popularity Isaias enjoyed among the fighters and the general public outweighed it by far.

Anecdotal comments, hearsay, and speculation about motive may all add up to circumstantial evidence but they were not explicit enough to infer what Isaias real motives were.

Then came a very explicit statement. In 1993, in a press conference in Addis Ababa, asked about the future relationship of Ethiopia Eritrea and possible integration of the two, Isaias Afwerki said,

> Why not is the answer I have given to this particular question. And if one can see deep into the agreement we have reached, we have not reached this agreement for the sake of domestic or international consumption. We're fully committed to this agreement. We believe the integration process might take a long time, it might take years, even decades, but full integration of Eritrea and Ethiopia, beginning with economic integration programs and ending possibly in some form of a political integration is a possibility. We need not have any bias; we need not have any reservations as to developing our bilateral relations toward that direction.

Again, it is only in hindsight and perhaps with the benefit of watching the YouTube video of the interview over and over again, that these words are reverberating today. At the time he said it, Eritreans were too euphoric celebrating the formal milestone of Eritrea being welcomed to the community of nations, to pay attention.

If there were any real concerns, they were likely dismissed by the fact that re-annexation by Ethiopia was totally out of the question for most and the Eritrean people and other leaders of the EPLF would not allow it.

However, one of Isaias' strongest traits is patience. In this case, if the people and his own organization are going to be in the way of this integration, then he will have to devise a plan that would neutralize the obstacles. But first, he must continue to consolidate his power. This power cannot be just authoritarian in nature, it must be systematically totalitarian; a one-man-totalitarianism based on a cult of personality.

After thwarting the constitutional process and using the pretext of war to jail, kill, disappear, or exile his opponents, by 2001, that goal had been essentially achieved. No electoral politics to speak of, no independent civil society, no private press, and the judiciary system under the direct control of the executive. It is as if there was a coup d'etat in Eritrea and Isaias was the victor, the last man standing.

For their own reasons, the TPLF who have been leading Ethiopia did not want Isaias to meddle in their own designs for Ethiopia. The border war of 1998-2000 gave them a perfect excuse to keep Isaias at bay. Even though they signed The Algiers Peace Agreement which formally resolved the disputes, they were creative enough to turn it into a no-war-no-peace standoff.

Surely, Isaias' former allies have become his nemesis. But the TPLF had a lot of enemies and all Isaias had to do is befriend and support them. Yes, even those who don't formally recognize Eritrea's independence.

Eritrea became the training and logistical center for a plethora of Ethiopian opposition groups, ranging from armed insurgency to political lackeys. A coalition of exiled activist parties like Kinijit (also known as the Coalition for Unity and Democracy or CUD) who frequently display maps of Ethiopia that includes Eritrea, to the anger of Eritreans became close confidants of the Eritrean dictator. The Washington, DC-based Ethiopian Satellite Television (ESAT), which promotes the idea of Greater Ethiopia and the zealotry of having access to the Red Sea became major propagandists for Isaias.

In return, it is believed that the Isaias regime is a major funder of the station.

Totalitarianism achieved at home and the colluding with anti-Eritrean independence groups in full force, the road toward reuniting with Ethiopia continued in full force.

Needless to say, this is tantamount to treason; Isaias the dictator is now Isaias the traitor. But who is going to formally accuse him of that? The EPLF has been gutted out and replaced by the PFDJ, a shell organization that does not have any mechanisms of power other than what Isaias wants it to be.

The cabinet is full of people who serve at the whims of the president. Any risk they take is brutally met with jailing and banishment. The army is controlled by generals who owe their allegiance to Isaias and not to Eritrea.

It is against this backdrop the jaw-dropping, dramatic confessions came … directly from the dictator's mouth.

After Abiy Ahmed came to power, In July 2018, at a speech he gave to a gathering in Hawassa, Ethiopia, Isaias blurted it out "anybody who says the people of Eritrea and Ethiopia are two peoples is someone who doesn't know the real truth." And if that is not shocking enough, he also added that he had repeatedly told the Ethiopian Prime Minister " …in any affair, if there is something that needs to be done, you are our representative. You are the one who is going to lead us."

The crowd at the Millennium Hall in Addis Ababa was even more jubilant as they celebrate a new era of Ethiopia going back to its glory days. The frenzy about Abiy Ahmed's "Medemer" ideology is now including Eritrea. It was a cleverly presented show. He adorned Isaias Afeworki with a traditional shawl, customary wedding wear that included a cloth-made crown. The message was noticeably clear: if you bring back Eritrea, we will treat you as royalty and as an emperor.

"We will share the port of Assab with Isu (term of endearment for Isaias)" Abiy declared.

The crowd cheered with joy. The normally stone-faced Isaias seems to suddenly melt with emotions. He could really feel the love. He felt he was in the right place and at the right time. Gently thumping his chest with blowing kisses to the audience he returned the love.

It was quite an ironic scene. On one side, here is a man who led a liberation war in which thousands were killed, maimed, and tremendously suffered, vowing to hand over his ill-gotten power to the leader of the rival country.

On the other side, people cheering the very rebel leader who is responsible for killing hundreds of thousands of their soldiers over four decades, as if he were incarnate of Mother Theresa. Politics makes strange bedfellows indeed.

Now that the stage is set for the victors to fully execute their plans, it is becoming abundantly clear that Eritrea's independence at risk. The dark clouds are gathering. Eritrea's sovereignty is in clear and present danger.

Resurgence of Expansionism in Ethiopia

For the past half a century, the world is probably tired of hearing about the conflict between Ethiopia and Eritrea. Without having the right perspective, it can be mistaken that the conflicts were about ethnic hatred, revenge, or other normal disputes between neighbors.

It is actually simpler than that. No matter how they were presented at what period of time, the tension has been always about the rulers of Ethiopia and their inability to control the urge of occupying Eritrea by force.

Landlocked from having direct access to the Red Sea, and perhaps feeling humiliated as a result of it, every now and then Ethiopians have been agitated towards war with Eritrea (they call them campaigns) that promises them that their fortunes will be reversed this time. Sometimes, this gets masqueraded as a campaign of "unity" to return home a runaway daughter, other times, to save a piece of Ethiopia from being sold to the Arabs, and most recently to prevent Eritrea from invading Ethiopia, which is absurd.

Consequences of the history of invasions by the Egyptians, Ottomans, Ethiopians, and Italians have forged the ethnically diverse people of today's Eritrea to be vigilant and fiercely independent. This yearning to be independent occasionally clashes with the desire of Ethiopia to encroach and expand her influence. This is why all the conflict between Ethiopia and Eritrea has always been fought inside Eritrea. In short, Eritreans have shown no desire to forcibly occupy Ethiopia but the reverse has been true ever since the founding of the Ethiopian empire.

Now, the tradition of that expansionism is about to unfold, now with the aiding and abetting of Eritrea's self-appointed leader who has repeatedly shown his wish for reunion with Ethiopia. While this is not unprecedented in Eritrea's history, as other leaders have also betrayed their position and handed it over to Ethiopia before, it would be the first time since the formal declaration of independence.

For almost 30 years, an ethnic-based federal system has been in place in Ethiopia. While it did not completely subdue the fervent hyper-nationalism that frequently blows out of proportion and itches to start yet another war of expansionism, it probably has lessened the risk.

But that cycle is now in the process of getting undone and the forces of the unitary state are gathering momentum. Instead of a county of many nation-states, Ethiopia can once again be a single state, with power concentrated with a central government pushing the agenda of a single culture, language and ideology masked as unity.

That call for unity always includes Eritrea by hook or crook. It is the crook kind that is most likely to unfold soon.

In yet, another disturbing speech, Prime Minister Abiy Ahmed announced that "… today, officially, President Isaias Afwerki has given me the responsibility of Foreign Minister." Which is to say, he will represent the interest of both countries and as if they were one – wink, wink – as if they were both Ethiopia and nothing else. He even hinted at closing Eritrean embassies as the need of both countries can be represented by the Ethiopian ones.

At the time of this writing, land-locked Ethiopia is revamping its naval force on the Red Sea. With direct and indirect influence over Eritrea's long coastline, yet one more dark cloud hovers over Eritrea's sovereignty. Conversely, thanks to Isaias Afwerki's ineptitude and grander goals, the Eritrea Navy is barely developed.

In any case, it will not be able to defend the country or itself.

If economic integration is a stop toward full assimilation, then that will also be based on a very lopsided scenario. With a population of over 110 million, Ethiopia is a humongous country. Hovering around 4 million,

Eritrea's population is relatively minuscule. The centrally planned and almost non-existent economy is no match for Ethiopia and its vibrant private sector. In this situation, unregulated open borders and free trade will hurt Eritreans who will be unable to compete, relegating them to be subservient to their Ethiopian counterparts.

The Solution

As long as Eritrea remains under the yoke of one man it will continue to suffer. Power corrupts and absolute power has corrupted Isaias Afwerki and is enabling him to do the unthinkable. To prevent this final act from happening, Eritreans must place the agenda of removing the dictator as their number one goal.

After all these years, a clear understanding of what is transpiring is not widely understood, especially inside Eritrea.

Eritrea's Diaspora-based opposition has been very vocal about this as they are the only ones who can speak freely but the opposition often lacks unity and credibility.

It can still play a role in educating Eritreans, Ethiopians, and the world community about the dangers of intermingling Ethiopia and Eritrea.

The real hope however rests with patriots within the Eritrean Defense Forces who have the wherewithal and the opportunity to take swift action to save the nation and save it from the jaws of defeat.

WHITHER ERITREA: NATIONHOOD, DICTATORSHIP, AND THE STRUGGLE FOR A DEMOCRATIC ERITREA

Ismail Omar-Ali

Introduction

Eritreans are in a quandary. After a long series of occupations that spanned a century followed by an independence that quickly turned into a mirage at the hands of a ruthless dictator, a gnawing question at the forefront of Eritrean people's minds today is: "when will it ever end"? Unfortunately, there is no end in sight though there is little doubt that the once mighty dictatorship that rose meteorically in the early years of independence has fallen equally dramatically in the last decade or so. Today, the regime is reeling in its final death throes. This raises a corollary question: Why is it still standing? It survives because the opposition in its fragmented state is even weaker and lacks the wherewithal to deliver the slight nudge needed to end it. All dictatorships collapse in the end with or without the help of an opposition, but it is the opposition's strengths or weaknesses that hasten or delay their fall.

It is important to remember, however, that even in its enfeebled state, a dictatorship can hobble along for many years lashing fiercely and frantically when it senses its end is near. Clearing the wreckage it will leave behind and erecting a democratic polity in its place will be a formidable challenge. As

Machiavelli once put it: "There is nothing more difficult to take in hand... than to take the lead in the introduction of a new order of things" (Machiavelli, 1532)[1]. Nonetheless, history and contemporary events attest that dictatorships are far from indestructible. Once fully aroused, a determined populace is virtually unstoppable and can quickly subdue even the mightiest of dictatorships. In recent years, we have seen this phenomenon unfold in several of Eritrea's neighbors with varying degree of success. Is it Eritrea's turn? It is increasingly looking that way.

Indeed, there are various signs that conditions in Eritrea and Diaspora are reaching a tipping point: The steady, skyrocketing rise in the number of dissidents both intra-and-inter the ruling party; the unmistakable erosion of the president's base of support; and the rapidity with which the status of the regime is tanking all point to a nation clamoring for fundamental change. Activism is also gathering steam on many fronts in Eritrea and the Diaspora as can be seen in the eruption of the "enough" movement and in the late Haj Musa's courageous defiance just to name a few[2]. Even international observers are taking note. Last year, the economist published an article that read "Eritrea's gulag state is crumbling." (Economist, 2019).[3] All this is good news for democratic workers, but a bumpy road lies ahead of forming a united opposition front, toppling the dictatorship, and safely

---

1 Niccolò Machiavelli, *The Prince*, trans. William K Marriott (Independently published, n.d.), p. 14.
2 Enough or Iakl movement was promising at first but was stymied in its infancy due to structural flaws and lack of diversity particularly in the leadership. It still has a great potential to galvanize Eritreans especially the youth once it overcomes this temporary hiccup.
3 "Eritrea's Gulag State Is Crumbling." 2019. *The Economist.* Accessed November 6, 2020. https://www.economist.com/middle-east-and-africa/2019/07/11/eritreas-gulag-state-is-crumbling.

transitioning towards democracy. This is the overarching theme of this chapter.

But before we delve into the specifics of toppling the regime and safely navigating a post-Isaias Eritrea towards democracy, we will briefly review important milestones in Eritrean history to provide a contextual framework. The first issue we will discuss is the crucial issue of nationhood and sovereignty. This is central to Eritreans because it was a firm and unshakable belief in their right to a separate nationhood that sustained them through many decades of immense suffering and it is this belief that will nurture them in the ongoing battle against dictatorship and beyond.

This will be followed by a discussion of the nature of dictatorship and the techniques it has used (still uses) to stay in power. How did one man and his clique manage to keep an entire nation hostage for so long? What past mistakes, if any, contributed to the current dismal state of affairs in Eritrea? Alarmingly, many Eritreans remain ill-informed about the nature and techniques of dictatorships and since such naivety has led to many catastrophes, the topic merits an in-depth look. We then review the issue of toppling the dictatorship where we attempt to answer questions about the best ways to conduct resistance and whether peaceful resistance could succeed in Eritrea. But as essential as toppling a dictator is, it is only the first step. New democracies can crumble, and a dictatorship can resurrect itself in new ways as it did in Egypt for example. We will therefore wrap up the chapter with a discussion of the challenges transition and consolidation of democracy pose in the struggle ahead. These are the interrelated subtopics we will also examine in this chapter.

Eritrea's claims to nationhood & Sovereignty

If there is one issue that has dogged Eritreans throughout their history, it is the question of nationhood and sovereignty. It has become less of an issue since independence, but every now and then doubts continue to be cast on Eritrea's right to a separate nationhood. President Isaias's bizarre ramblings about being "one people" with Ethiopia is a recent case in point. This is unwarranted in view of the more than a century of shared experience Eritreans have had together. Eritrea's quest for a separate nationhood can be traced as far back as the Italian colonization (some say even earlier) though it took concrete form as an organized effort during the peaceful and armed struggles for independence in the 50s and 60s respectively.

In many ways, Eritrea's independence history is an anomaly among African countries. First, while many African countries were joyously celebrating (or about to celebrate) their independence from European powers in the 60s, Eritrea was freshly conquered by Ethiopia. It was exactly a year after 17 African countries gained independence in 1960 (a year that became known as a "year of Africa") that Awate, the founder of Eritrean Liberation Army fired his first shot. Second, Eritrea is the first country to successfully gain independence from another African country. South Sudan did the same about two decades later[4]. Third, Eritrea's struggle for independence was the longest in Africa and arguably the toughest. Fourth, Eritrea's struggle started during the "Golden Age of high pan-African ambitions" when Nkrumah, OAU, and other notable African intellectuals were passionately rallying for African unity. Together, all these factors made it seem that Eritrea was marching against the tide of African unity & seeking "secession" instead of "integration" with African countries.

Why then did Eritreans wage such a protracted war against another African country instead of coalescing with it? What is the basis for their claim to a separate nationhood or statehood? To answer such questions adequately requires an understanding of nation-states particularly African nation-states.

---

4 Two decades after de facto or 18 years after de jure independence.

Nation-State

Socrates once reportedly declared: "I am not an Athenian or a Greek but a citizen of the world". Two millenniums later, Thomas Paine, the eminent American political activist, expressed a similar sentiment when he asserted "my country is the world, and my religion is to do good." Many other philosophers, religious leaders, and thinkers have expressed similar thoughts. The vision of one humanity, one Government, and one world is a powerful ideal that humanity will hopefully attain at some distant future. At present (and for the foreseeable future), however, the world follows a territorially based paradigm of structuring society that political theorists refer to as nation-states.

What exactly is a nation-state? Comprising of two terms (nation and state) that are themselves hard to quantify, a nation-state is a highly abstract political concept that defies easy characterization. Political theorists and social scientists have debated and continue to debate the precise definitions of a "nation-state". Some have hypothesized that the term should be restricted to those states with homogenous ethnicity and culture (one people, one nation). Such a definition, however, would preclude the overwhelming majority of modern states including Eritrea which comprises of several religions and ethnicities. Encyclopedia Britannica defines nation-state as "a territorially bounded sovereign polity—i.e., a state—that is ruled in the name of a community of citizens who identify themselves as a nation." (Encyclopedia Britannica, 2020)[5]

This is a more accurate rendering and a better workable definition for modern nation-states because immigration, intermarriage, and many other factors have made it virtually impossible for nations to remain homogenous. With slight variation, this definition of nation-states is what supra-national organizations like the United Nations have adapted.

---

5 *Encyclopedia Britannica Online*, 2020, s.v. "Nation-State". https://www.britannica.com/topic/nation-state.

Accordingly, Eritrea's claim to a separate sovereignty over its territory is an internationally justified contention. As we shall see shortly, it also conforms to Africa's specific guidelines for border delineation.

In considering the case of Africa and how Eritrea's case relates to it, we should first bear in mind that the entire map of Africa is a post-colonial construct. African nation-states were created by Europeans for European interests. So, when African countries achieved independence in the 50's and 60's, they faced a dilemma of what to do with such arbitrarily drawn territorial boundaries. A lot of discussion and debates ensued but finally, fear of widespread conflicts swayed the discussion towards accepting all post-colonial borders as sacrosanct sovereign states. Eritrea's current borders originate in Italian occupation; moreover, as we alluded to earlier, Eritreans' sense of collective identity was shaped by eighty plus years of Italian, British, and Ethiopian occupations whereby their communal bond was forged in blood and tears. Few, if any, African nation-states can boast such an irrefutable basis for nationhood. Thus, Eritrea's claim to territorial sovereignty among African nations also rests on iron-clad foundation. But despite the incontrovertible legitimacy of their claim on both African and international standards, Eritreans' aspirations were destined to be obstructed again and again.

When Italians left Eritrea in 1941, Eritreans were eager to be independent. They staged various forms of protest to express their wishes. Lamentably, foreign intrigue coupled with Ethiopia's duplicity, forced them into a federation with Ethiopia which granted Eritrea a limited autonomy over its administrative, judicial, & other institutions. In less than 10 years, Emperor Haile Selassie of Ethiopia, summarily annulled Eritrea's autonomy, dissolved the federation, and finally annexed Eritrea in 1962. Once again, Eritreans vehemently protested this unilateral violation of the federation only to be repeatedly snubbed by the international community.

Struggle for Independence

After peaceful protests failed to produce results, Eritreans launched an armed struggle for independence in 1961 under the leadership of Idris Hamid Awate. Revered as the indomitable father of the Eritrean revolution by Eritreans of all walks of life[6], he and his handful followers were instrumental in imbuing the movement with revolutionary zeal from the get-go; they set a powerful precedent when they stood up defiantly and resolutely to take on the mighty behemoth of an Ethiopian army. From thereon, the revolutionary period would go through many trials and tribulations and become embroiled in petty ethnic fights every now and then, but courage and fortitude would remain the hallmarks of both ELF[7] and EPLF[8] fighters. Awate's first shot would fly precariously for 30 years like a rocket with no breaks or a fire that would not be extinguished to finally hit its target in 1991. Awate (and many other early pioneers) would not live to see it but on May 24, 1991, their mission was accomplished when Eritrea became a sovereign state.

Independent Eritrea

For long suffering Eritreans, independence was a breathtaking event that will remain etched in their memory. Throngs upon throngs of cheering and dancing Eritreans poured into the streets of Asmara, Eritrea's capital, to greet their saviors and to salute their long-sought independence. At home and abroad, Eritreans were ecstatic and delirious with joy. Isaias and EPLF became instant heroes. If Awate was the father of the liberation

---

6   The Kunamas are a notable exception as some in their ranks accuse Awate of crimes against their people
7   The term ELF or Jebha is being used throughout the chapter to mean all people who were either veteran members of ELF proper or belonged to one of its offshoots
8   The terms EPLF, PFDJ, GOE, Shaebia will be used interchangeably throughout this chapter to denote the entire political culture that Isaias presides over or has presided over.

movement, Isaias became the founding father of independent Eritrea. The optimism was so universal that even those who knew EPLF's authoritarian tendencies began to hope for a bright future. Numerous expats and former rivals (ELF veterans) returned to Eritrea after years in exile with high expectations that old grudges would be forgiven, and healing would commence. Few Eritreans at the time had an inkling of the grim destiny that awaited them: a dictatorship, to which we turn next.

The Dawn of Dictatorship

In fortunate countries, independence is followed by an era of freedom and prosperity. For a brief period after independence, such a scenario had indeed seemed possible in Eritrea when EPLF, firmly ensconced in power, declared:

"The people of Eritrea have forever altered the course of Eritrean history and launched a new phase in the struggle for democracy, equality and freedom" (Eritrea: Birth of a Nation, 1993)[9]

In just about a year after the above pronouncement, disabled veteran protestors would be shot at Mai Habar and countless number of Muslim teachers, Jehovah Witnesses, and other civilians would be held incommunicado or killed extrajudicially throughout Eritrea. In subsequent years, the list of victims would expand or shrink, and the severity of despotism would wax and wane, but the pattern of oppression would continue unabated. The regime's tyranny, it should be noted, is no garden-variety dictatorship but of a full-blown totalitarian[10] monstrosity that not only wields infinite powers over the executive, judiciary, and legislative bodies, but also has the last word on every financial venture, every domestic policy, every educational strategy, every social program, and every

---

9 Eritrea: Birth of a Nation. Eritrea: Government of Eritrea, Department of External Affairs, 1993.
10 Eritrea is one of the only two totalitarian countries in the world. The other is North Korea.

cultural initiative. It imposes heavy taxes haphazardly, locks up people whimsically, appoints and fires public servants at will, and declares war and breaks alliances without any rhyme or reason.

Unfortunately, it would take close to a decade and a devastating war for many Eritreans to recognize the dictatorship thereby enabled it to entrench itself deeply into every facet of Eritrean life. The 1998 war with Ethiopia was thus a watershed moment. Before the war, few thought of the regime in Eritrea as a dictatorship and dissenters were few and far between, and for the most part confined to certain regions. After the war, perceptions abruptly changed, and many Eritreans started to see the regime for what it has always been: a dictatorship.

The above analysis is sometimes disputed by current or former EPLF supporters who point to a brief period in the late 1900s when a seemingly 'freer Eritrea' with private press was burgeoning and active. In my view, this is a misguided perception. It is true that Eritrea had what faintly resembled a democracy with press freedom, but the facade was more of an optical illusion than real. This will become clear when we consider several points. First, Eritrea never had elections of any sort since independence, not even mock elections and *there can be no democracy without elections*. In contrast, almost all African countries have had multiparty elections of some sort. Second, post-independence Eritrea was, is, and remains a single party dictatorship where the formation of other political parties is permanently banned. Third, Eritrea never did and still doesn't guarantee basic democratic rights such as freedom of religion, speech, the right to assemble, and other fundamental civil liberties. Furthermore, throughout the period in question, innocents were pining away in various detentions and dungeons all over Eritrea without being charged or tried.

Similar was the case with the simulated free private press because a freedom that can be offered and retracted at the whim of a tyrant is no freedom at all but is analogous to crumbs that are tantalizingly proffered and withdrawn from a servile subject. Thus, the whole "democracy" episode was a charade to enable the dictator to sift his loyal followers from would-be enemies or detractors. Many other examples could be given but that should suffice to show that post-independent Eritrea has always been a bona fide dictatorship without any letup since independence.

What some Eritreans mistook for democracy and freedom was nothing but Isaias's carefully timed sleight of hand. To appreciate this, one needs to recall that this happened in a post-soviet world when the demand for democracy was intensifying globally. Isaias had to put on a show of democracy to the world at large as he simultaneously kept an eye on Eritreans to see who would agitate for democracy, so he can crush them expeditiously. For extra insurance, he also needed a diversion and the 1998 war with Ethiopia provided him with the perfect pretext. Unfortunately for him, it ended in defeat that cost the lives of tens of thousands of Eritreans. This dealt a deathblow to his and EPLF/PFDJ's mystique of invincibility. It also convulsed many of his followers into a rude awakening who belatedly realized that they have been following a trickster all along. This led to the G-13/15 rebellion. Isaias pretended to listen to the grievances for a while but was in fact biding his time and when an opportune moment presented itself during the September 11 tragedy, he struck decisively and swiftly to nip the movement in the bud as is his wont. The G-15 committed a cardinal mistake when it attempted to reason with a dictator instead of staging a coup, calling for his resignation, or orchestrating a mass protest[11].

Two decades after the tragic purge, Eritreans are still chafing under a tyranny and remain as perplexed as ever. How and when did Eritrea, a jolly innocent new nation with great

---

11 Regrettably, this was because the G-15 naively believed the issue was a negotiable internal PFDJ matter that could be resolved without removing the oppressive regime. In other words, they sought to reform not to overhaul the oppressive regime.

promise and potential, morph into one of the most despotic countries in the world? What factors led independence to be subsumed so quickly by tyranny and terror? What led Isaias, a liberation-era protagonist, to become one of the most ruthless dictators in Africa? And why didn't Eritreans rise against his oppressive regime as they did so heroically against foreign occupation? Above all, how did he (one man) manage to defraud a nation of about 4 million people for almost 30 years and counting? Was he a lifelong demagogue or did he change stripes after independence?

Some of these questions are easy to answer, others are not. The answer to 'how did one man (Isaias) succeed in tyrannizing an entire nation?', for example, is straightforward: he didn't. No doubt he was/is the chief architect but irrespective how shrewd he was or how diabolically crafty he had been, he could never have done it without the consecration and substantial backing of many Eritreans who actively fanned his megalomaniac propensities cheering him along, fibbing for him, and sacrificing for him throughout his quixotic escapades. Nor could he have succeeded without the organization (EPLF & its various reincarnations) he gave birth to decades ago[12]. As we read in the bible "a good tree cannot bear bad fruit, and a bad tree cannot bear good fruit."

"There were some commendable positives we all know; the discipline, the selflessness, the sacrifice, and camaraderie that EPLF fostered but far more important in a pluralistic democracy is an open and tolerant attitude towards others which EPLF central command never had. Now, why is it important to recognize or identify EPLF for what it was/is: an aberrant outgrowth of the liberation movement?

First, it will facilitate dialog and reconciliation because if Eritreans continue to mythologize EPLF, they will be ill-equipped to engage in cool-headed democratic dialog. It should

---

12 It should be noted that we are referring here to the militaristic infrastructure of EPLF not the rank and file innocents.

be remembered that EPLF was/is a large storehouse of misinformation and propaganda. If you are an EPLFer, think of the elaborate tales you were told and believed starting from Isaias' incorruptibility to EPLF's invincibility. Think also of all the lies you were told about the ELF/opposition and how you slandered them as sellouts, traitors, jihadists, and weyanes and how similar epithets are now being used to describe *you*. Think also of how parochial you were in your thinking about Eritrea (equating it with EPLF), about nationalism, religion, ethnicity, and the world. Isn't it time to break free from this strong compulsion that continues to hamper your efforts to relate to others on equal terms?

Second and more importantly, such glamorized notions about EPLF will have far-reaching ramifications on how we go about dismantling the current regime. Will we go for a deep surgical removal of the entire EPLF/PFDJ/GOE colossus or for a mere cosmetic touch here and there that leaves the regime and its core political culture basically intact? The latter would be a fool's errand because a dictatorship that is not uprooted has a way of reconstituting or regenerating itself even from a tiny severed part of itself. We see this phenomenon over and over again in many countries in Africa and elsewhere where one dictator is replaced by another or by a fake democracy. A totalitarian regime that is so deeply embedded in the fabric of every part of society as Eritrea's dictatorship is would soon relapse into a new dictatorship if care is not taken to demolish it firmly and decisively. "[13] Sun Tzu, the ancient Chinese military strategist, believed that success in battle hinges on knowing the enemy. The same is true of a dictatorship. A sound understanding of a dictator's mind and techniques is the first step towards overcoming him which brings us to our next segment.

---

13 The two quoted paragraphs are from the following article I wrote on Awate: http://awate.com/elites-isaias-eplf-and-the-eritrean-people/

Understanding Eritrea's dictatorship: the mind of a dictator

"This is the miracle of our age", Hitler once thundered, "... that you have found me among so many millions! And that I have found you, that is Germany's good fortune!" About half a century later, Eritrea's mini-Fuhrer, gloated:

> Our army has no sophisticated modern arsenal. In fact, it hardly possesses weaponry up-to-date enough to be called an army; what distinguishes our army and what is responsible for its many wonders and miracles, is the political consciousness of each combatant.

The above words (a rough translation from Tigrigna) were spoken by Isaias decades ago. Note in the quotations above how both Isaias and Hitler refer to miracles thereby arrogating themselves supernatural prowess. The intention here is not to compare Isaias to Hitler but to illustrate the nature of all dictatorships. A propensity to delusions of grandeur is characteristic of all despots and is key to unraveling the seemingly paradoxical knack of dictators for both notable deeds and suicidal recklessness. Since familiarity with the nature of dictators is crucial to preventing their recurrence, we will explore the topic in a little more detail. It is my contention that many errors in the past (including the G-15 tragedy) may have been averted if the nature and ploys of dictators were widely known by Eritreans.

Considering the high status of the G13/15 members, some may challenge my assertion; others may disbelievingly wonder if it is really possible for a dictator to bewitch and hoodwink the learned elites who knew him so intimately. Sadly, the answer is in the affirmative. It clearly happened in Eritrea and it has happened in many other countries. Sustained and pervasive propaganda is so powerful and so enchanting that even otherwise shrewd intellectuals find it difficult to escape its influence. An Egyptian intellectual once confessed about Nasser that he "stripped us (intellectuals) throughout the years

205

of every independent thought and every strong personality other than his own". At various times, Professor Bereket Habte Selassie and Mesfin Hagos[14] have also acknowledged that they were similarly conned by the dictator which raises the question: What drives dictators? How do they do it?

A dictator is a leader who, through subterfuge, propaganda, and intimidation bends multitudes to his will. This ability to dominate and mold masses to do one's bidding (often against their best interests) is so powerful an intoxicant, so an exhilarating tonic that a dictator will gradually start to believe that he is indeed invincible. It is this powerful feeling of impregnability that drives dictators like Isaias to take reckless risks and wage wars even when it is no longer necessary to do so. Like the feverish gambler whose ravenousness redoubles with every win, each victory feeds the dictator's appetite for preeminence and glory.

Nor is the dictator's dream confined to military ambitions. Surrounded by 'yes men' who ostensibly accept his verdict on every issue, he starts to believe (and persuades others to join in his delusion) that he is omniscient or that his judgment is impeccable. How else did I prevail, he will reflect, over so many people and over so many insurmountable obstacles all these years? All the men and women who died bravely to make him seem 'great' are inconsequential to him. In his mind, He deserves all the credit. The fact that many individuals with better intelligence and erudition happen to eagerly kowtow to his 'wisdom' intensifies this feeling of all-powerfulness and convinces him that he is grander than all others. Eventually, this grandiose feeling turns into uncontrollable urge that must be satisfied at all costs. Be that as it may, a dictator intuitively realizes that mass delusion cannot be sustained indefinitely if it is not constantly reinforced with a slew of techniques which is a topic we discuss next.

---

14 See Bereket Habte Selassie, *Wounded Nation: How a Once Promising Eritrea Was Betrayed and Its Future Compromised* (New Jersey: Red Sea Press, 2011), 61

Eritrea's dictatorship: Isaias's techniques explained

We indirectly alluded to one of the techniques when we discussed the sham democracy but there are many others. Here, we will confine ourselves to only three of the most common ploys that Isaias has used.

Legitimacy

A famous line from Shakespeare's Twelfth Night reads "some are born great, some achieve greatness, and some have greatness thrust upon them". Monarchs are born great[15] since they inherit their status, but modern dictatorships rarely are. They instead achieve "greatness" and legitimacy through years of painstaking effort championing honorable causes. Isaias earned his legitimacy by joining the armed struggle for Eritrea's independence in the 60's where he quickly rose to prominence. This gave him a base of support and helped establish him as a zealous patriot. But Isaias, who had bigger ambitions, came to perceive the Arabized culture of Jebha as an obstacle to his long-range objectives. This coupled with his innate dislike to playing second fiddle to others finally drove him to break away. This accorded him two rewards: first, he became the supreme undisputed leader albeit over a smaller and totally homogenous group. Second, it enabled him to propagate his religio-cultural mission of de-Arabizing and de-Islamizing a subset of Jebha (and subsequently Eritrea). To his dismay, things did not run smoothly even among his carefully selected followers. The most serious threat came (in the ever-paranoid eyes of Isaias) from the Menkae movement. Quick as a wink, he dealt with them as he would all future threats to his rule: by nipping it in the bud which brings us to another of Isaias's tactics.

---

15 Shakespeare's usage of the word "great" should not be taken too literally here but rather in the general sense of leadership. Furthermore, though monarchs are technically dictators, they are irrelevant to our discussion since they are almost extinct in the modern world

207

Ruthlessness

Isaias demonstrated his readiness to use deadly force to eliminate all opposition on numerous occasions throughout his years as the leader of EPLF. We just alluded to Menkae movement but all protests that arose after independence were similarly dealt with. Anyone who shows the slightest sign of dissension is immediately crushed. He is equally brutal towards the young (e.g. Ciham) and the very old (eg. Hajj Musa). To this day, weeding out opponents and castigating insubordination before they gain momentum continues to be his trademark and is one of the secrets to his longevity. But as effective as ruthless suppression of opponents can be, it sometimes generates sympathy for the victims and may eventually trigger a revolt if it is not supplemented with another powerful weapon.

Propaganda

EPLF under Isaias used propaganda for two goals. 1)To glorify and canonize itself as the only genuine nationalist movement and 2) to demonize all others as working against national interest and unity. Supporters are portrayed as the only genuine patriots, Shaebia as the ultimate miracle worker, and Isaias as a genius who can do no wrong. In sharp contrast, critics are repeatedly maligned as sellouts, losers, and traitors and ostracized as enemies of national unity.

Looking back, we can say that Shaebia's propaganda at the gutter level was terrifyingly effective in both respects (i.e. in aggrandizing itself and in demonizing its enemies). Nothing speaks more eloquently to its eerie effectiveness than the fact that it took a devastating war and almost a decade for any of his core followers to even whisper a mild protest! Its power can also be gauged by the fact that until recently Shaebia had significant followers despite its colossal failures at multiple levels. I believe many ills of the opposition such as mutual distrust and fragmentation are traceable to shaebia's powerful propaganda.

Of course, shaebia did not originate propaganda nor is it the only entity in the world to apply it. On the contrary, propaganda has become the most ubiquitous phenomenon in the modern world that all nations including countries with stable democracies practice. So, why should Eritrea (GOE) be deprived of it? Well, it shouldn't, and no one is suggesting it should but as we all know propaganda can be used for good or ill. Some examples of good propaganda are those that seek to inform, to educate, and to warn of dangers while bad propaganda brainwashes, misleads, and forces conformity. PFDJ/GOE's propaganda is of the latter form. Moreover, propaganda in dictatorships is quite different from those in democracies because in the latter, people can have access to a variety of opposing views without suffering dire consequences.

The goal of dictators, on the other hand, is to straightjacket the thinking of their people within carefully defined boundaries. To this end, they subject their people to the same identical message day in and day out, harping on the same issues systematically and incessantly. The public is constantly kept charged so to speak with uplifting and impassioned rhetoric of dignity, nation, blood, martyrs etc. on the one hand and the dictatorship's half-truths on the other. As a result, the lofty feeling one experiences when contemplating nationalism becomes firmly associated with the regime. Over time, this bastardization of nationalism with dictatorship causes people to lose their faculty of discernment – their capacity to disentangle the dictatorship from a nation and its people.

The effects of Shaebia propaganda was not confined to its staunch supporters. Indeed, it may have been more damaging to non-Shaebians than Shaebians. The former were so thoroughly maligned and demonized that they eventually lost confidence in themselves and in their ability to bring about change. EPLF's propaganda thus led to psychological emasculation across the board. This is its ultimate achievement and its most egregious crime[16]. But time marches on and as unmasked lies kept piling up, its effects finally wore off. As the Quran asserts, "falsehood by its very nature is bound to perish". Eritreans have finally broken the spell that bound them to the dictator's canard and are now ready to defeat the dictatorship itself and march towards democracy, but they must first learn to work together to which we turn next.

Uniting the opposition

As was stated in the introduction to this chapter, only a united opposition can hasten the defeat of a dictatorship. The ability to mobilize the masses under one banner is a feature that is common among all successful movements. To succeed, Eritrean opposition must not only be able to attract and retain a large group of people, it must also be able to garner a consensus around a set of core principles. The latter requires a great deal of intensive campaigning and dialog but in the case of Eritrea, this should now be a little easier because there is already a consensus within the opposition and among the general population at large about the primary goal; the overwhelming majority wants the dictatorship out, dismantled, and replaced with a just system. All are also agreed (except for a handful intellectual oddballs) that Eritrea should have a representative democracy.

So, what is preventing the Eritrean democratic forces from making noticeable progress? There are many factors, of which the most important causes are the dictator's ploys that we discussed in previous sections whose cumulative effects produced a long-lasting culture of fear, inferiority complex, and mutual mistrust. This is not unique to Eritrean society but is a malady that afflicts all people who live under modern dictatorships. In his seminal book, 'From Dictatorship to

---

16 Isaias uses many other ploys such as cabinet shuffle, career freeze, fear mongering etc. He also deliberately perpetuated the myth that the entire world is against Eritrea etc. but to itemize them all would require an entire book

Democracy", the celebrated guru of non-violence, Gene Sharp insightfully sums up the plight of a population under authoritarianism who become "unable to work together to achieve freedom, to confide in each other, or even to do much of anything at their own initiative... People are often too frightened to share their hatred of the dictatorship and their hunger for freedom even with family and friends." (Sharp, 2012)[17]

This aptly depicts the current state of Eritreans and the Eritrean opposition. So democratic forces face an uphill battle as they seek to reverse this psychological barrier. Hopefully, the current devastating civil war in Ethiopia[18] and the real danger it poses to Eritrea will galvanize Eritreans to save their country from total ruin. To say time is running out is an understatement. Eritreans are truly surviving on borrowed time.

Another major impediment to abiding unity is the slanted and dubious historical records (oral and written) that have accumulated over the years. The history of the noble struggle for Eritrean independence is also the history of hate propaganda, mutual mistrust, and mutual demonization. Reciprocal rivalry and enmity in turn spawned all sorts of anecdotal records that both sides swear by. As a political historian once put it, 'political perspectives are not immaculately conceived' which is a fancy way of stating that our political views are largely determined by our past experiences. The political views of most Eritreans seem to originate directly or indirectly in these politically motivated records. I consider this to be the crux of the problem because these ambiguous narrations are at the back of people's mind whenever they try to collaborate with one another.

---

17 Gene Sharp, *From Dictatorship to Democracy: A Conceptual Framework for Liberation* (New York: New Press, 2012),5
18 As of this writing, November 15, 2020, indications are that Isaias, the dictator, is not only involved in the raging battle but may be the strategic mastermind behind the conflict though there is no hard evidence at this time.

In the eyes of EPLF supporters, for example, ELF was, and its offshoots continue to be motivated by sectarian and regional goals. Since its inception, ELF was, according to many Shabians, a criminal organization that massacred many innocent Eritreans for political and religious reasons. True to its evil nature, ELF slept with the enemy (Weyanes) after independence when the very survival of our nation was at stake. The goal of such groups, EPLF supporters maintain, is to divide Eritrea along tribal and religious lines. The charge continues that former and current ELF supporters want to secretly Arabize and Islamize Eritrea by working with neighboring Arab countries, and so on and so forth.

Seen from ELF's and other opposition groups, the issue assumes a completely different cast. In their eyes, it was Shabia that broke away from ELF to form a parochial, regional, and repressive party. Since then Shabia has consistently worked to undermine the Eritrean revolution by thwarting ELF's effort to unite the country. It is accused of cooperating with Ethiopians (the TPLF) to attack the parent organization, the ELF, during armed struggle for independence. ELFers also remind us that it was Isaias Afeworki and his group (not ELF or Ahmed Nasser) that secretly eliminated many intellectuals who did not agree with their vision. Glossing over all these historical facts, ELFers would passionately retort, Shabians have the audacity to accuse us of sleeping with the enemy. If anyone is culpable of this heinous crime, it was the EPLF that befriended these enemies at the expense of Eritrean people in the most trying period of our history. Shaebia is the malignant tumor that ate away at the heart of our revolution; the enemy from within; the scourge that crippled our struggle etc..., etc..., etc...

These are some of the historical baggage people carry around and swear by as solemnly as a witness giving sworn testimony in court. When such thoughts take residence in people's minds, mutual trust and respect is hard to come by because ordinarily, people do not want to negotiate or unite with groups they think harbor a hidden agenda. How much of what EPLF and its affiliates narrate is true and how much of it is false? What percentage of ELF's claim is fact and what portion fairy tales? I am inclined to think that we will never know. We should therefore leave the matter for future historians to sort out while we concentrate on the future. This is not a call to forget the past, the heroes, or the martyrs but rather an acknowledgment that we can struggle against the entrenched dictatorship better if we dwell less on the past & more on creating a new future. This is important because if the demise of the dictatorship is not accompanied by a parallel demise of prejudice and if this in turn is not cushioned by the cultivation of mutual tolerance, then the democracy we seek to establish will be in great peril and will soon wither away before it even stands on its feet.

Once the opposition overcomes its tendency to assess the present through the lens of the past, genuine unity will be within reach. Finer details aside, the path to unity can be achieved in three phases. In the first phase, organizations and civil associations with similar platforms should come together to form larger groups. In the second phase, a diverse group of highly respected individuals should be selected or elected to facilitate the merging of these large groups. In his book, "Defeating Dictators", professor Ayittey advises the formation of an umbrella group "to coordinate the activities of all opposition groups to achieve focus and impact." (Ayittey, 2011)[19] The third phase will be achieved when the opposition is finally united under a single leader or leadership. The goal is not to establish a uniformity of views (which is usually impossible anyway) but rather, a unity in action and strategy.

I am presenting nothing new here. To its credit, the Eritrean opposition did not only deliberate over all these ideas at length but has made several attempts to put it in practice. Some of its efforts failed probably because no safeguards were

---

19 George B. N. Ayittey, *Defeating Dictators* (New York: St. Martin's Griffin, 2011), 165

placed to make the coordinating committee truly independent. Ghana's 1995 version of an umbrella group, the Alliance for Change (AFC), for example required its members to sign a covenant that required them to totally renounce political ambition, and to eschew advancing "their own personal, political, or sectarian interest and to hold the interest of Ghana supreme above all others."[20] Eritrean opposition should consider inserting more preconditions like these in current or all future such ventures. I would add one more prerequisite to the list: the group should be ethnically and religiously diverse to avoid actual or perceived bias.

To further buttress the unity, the umbrella group should eschew delving into details about the constitution (whether to start-over or amend), the exact form of government (federal, unitary, decentralized etc....) a post-Isaias Eritrea should adapt. Academics can (and should) study and wrestle with such issues in-depth and from all angles. So, should political groups. This is not only desirable but should be considered mandatory for organized groups. Ordinary Eritreans can also discuss and provide their views freely on all issues. The only entity that should not take part in such detailed discussions and deliberations is the elected umbrella group because it needs to scrupulously maintain its neutrality which may be compromised (or be suspected of favoritism) if it engages in such deliberations. It should instead focus all its energies and resources exclusively to defeating the dictatorship by consolidating the resources and talent of all Eritreans to form a united front.

Toppling the regime

After an independent overseer to coordinate and facilitate opposition activities is successfully created, the battle against the regime can commence in earnest. Dictatorships are toppled in various ways: coups, assassinations, violent revolutions,

---

20 Ayittey, Defeating Dictators, 167

international intervention, or through massive protests. Of these, a coup is usually the fastest while toppling through peaceful massive protests is the most preferred. Unfortunately, both options have now become difficult for Eritrean revolutionaries. Those who were best positioned to stage a coup (the G-15) have been purged and forewarned, Isaias will be even more vigilant than he ever was. Peaceful mass protests in Eritrea will likewise be difficult for reasons we will discuss in a later section.

So how should the struggle against the dictatorship be conducted? In discussions about this topic, one controversial issue has been whether to use exclusively nonviolent methods or armed resistance. Some favor nonviolent struggle arguing that it will result in less fighting and fewer casualties while others believe only armed resistance can dislodge the regime since it is less likely to respond to nonviolent methods. My own view is that democratic fighters should use both. The opposition should not a priori constrain itself exclusively to peaceful or armed struggle. Its supreme goal is victory with the least number of casualties and it should use whatever tactic works at different stages of the struggle. The initial Eritrean infatuation with peaceful resistance has largely abated now as many of its former advocates started to realize how futile purely nonviolent tactics would be against Isaias. So, I will only briefly touch on the topic.[21]

A non-violent movement would never mushroom or grow into an effective force in Eritrea without the support of a military component because the regime would never countenance it. In the current political climate, it would be insanely suicidal to stage even a simple march inside Eritrea let alone wage a full-fledged non-violent struggle. The movement leaders would either be executed or thrown into a dungeon

---

21 I have expressed my views on the topic in more detail in my column 'pointblank' at awate.com which can be retrieved at: http://awate.com/eritrea-peaceful-resistance-or-peaceful-surrender%e2%80%94the-new-non-violence-mantra/

which reminds us of Orwell's very astute observation: "It is difficult to see how Gandhi's methods could be applied in a country where opponents of the regime disappear in the middle of the night and are never heard of again." Sounds familiar? He adds that "Without a free press and the right of assembly, it is impossible not merely to appeal to outside opinion, but to bring a mass movement into being, or even to make your intentions known to your adversary."

Instead, the opposition should conduct a carefully calibrated series of armed and nonviolent engagements. At this stage in the struggle, the Diaspora opposition should assume the leadership role since those in Eritrea cannot even congregate freely let alone fight under a central command. The united opposition should start forming secret cells inside Eritrea that mirror its efforts abroad. It should also assemble a united armed force to conduct coordinated guerilla style military strikes along the porous borders that surround Eritrea. At first, the resistance army should strike at easy targets. This is to bolster confidence and gain experience. Gradually, as its forces grow, it can start attacking targets throughout Eritrea. Such operations will necessarily be organized and executed by Diaspora leadership but those inside Eritrea should simultaneously wage a low intensity non-violent resistance, secretly at first, openly as its numbers grow.

In addition, Diaspora leaders should do their utmost to inundate Eritrea with revolutionarily appeals/slogans using a variety of communication channels including smuggled leaflets, social media, satellites, letters etc. The main target of such educational materials should be the armed forces, top-notch military commanders and security officers in particular. Soldiers and military commanders are likely to defect in masses if they judge victory might be possible. They will not take risks if they don't see progress in the opposition. If no organized armed resistance exists, our forcibly recruited children will have fewer opportunities to defy the oppressive regime. Having seen the regime's brutality first hand, many of them would never

216

endanger their lives on non-violent resistance if they see no prospect to prevail over the enemy. The presence of an armed resistance nearby will give them courage knowing that they can at any time join their brothers and sisters and a gun will be placed in their hands to repulse the oppressor instead of dying for him. But if the opposition was to resort to non-violent only strategy, the only way open to them would be to continue the unarmed trek across the border risking being arrested or killed.

That is why a series of successful military strikes (even on a small scale) is imperative. When Eritreans (including the military) hear about them, they will be emboldened to rebel and form their own group to fight the regime just as was the case during struggle for independence. Sharp lists 198 methods of nonviolent actions that resistance movements can use[22]. Eritrean democratic workers should study them carefully and intelligently to derive tactics that may be useful at various stages of the struggle for those inside Eritrea. Sharp is an advocate of pure non-violence but if we were to adapt his methods blindly, a massacre like that of Tiananmen Square will be likely but if we selectively and prudently adapt what we judge will work in our situation, then we can benefit a great deal. That is exactly what Sharp himself might advise because he candidly acknowledges that he cannot give "prescription for a particular country". As was noted in the introduction, all dictatorships eventually collapse with or without the opposition, so the latter should prepare for such an eventuality in tandem with its struggles to topple the regime. In other words, it should be ready to spearhead the transition period at a moment's notice to which we turn next.

---

22 Sharp, *From dictatorship to democracy*, 79-86

Transition[23]

Whether Eritrea's victory will come about through mass protests, coup, or a military confrontation, it is the actions that Eritreans will take immediately after takeover that will be the most consequential for Eritrea's future and its prospects of establishing a stable democracy because it is during this period that the seeds of democratic institutions are sown. It is also during this period that the socio-political culture would be transformed or molded to align it with democratic ethos.

After taking over the reins of government, the interim government should immediately set a time frame during which it will complete all transition related tasks upon completion of which, it would promptly step down. It should provide a detailed list of projects it seeks to accomplish, approximate completion dates, and submit periodic updates. The transition committee should also stipulate clearly under what condition its mandate to rule can be extended. Reasonable allowances can be made as long as the transitional government remains fully transparent and accessible to the people.

At the minimum, the transitional government should accomplish the following tasks: 1) Dissolve the PFDJ cabinet, detain its members including the president, and introduce itself and its mandate 2) Protect and secure vital government records and property 3) Establish law and order 4) set up an election committee. For the very first election, it should consider inviting domestic and international observers to lend transparency and legitimacy to the process. 5) Appoint a constituent assembly to draft a new constitution or amend the 1997 constitution. 6) Secure the border to prevent serious criminals from fleeing the country and to ward off foreign interference. Border patrol at airport, seaports, and land routes should be given the identities of all high-ranking officials of the

---

23 This section is a highly abridged version of the following article I wrote at Awate: http://awate.com/eritrea-the-fall-of-dictator ship-and-consolidation-of-democracy/

ousted regime to keep them from leaving the country. 7) The interim government should also prohibit placement of former collaborators of the regime in vital and sensitive positions. 8) Set up a committee to study repatriation of refugees and provide recommendations.

To forestall restiveness, the interim government should assure all government employees and other civilians that their jobs are secure and that they will continue to receive their paychecks uninterrupted provided they haven't committed serious crimes or willingly abetted the regime in its crimes. Likewise, the police force should continue its law enforcement duties uninterrupted but with new guidelines that requires them to respect the basic rights of citizens.

Top military officials who are suspected of gross human rights violations should be detained to prevent their disappearance before apprehension, but the rest of the military should be left alone though partial demilitarization will be needed. The military's primary task should be to safeguard vital government assets and to protect the borders. Prosecution of criminals is necessary for many reasons. First, the victims and families of those who suffered injustice under the regime deserve justice. Second, if denied justice, victims and their families might take the law into their hands leading to a chaotic situation that can pose a serious threat to the embryonic democracy. Third, setting criminals free will encourage future violations while prosecuting past crimes will send a strong signal that we are dead serious and will not tolerate future violators and offenders. It is important to keep in mind however that the primary goal is not retribution but justice. As a sage once put it, "for good, return good; for evil, return justice".

To summarize, the goal of the transitional period is to take down the dictatorship and prevent its return in any shape or form and to institute a firm foundation upon which a representative democracy can be established. The triumph of democracy and liberty must be final and absolute. Among other things, this requires that we prosecute criminals to deter future offenders and to send a strong signal that we are resolute about implementing the rule of law. It also requires the removal of former collaborators of the regime from critical and top positions. They should also be banned from applying for high offices for a set number of years. The goal is fortification of the budding democracy, protection of human rights, and keeping the rule of law, not retaliation. As we raze the old system, we concurrently build democratic institutions, form a representative government, revamp the economy, and reeducate the public. All these will facilitate successful consolidation of democracy which is a topic we turn to next.

Looking ahead: Consolidation of Democracy

A saying variously attributed to Woodrow Wilson, Billy Graham, and an Italian proverb goes like this:

> "When wealth is lost, nothing is lost
> When health is lost, something is lost
> When character is lost, everything is lost."

Political theorists have written volumes on this topic but at its core, consolidation of democracy is principally about character. This should not be surprising since the entire edifice of democratic governance is built on the presumption that citizens will behave responsibly and with integrity. Erecting the most magnificent set of sophisticated democratic institutions full of bells and whistles featuring a flawless constitution, governmental checks & balances, an independent judiciary, an egalitarian economy etc. will have little worth if most citizens are crooks. What value can we derive from institutions (democratic or not) if those we appoint to manage them happen to be corrupt? In other words, if an official can be bought or lobbyists can sway lawmakers, it vitiates the vitality and reliability of democracy. Political laws and courts are toothless if politicians and judges can be bribed for favors.

220

When liars and scoundrels are rampant, they can derail elections, rig ballots, engage in nepotism, and in a host of other vices. A lot of the chaotic scene we witness in Africa, Asia, and in other parts of the world are often the result of a society plagued with unethical or weak-willed individuals. Fix the individual (elevate the overall moral fiber) and you will fix society which in turn leads to a stable, vibrant democracy. So, morality is not a 'nice to have" prerogative for democracy but a 'must have' prerequisite.

Intersection between Democracy, Morality and Religion

Discussions about morality inevitably brings the topic of religion because it is often from the latter that we derive an ultimate basis for ethics and values. The illustrious enlightenment thinker Immanuel Kant believed "morality leads ineluctably to religion" (Kant, 1960)[24]. He postulated that even if we cannot demonstrate the value of religion on the basis of theoretical thought alone, we desperately need to do so for pragmatic reasons. Even Voltaire, a strong critic of religion famously quipped that "If God did not exist, it would be necessary to invent him".

In the case of Eritrea, the place of religion is even more pivotal. Eritreans are a deeply religious people. For centuries, they have believed in certain mores and values derived from their religion and have evolved a unique culture that is a blend of high moral principles and mysticism. The life of the average Eritrean revolves around religious rituals. There is hardly any event to which Eritreans do not attach religious significance. The birth, the marriage and the death of an individual are solemnly contemplated with prayers, supplications, and thanks giving. Even routine activities like eating and sleeping are

---

24 Immanuel Kant, *Religion within the Limits of Reason Alone*, trans. Theodore M. Green and Hoyt H. Hudson (New York: Harper, 1960)

followed by thanks to the source of these amenities. In my view, such cultural anchors are awesome and should be encouraged to flourish if for nothing at least as a bulwark against corruption and excessive materialism.

"There is no easy walk to freedom anywhere, Mandela once warned echoing Thomas Paine's observation, "...it would be strange indeed if so celestial an article as freedom should not be highly rated." In a similar vein, the distinguished historian, Arnold Toynbee opined that human history can be distilled into a single formula: challenge and response. The path to liberty, no matter how easy the initial steps, is a difficult one but never a futile undertaking. The opposition is at a momentous crossroads and faces a weighty challenge. Will it rise to shoulder its historical responsibility as a resistance force to meet the challenges outlined in various places in this chapter? Will it transcend stereotypes and prejudices to work together with discipline, courage and dedication to save Eritrea from the impending doom? Only time will tell but there can be no doubt that its actions today will have far, far-reaching repercussions for posterity and the future of Eritrea.

Bibliography

Ayittey, George B.N. *Defeating Dictators*. New York, NY: St. Martin's Griffin, 2011

Encyclopedia Britannica. "Nation-state." Accessed November 2, 2020. https://www.britannica.com/topic/nation-state.

Government of Eritrea, Department of External Affairs. *Eritrea: Birth of a Nation*. 1993

Kant, Immanuel. *Religion within the Limits of Reason Alone*. Translated by Theodore M. Green and Hoyt H. Hudson. New York: Harper, 1960

Machiavelli, Niccolò. *The Prince*. Translated by William K Marriott. Independently published, 2019

Omar-Ali, Ismail. "A Critical Look at the EPLF/PFDJ/GOE Saga": A Half Century-10 Epic Drama". Accessed

November 17, 2020. http://awate.com/a-critical-look-at-the-eplfpfdjgoe-saga-a-half-century-10-epic-drama/.

Omar-Ali, Ismail. "Elites, Isaias, EPLF, And the Eritrean people". Accessed November 13, 2020. http://awate.com/elites-isaias-eplf-and-the-eritrean-people/.

Omar-Ali, Ismail. "Eritrea: Peaceful Resistance or Peaceful Surrender—The New Non-Violence Mantra". Accessed November 17, 2020. http://awate.com/eritrea-peaceful-resistance-or-peaceful-surrender%e2%80%94the-new-non-violence-mantra/.

Omar-Ali, Ismail. "Eritrea: The Fall of Dictatorship and Consolidation of Democracy". Accessed November 1, 2020. http://awate.com/eritrea-the-fall-of-dictatorship-and-consolidation-of-democracy/.

Selassie, Bereket Habte. *Wounded Nation: How a Once Promising Eritrea Was Betrayed and Its Future Compromised.* New Jersey: Red Sea Press, 2011.

Sharp, Gene. *From Dictatorship to Democracy: A Conceptual Framework for Liberation.* New York, NY: New Press, 2012.

The Economist. "Eritrea's Gulag State Is Crumbling", Accessed November 6, 2020. https://www.economist.com/middle-east-and-africa/2019/07/11/eritreas-gulag-state-is-crumbling.

CONCLUSION

Bereket H. Selassie

Our Sovereign Statehood Under Threat: Challenges and Opportunities

A Timely Response to a Clear and Present Danger

This book represents the intellectual version of the national struggle for Eritrea's right to self-determination and sovereignty, as already noted. All the writers of the various chapters of the book have been part of the inspired devotion, in one way or another, to help attain the independence of Eritrea. They have been involved in different activities, be it as members of the ELF or the EPLF, or as supporters engaged in providing support of different kinds in pursuit of the sacred goal of national independence.

When the book writing project was conceived, there was a common concern among us all as well as of all other patriotic Eritreans that the dictatorial regime of Isaias Afwerki was flirting with the idea of joining Eritrea with Ethiopia in one form or another. His infamous declaration of Aykessernan and his treasonous invitation of Abiy Ahmed to "lead us(meaning lead a unified Eritrea and Ethiopia) had caused a lot of anxiety and fear among all patriotic Eritreans. The participants of the book project then hurried to mobilize the appropriate response to the emerging secret diplomacy between the two leaders of the two countries, presumably working out a strategy to present us with a fait accompli—a finished and irreversible situation compromising Eritrea's sovereignty.

Since then, on November 4, 2020, war broke out between the federal government led by Prime Minister Abiy and the Tigray Region. This devastating war has, by some reliable accounts, involved Eritrean Defense forces on the side of the Federal government of Ethiopia. The war and the involvement of huge Eritrean defense forces has profoundly negative implications for the politics of the region including Eritrea and Ethiopia as well as the entire sub-region of the Horn Africa. What this altered situation would mean in terms of the future politics in Eritrea, including its potential for facilitating or hindering the prospects of changing the dictatorial regime remains to be seen. To repeat what experts of the Chinese language say explaining the meaning of the word crisis in Chinese, the word in the Chines alphabets represent two pictures—danger and opportunity. If the impact of the post war in Tigray might present us with a crisis situation, will it pose a potential danger to our sovereignty? Might it also have the potential of an opportunity for changing the dictatorial regime?

The question is what do we do to use such opportunity.

For most of the years of its existence, our Sovereign State has been facing a Clear and Present Danger, as one of the chapters of this volume has headlined it. The source of the danger—indeed its one and only cause—is the very person that is supposed to protect it and guarantee its well-being in all respects.

Under the ratified Constitution of Eritrea (1997), it is provided that "…The President shall ensure respect of the Constitution; the integrity and dignity of the State; the efficient management of the public service; and the interests and safety of all citizens, including the enjoyment of their fundamental rights and freedoms recognized under the Constitution." The crisis facing Eritrea, which has been sadly a fact of life experienced by Eritrean citizens and known by all interested observers, can be traced to the fact that the man acting as the country's President has not performed the duties prescribed under the above-cited article of the Constitution. Indeed, incredible as it may seem, far from performing his duties under the Constitution, he has been doing the opposite. It is as if he swore not to do what the Constitution ordains, but to do the exact opposite.

A Rude Awakening

For those of us that originally embraced Isaias as a competent leader and supported him for much of his earlier leadership of the EPLF, despite stories of crimes he had committed in the Field, his post-liberation act of betrayal was a rude awakening. When stories of the crimes he had committee earlier were raised in opposition to his leadership, most Eritreans gave him the benefit of the doubt advocating the need to separate the issues and recommending that such charges will be examined in due time and that he would be held answerable for any crimes that could be proven beyond reasonable doubt. There were even those who had claimed that Isaias was an enemy agent, from the beginning, chosen and charged to infiltrate the Eritrean liberation struggle by Ethiopian authorities in collaboration with the CIA. Most Eritreans rejected this claim and gave him coverage and enthusiastic support for over thirty years.

Now he has blown his thirty-year old cover and revealed himself to be an enemy of Eritrea. He has embraced the Ethiopian imperial project that he pretended to hate for thirty years. Reflecting on this astounding reality of the betrayal of Isaias, it is not unreasonable to speculate that his imperial dream of being the new Emperor on the back of the new Ethiopian Prime Minister will turn out to be "*Hilmi Derho*" as we say in Tigrigna, a foolish dream. The factor uniting Isaias and Abiy is their common hatred of the Weyane, the Tigray Peoples Liberation Front (TPLF). The TPLF beat Isaias defeating him in the 1998-2000 war, inflicting a bitter humiliation from which he has not recovered. Evidently, Isaias is a creature that nurses a memory of a bitter experience, burying it for a long period, carefully hiding his rage but hoping for possibilities of wreaking vengeance one day. He waited twenty years following the 1998 humiliating defeat at the hand of the TPLF. The opportune moment he had been waiting for came with the rise of Abiy Ahmed as Prime Minister of Ethiopia.

In summary this is what happened. When the newly elected Prime Minister Abiy Ahmed announced that he would be willing to resolve the so called no-war-no-peace situation of tension between Ethiopia and Eritrea by implementing the Hague decision on the territorial dispute between the two countries, and sent an emissary to Isaias to assure him that he would fulfill his promise, Isaias saw a wonderful opportunity. What followed was an extraordinary series of events that included several exchange of visits of Abiy and Isaias to their respective capitals, as well as declarations by both about their readiness to work together on a number of issues of common interest. Abiy had ordered the release of all political prisoners in addition to his proposals of peace and friendly relations. One of the released prisoners was one Andargachew Tsige, a member of a groups opposed to the TPLF rule. Andargachew, an Ethiopian of the Amhara ethnicity and a naturalized British subject, had worked for his political group in Eritrea obtaining help from the Isaias government. He was caught while traveling from Yemen because the air flight was diverted to Ethiopia where he was instantly arrested by the TPLF security.

Abiy knew about Andargachew when he was working in the military Intelligence of the EPRDF (in reality for the TPLF) government. He decided to send him to Isaias on a mission of reconciliation. It has been reported that Isaias was suspicious, at first, telling Andargachew that Abiy was a creature of the TPLF, to which Andargachew responded by assuring Isaias that he could trust Abiy as authentic, even telling him that he had connections with external powers (presumably the Americans) and that he had secretly revealed secrets to Ethiopian Opposition groups working to overthrow the TPLF government. In other words, Abiy had been a double agent, working both for the TPLF and the Americans (presumably through the CIA).

Isaias was thus persuaded that he could trust Abiy and work with him against the TPLF that was thus a common enemy. One can imagine the exultation that Isaais must have felt with this discovery, which partly explains his astounding behavior, as already mentioned, smiling at the Ethiopian crowd thumping his chest with pleasure and blowing kisses to the amazed crowd. A little under two years later, things happened that have transformed the history and politics of the Horn of Africa and leading to enormous loss of life and devastation of property mainly in the Tigray Region of Ethiopia and in Eritrea.

As pointed out in the Foreword of this book, a dispute that, according to all commentators, could (and should) have been resolved by discussion at the conference table, was decided instead by a devastating war waged between the Abiy government and the TPLF. Both sides accuse each other for starting the war, but it appears that both were gearing up for a decisive confrontation. The result is the usual horror of war—death and devastation on a large scale.

Eritrean Involvement on Abiy's side

One feature of the war that took one month to be the subject of international condemnation and censure is the involvement of the entire Eritrean armed forces in the war in Tigray on behalf of the Ethiopian government led by Abiy . A US State Department statement issued on December 10 demanded that the Eritrean defense forces must withdraw from Tigray immediately. It also condemned alleged abduction ordered by the Eritrean President of Eritrean refugees who had been living in Tigray. It is impossible for the Eritrean government to deny the massive involvement of Eritrean armed forces, including mechanized brigades, tanks and the entire infantry. The international community's censure may eventually include charges of war crimes and crimes against humanity, particularly as it pertains to the issue of the handling (or abduction) of Eritrean refugees. If Isaias is charged with the said international law crimes, Abiy may also be cited as a co-defendant enabling the commission of the crimes. One wonders how the Nobel Committee of Norway might be feeling as they learn of the war in Tigray and Abiy's role in it. An Ethiopian who had been one of those who recommended Abiy for the Nobel Peace Prize, has been heard expressing his bitter disappointment and regrets for making the recommendation. But that is another story.

The most significant element of the story concerns the devastating war In Tigray and the emerging Isaias-Abiy Alliance with its implications for the future politics of the region and especially its impact on Eritrea and its sovereignty. We will now deal with this subject.

Conspiracy to End Eritrea's Sovereignty?

During the earlier period following the Isaias-Abiy *rapprochement,* the two leaders signed agreements that, at least on Eritrea's side, were not the subject of approval by the National Assembly as required by the Eritrean Constitution. *According to the Constitution, all international agreements must be ratified by the National Assembly.* (Article 32(4)). Eritreans heard or read about the signing of agreements between Ethiopia and Eritrea from public statements issued by the two leaders. The veil of secrecy surrounding the events of signing the agreements naturally led to speculations that some secret bargaining was taking place that conceivably involved the fate of Eritrea. This was before Isaias made the incredible declaration that "from now on Abiy will lead us" and that "the Eritrean and Ethiopian people are one people." He also declared "Aykessernan" (we have not suffered loss), referring to the war of 2018 fought with with the TPLF which he had lost, as already mentioned.

Judging by the statements made by both Abiy and Isaias regarding their growing closeness and their frequent meetings, as well as the astonishing declarations of Isaias referred to above, it was clear that they had been planning something big together. The events of the few days before the outbreak of war on November 4 of this year, and the war that followed make clear that Isaias and Abiy have been planning to end the independence of Eritrea and join it with Ethiopia.

In addition to their common interest in either eliminating the TPLF or at least considerably reduce its military capability, there is the implicit objective of Isaias, namely revenge on the one hand, and imperial yearnings on the other. As a former military officer in charge of Military Intelligence, Abiy must have had inklings of Isaias' desire for bigger things beyond Eritrea.

A close examination of the manner in which he addressed Isaias ingratiatingly during their meetings in public, using the term of endearment, *Issu and Wedi Afom,* with which Isaias is known to his Eritrean admirers, Abiy launched his seductive appeal and seems to have won him over. The question is: what is the ultimate end of these public "courtings?" What is the endgame? The decision by Isaias to be involved in the war in Tigray deploying the entire armed forces of Eritrea, aimed at destroying the TPLF, must have been an incredible gift to Abiy, for the TPLF had been a thorn on his side. Therefore, Eritrean massive involvement in the war in Tigray is obviously a big prize for Abiy who had been trying to tame the TPLF without success.

And what is in it for Isaias, apart from the revenge wreaked on his "enemies." To answer this question we have to consider the complex personality of Isaias Afwerki with his gigantic ego, ever contemplating bigger targets, with overpowering ambition; (*"his vaulting ambition"* that *"overleapt itself, falling on the other side,"* to borrow from Macbeth). Abiy's flattery and terms of endearment answered the thirst for adulation that Isaias Afwerki's narcissistic personality craved. And as was hinted in this book's Foreword, it all led to the fulfillment of his imperial yearnings. Therein lies the real danger to Eritrea's Sovereign Statehood.

There, too, lies the key to explain Isaias Afwerki's betrayal, forsaking the cause for which he had spent the best part of his youth in the desert; betrayal also of the trust on whom his martyred comrades had reposed. But that apparently means nothing to Isaias Afwerki, this cold-blooded creature with his blood-stained hands and his sociopathic need of sacrifice, a sacrifice that meant abandoning the cause for which thousands perished.

Eritrean Nationalism and the Present Danger

Many non-Eritreans are puzzled by the fervent expression of Eritrean nationalism, often wondering what makes it tick. Ethiopians, in particular, are obsessively intrigued by it wondering about what is so special about it that generations of Eritreans have been willing to die for it. They naturally wonder what is it that compels Eritreans to make so much sacrifice in blood and treasure in succeeding generations. Such queries may involve an element of envy if not disdain.

Provoked by such inquiry as well as what seemed to be general hostility to Eritrean pride and tenacity, the late Tekie Fessehaitsion, in a moment of poetic insight (unusual for one who taught the dismal science), wrote the following:

"The world and especially the US might as well accept the reality of Eritrea. It has to be said for the umpteenth time that Eritrea is not just a place; it's one big heart that embodies the indestructible spirit of brave people. Surely Eritreans are accustomed to being betrayed but, as is often the case, they always come through, stronger and more determined than ever to make sure that Eritrea lives. For an Eritrean the country is more than a piece of land: it's a sacred trust that must be passed from one generation to the next, whole and indivisible...No one except her people wanted Eritrea to be born. Not the UN. Not the OAU. And definitely not the US. Yet Eritrea was born in defiance of all the powers that be. Who could forget John Foster Dulles's unforgettable remarks about justice being on Eritrea's side but expediency dictating that Eritrea had to be handed over

to Ethiopia..."(Tekie, Shattered Illusion, Broken Dreams. Red Sea Press, 2002 pp.232-233).

Tekie was a gentle soul with a sharp pen, if not a sharp tongue. He deployed his pen for the patriotic cause. Both his gentle soul and his sharp pen are sorely missed. As part of his moral outrage at the duplicity of the US policy concerning Eritrea, Tekie wrote, "*Those who did not want to see Eritrea born should not now be expected to do a thing to see it live. Yet Eritrea will live, simply because its people will make sure it does. In the end it matters not whether the world likes it or not. Eritrea is here to stay. Eritrea lives.*"(Page 232).

It is this kind of passionate affirmation of one's patriotism that **both amazes and** puzzles our non-Eritreans friends, especially Ethiopians. Coming from a cool dude like Tekie, who is usually calm and measured in his remarks, asserting his undying belief in Eritrea with such zeal and fervent sentiment is naturally bound to lead to inquiry as to the root cause of such passion and faith. Is it based on a belief in Eritrea's exceptionalism? If so, such claim of exceptionalism usually provokes skepticism. That Eritreans succeeded in securing their independence against overwhelming odds is indeed a matter that induces a special pride including the temptation to entertain a sentiment of exceptionalism among Eritreans.

Will such sentiment endure in the face of the impending danger posed by the imperial machinations of the Isaias-Abiy conspiracy? If the history of Eritrean liberation struggle and the incredible story of survival of a people's desire to be free in the face of what seemed to be insuperable enemies is any guide, the answer to the question is a resounding yes.

The Pillars of Eritrea's Sovereign Statehood

As the Introduction to this book tried to explain, the source of Eritrean sovereignty is more—much more—than just a fancy nationalist sentiment, the momentary expression of pride of a people historically wronged by what must have seemed to them a general feeling of being singled out for injustice by the world community. The fact that in their demand for justice Eritreans were abandoned in favor of Ethiopia and that the two super powers—The United States and the Soviet Union—alternated in favoring Ethiopia against Eritrea was proof positive confirming their suspicion that the world community had ganged up against them.

But this sense of betrayal did not lead to despair and despondency. To the contrary, it steeled them to fight on depending on their own inner strength as a people. The structure and articulation of this book project is based on such unique story of self-reliance in the search for self-determination. The struggle was long and hard but the victory of national independence scored in the Spring of 1991, thirty years after the first shot were fired in the hills of Western Eritrea by a small group led by the national hero, Hamid Idris Awate, was a vindication of such self reliance and resilience. Hence the structure of this book project and the descriptions and analyses of each chapter.

First the Historical Basis of Eritrea's sovereignty.
By Awet Weldemichael and Samuel Tsegai
That this book is a timely work that will help in organizing Eritreans' response to the current development is beyond question. So, cherished compatriots, we should all be proud in being part of this important process.

The chapter on the Historical Basis of Eritrea's Sovereign Statehood documents specifically the consolidation of the formal Italian colony of Eritrea including its being passed from one foreign, rule to another, against the backdrop of novel African and international norms on accession to sovereign statehood. The chapter records Italy's takeover from the Rubatino Copany's concessioanry land grant along Southern Eritrea's Red Sea shore in 1882. Then in 1889, the Treaty of Wuchale was signed between Italy and Emperor Menelik of Ethiopia who had succeeded Emperor Yohannes, following his death in the war against the Sudanese Dervishes at the battle of

Metemma. Menelik welcomed Italy's expansion and even ceded the rest of the land of what became Eritrea.

Ironically, Yohannes had defeated Italian attempts of encroachment of areas in the Eritrean highlands, immediately before he was summoned by Gondar's Clergy and nobility to come to the rescue when the Dervishes attacked the historic city of Gondar, pillaging its Churches.

Fast forward by decades...

As Italian rule in Eritrea was nearing its end, in what became a serious bone of contention, Eritreans did not rely on international norms or trust the British in their promises to help Eritreans attain their national aspirations of self determination. Convinced of being betrayed, Eritreans began organizing politically; that was why *Mahber Fiqri Hager* (Love of Country) was created in May 1941. The writers of the chapter, both historians, contend that this party was a "prototype" nationalist organization out of which Eritrea's first political parties emerged demanding an immediate break with European rule. Between 1946 and 1947 political parties espousing different political options emerged out of the Association of Love of Country.

The Unionist Party sought to end European rule by joining with Ethiopia. The Liberal Progressive Party (LLP), also known as Party of Eritrea For Eritreans, and the Muslim League (ML) demanded independence.

The chapter traces the impact of the Cold War politics as well as the fragmentation of Eritrean political parties, giving Ethiopia and their US supporters an opportune moment to press for the merger of Eritrea with Ethiopia. The US government lent support for Ethiopia having concluded that its strategic interest in the Red Sea Region would be better served by supporting Ethiopia's claim. And the British "Care-Taker Administration" did all they could to facilitate the merger, despite their earlier attempt to carve Western Eritrea and join it with the Sudan, which was ruled by them at the time.

The Legal Basis of Eritrea's Sovereign Statehood

By Bereket Habte Selassie

Law is the be-all and end-all of human and social affairs, be they at the local, regional, national and global levels. That is why the Supremacy of the Rule of Law is the highest principle of organized society, and peace and stability is grounded on it. Hence the need to keep referring to it constantly by people carrying responsibility delegated to them by society. At its most fundamental level law (and the Constitution as the highest law) is a crucial source of sovereignty.

Thus this chapter as well as those on Historical and Economic bases of Eritrea's Sovereign Statehood will hopefully contribute to a better understanding by all Eritreans and encourage them to make their due contribution in the on-going struggle for democracy and the Rule of Law.

Retaining and maintaining Eritrea's sovereignty is a critical part of that struggle. The spirit and letter of this book project is also, in essence, an important part of that struggle.

The Economic Basis of Eritrea's Sovereign Statehood

By Dr. Assefaw Tekeste

Dr. Assefaw Tekeste, the writer of this chapter, is a physician (an MD) by training, and his contribution with this gem of a chapter (concise, yet brilliant in conception and execution) is, therefore, especially welcome. The origin and provenance of this chapter is also of interest; it was based on an interview Assefaw gave to EriSat, which many liked and admired, including the editor of the present book, who prevailed upon his friend to turn the interview into a chapter for this volume. Assefaw, at first was reluctant due to other commitments, but eventually graciously agreed—to his credit.

It is trite to say that the economy of a nation is the mainstay of its life. It is the anchor on which all human and social activities are grounded. You don't have to be a Marxist to appreciate the centrality of economics in the life of a nation. In terms of symbolism, the currency of a nation represents its sovereignty. And the currency embodies the store of value and

236

acts as the mode of exchange in all financial transactions.. Hence its critical importance; hence also the sad story of concerning the confrontation between Eritrean and Ethiopian experts when negotiating the rate of exchange between the Ethiopian currency (the Birr) and the newly issued Eritrean currency, the Nakfa.

When Eritrean government agents were engaged in negotiations with their Ethiopian counterparts on the issue of the common currency, which was the Ethiopian Bir, following Eritrea's independence, they confronted a wall of stiff resistance on the part of the Ethiopian negotiators concerning the basis of the rate of exchange between the Ethiopian Bir and the newly proposed Eritrean currency, the Nakfa. One of the Eritrean negotiators, who had been trained in Ethiopia and was aware of the niceties of the Amharic language and its capacity to be wielded as a weapon in any interaction, could not help noticing the crass prejudice and hostility toward things Eritrean, including the Ethiopian negotiators resentment of the use of the name Nakfa, a symbol of national aspirations and pride. The fact that the proposed Eritrean currency was named Nakfa, the town in the EPLF's base area where a life-and-death struggle had been waged between Ethiopian forces and the valiant Eritrean resistance forces, was a non-starter in the negotiations.

Leaving the technicalities involved in the negotiations aside, it became abundantly clear to the Eritrean negotiators that the Nakfa factor was a stumbling block in terms of arriving at a reasonable solution on the rate of exchange. It is worth reiterating that a nation's currency is a powerful symbol of its sovereignty and this cardinal fact was not lost on the negotiators on both sides. And at a time when the top and middle civil servants of Ethiopia holding the crucial positions, most of whom happened to be Amhara nationalists passionately opposed to Eritrea's independence, it did not augur well to arrive at a reasonable solution on the rate of exchange that was being negotiated.

So, despite the good will on the part of the top leadership at the time, on the economic and financial policies (as well as their wholehearted support of Eritrean independence), the prejudiced views of the top negotiators prevailed. The result was that the two countries went their separate ways on the issue of currency and related financial (and trade) policies. This fact would become one of the causes of the misunderstanding leading to conflict between the two countries. It bears emphasizing that this was only one of the causes; there were other perhaps more critical issues having to do with the personality of the Eritrean leader that became the cause of the conflicts.

Please note the title of Dr. Assefaw's chapter: *Poor Populations in a Wealthy Country.*

And also note the introduction which lays down the argument for Eritrea's economic independence, contrary to what Isaias has lately taken to denigrating presumably as a sign of his fealty to Ethiopian expansionist dreams and designs. Much of the chapter is anecdotal, and all the more convincing in terms of providing precious historical data of how promising the Eritrean beginning was with its gifted and dedicated leader, Chief Executive Tedla Bairu, who was eventually pushed out by Emperor Haile Selassie with the assistance of Eritrean Unionist leaders, beholden to the Emperor's Representative. Tedla, who had been a leader in the Unionist Party, had become too much of an Eritrean patriot for the imperial machinations designed to undermine its regional autonomy, contrary to the Federal arrangement ordained by the United Nations.

In addition to the valuable anecdotal evidence, the chapter is also filled with valuable data demonstrating Eritrea's economic potential not only to take care of its populations, but also to produce surplus for export, thus putting to rest all false claims of Eritrea's lack of self sufficiency.

The chapter ends with a firm belief that all that "the population living in a wealthy country" needs is a State governed by the will of the people.

It is a conclusion that leads to the remaining chapters whose analyses and conclusions are in accord with Assefaw's conclusion, as we shall see presently.

A Museum of Peoples...
By Mohamed Kheir Omar

Mohamed Kheir Omar's chapter is an ethno-geographic marvel concisely portraying Eritrea's richly variegated peoples that populate mainly two geographic regions—the Central North and South Highlands, on the one hand, and the Eastern and Western lowlands on the other. Mohamed Kheir is a scientist who is apparently deeply interested in the history and geography of his different peoples. His ethnographic scheme considers the highland civilization of the Axumite-based "Abyssinian" complex of the Tigrigna and Tigre people, on the one hand, and the lowland communities, on the other. The former, found in the highlands are engaged in agriculture with a few also raising livestock. The latter are mainly nomadic communities and a few engaged in farming, inhabiting the Eastern and Western Lowlands.

The chapter is well-researched and informative, particularly to readers with no previous knowledge of Eritrean history and ethnography.

The Rise and Fall of the Eritrean Liberation Front (ELF)
By Anghesom Atsbaha and Ghirmai Negash

The ELF's birthing of the Eritrean struggle for independence had helped intensify Eritrea's national consciousness politically. Militarily, as the first armed political movement in Eritrea, the ELF developed the idea of protracted war as a strategy of liberation of the country. From 1961-1971, the ELF was the sole organization to wage war effectively against the Ethiopian imperial State. Between 1970 and 1980, the ELF was instrumental in liberating a wide swath of the rural countryside.

But the emergence of the EPLF in 1970 presented a challenge to the ELF. The first response was to wage a campaign of vilification of the EPLF, including claims that it was a weapon of the enemy, that its leadership was a mercenary sent to sow dissension and division in the Eritrean armed struggle. The ELF leadership even passed a resolution at its First organizational Congress authorizing its armed units to launch attacks on the fledgling EPLF. A "civil war" thus started lasting a few years, until 1981, with intermittent "peace" intervals lasting a few months. During such peace interval the two organizations fought the enemy forces together in several battles, liberating many towns. But the rivalry and accompanying animosity culminated in a final confrontation that led to the demise of the ELF as a united liberation organization. The ELF left the Field in 1981, leaving control of the liberation struggle to be carried on by the EPLF.

The authors of the chapter argue, by way of conclusion, that if any lesson can be drawn from the history of the ELF, it is that despite the internal weaknesses, the ELF's final fall ultimately came from the machinations of the EPLF. They also state that the fate of the ELF reflects the recurring differences and conflicts between Eritrea and Ethiopia, which "have seldom been managed or negotiated peacefully by their respective leaders."

Three Decades of Authoritarianism: Challenges to Eritreanism, National Identity and Sovereignty
By Abdulrazig K. Osman

The author of this chapter, Abdulrazig Osman, is like Dr. Assefaw, a new-comer to the original group of eight participants. Abdulrazig performed a miracle in completing his chapter three weeks after he volunteered to join our group. He not only accomplished his task in record time, but acquitted himself admirably by producing a well-researched and well argued, scholarly work. It is worth emphasizing that the various chapters of this book support one another thus enriching the reading experience of the potential readers of the book and making the book a well-rounded work that will provide rich material for readers, as well as stimulating them and also, of course, encouraging them to make their specific contributions in the struggle for democracy and the Rule of Law, and preserving our hard-won Sovereign Statehood.

Abdulrazig's crucial concern

According to one of Abdulrazig's theses, Eritreanism is based on: (1) the existence of Eritrea as an autonomous territory that had been created as an Italian colony; and (2) the desire of Its people to negate Ethiopianism. More to the point and relevant to the theme of this book, Abdulrazig states that Isaias worked hard to make Eritrea an unviable State. And history shows, he argues, that when a State becomes unviable, it becomes susceptible to any project antithetical to its existence as a political entity. It is up to Eritreans, he asserts, from all walks of life, creeds, political affiliations, or ideological inclinations to fully grasp the ramifications of the current development and urgently prepare to meet the challenges to "restore Eritreanism" and preserve Eritrea's sovereignty.

In three decades, Abdulrazig cautions, Isaias had depopulated Eritrea, impoverished its people, messed up its social fabric and weakened its military.(emphasis added by editor). The conclusion he reached that is irresistible, was that Isaias has been doing this in front of our very eyes, with the aim of eliminating our country's identity as a sovereign nation and mix it with Ethiopia. His hidden desire is to be either the king or, failing that, a king maker in the affairs of Ethiopia and possibly the entire Horn of Africa region.

This book being a carefully researched with much detail of information concerning his central argument summed up above, we welcome Abdulrazig's Chapter as an important addition to the other chapters.

Clear and Present Danger
By Daniel Teklai

Daniel starts this chapter by reminding us of the National Anthem, and its evolution from the time of the struggle framed

241

in the form of prophesy to the post-liberation period. In its post-independence version, the Anthem proclaims: *"Eritrea has taken its rightful place in the world."*

The author declares that the years of yearnings of Eritreans is felt in these simple words. And "taking its rightful place in the world"means that one day Eritrea would be governed in accordance with the will of its own people. In principle, and by popular desire, this basic political (democratic) end was supposed to be attained. The fervent hope of Eritreans was that their popular and charismatic leader would lead to such objective. Isaias Afwerki seemed to demonstrate his special leadership qualities in May 1993 when he addressed the Organization of African Unity (OAU), shaming and blaming them for their notable failures, including their negative record with respect to the just struggle of the Eritrean people. His popularity continued for some six or seven years, until he unilaterally involved the country in an unnecessary war with the TPLF. Many believe that he took this disastrous step partly (some believe principally) in order to justify his decision not to implement the Constitution that his own government initiated and which had been ratified by the National Assembly and a Constituent Assembly.

Daniel continues his narrative by stating that things went from bad to worse until a critical point was reached when the country's sovereignty faced "clear and present damger," as the chapter's title signifies. Such clear and present danger can be explained in terms of two "intertwining phenomena," first is the unchecked authoritarian power of Isaias Afwerki; and secondly, the rise of Ethiopian expansionism. The two phenomena became closely related when it appeared that Isasas and Ethiopia's new Prime minister, Abiy Ahmed, became close allies with a common cause centered on their common enemy, the TPLF. It all became cleat when in the Summer of 2018, Isaias declared Abiy "our leader" and they met several times in the two years following that declaration culminating in the war against the TPLF declared by Abiy on November 4, 2020.

There is no doubt that the war strategy was designed jointly, involving Eritrean armed forces in the Tigray war. In a section titled, From Dictator to Traitor, Daniel traces the trajectory of Isaias toward "becoming an Ethiopian," and stating that henceforth he would not remain uninterested in the internal affairs of Ethiopia. The chapter's conclusion is that Eritreans must focus entirely on removing Isaias from power, if Eritrea's sovereignty is to be guaranteed.

Whither Eritrea, etc.
By Ismail Omar-Ali

Ismail's chapter with its timely title, begins by stating that just as Hamd Idris Awate was the father of the start of Eritrea's armed struggle, Isaias Afwerki may justly be recognized as the father of independent Eritrea. But his fatherhood ends there, for it did not take him long before he showed character and personality traits that negate that hallowed title of Fatherhood.

Ismail notes that the propensity to delusions of grandeur is a characteristic of all despots and that Isaias suffers from this malaise. He adds that this characteristic is the key to the unraveling of despots, involving as it does the knack of despots for both horrible deeds and suicidal recklessness.

Doesn't this phenomenon seem familiar, as we witness the outcome of unholy alliance between Abiy and Isaias under which Isaias agreed to involve the entire Eritrean military forces in Tigray committing horrible deeds? What Ismail calls suicidal recklessness was demonstrated in Isaais' decision without consulting with his cabinet in the so called Badme war, which cost Eritrea thousands of dead and wounded and Eritrean territory was occupied by Ethiopian forces. Isaias was forced to accept the defeat, which is the reason why he agreed to aid Abiy in waging war against the TPLF by committing the entire Eritrean Defense Forces to invade Tigray, and fight against the TPLF.

One of the specific contributions of this chapter to the whole project of the book is its focus on the psychological makeup of a despot like Isaais, including the hidden mental dynamics pushing him to perform incredible acts of cruelty as well as cause widespread desolation people's lives and livelihoods. In all his actions in which other people, men and women, perform useful deeds enabling him to achieve his desired objectives, be it the independence of the country or other objectives, he does not stop to give them any credit and recognize their contribution. All the men and women who sacrificed "to make him seem great are inconsequential to him," Ismail writes. He adds that when many highly educated people, people of erudition, kowtow to "his wisdom"such behavior intensifies his feeling of all-powerfulness and convinces him that he is grander than all others. No one can advise him because he is superior in intelligence and knowledge and needs no other person to advise him. Under such psychological makeup, the hidden script is written by him to do all things without any advise or consultation. It was thus that he decided to launch the so-called Badme war in 1998, which is the basis of all the subsequent problems that has landed Eritrea to the present crisis.

This summary review does not do justice to a chapter that was well thought out and well argued, an altogether sophisticated piece of writing. The chapter ends the same way Daniel's chapter ended calling for change of regime.

A Summing Up

Conceived in serious concerns about Eritrea's future, facing as it has been with the destructive policies and practices of Isaias Afwerki and his authoritarian rule as well as the surge of Ethiopian expansionism, this book covered several pertinent topics. With the fervent patriotic passion combined with the intellectual acuity and vigor of the various authors, the book covered important subjects that may be justly considered to be the pillars of Eritrea's sovereign statehood.

The declaration of war by Ethiopian Prime Minister against Tigray and the involvement of Eritrean armed forces in the war on the side of Ethiopia, invading Tigray not only justified the project of writing the book and the concern of the originators and authors of the book project, and rendered the serious concern even more urgent. It was the last straw that would break the (Eritrean) camel's back.

So, what is to be done? The short answer to the question of what is to be done to avoid the demise of Eritrea's independence is for Eritreans to unite in the urgent task of removing Isaias and his totalitarian regime and reinvigorate democracy and the Rule of Law. To that end, implementation of the ratified 1997 Constitution with the necessary amendments must be a primary objective. And to those ends, the publication and wide distribution of this book is an imperative. In this task all Eritreans should forget their differences, whatever their origin and reason for existence. What is at stake is the very existence of our nation, this nation of heroes and martyrs. Fellow Eritreans please forget your differences and unite to save your nation!

APPENDIDX

ጥብቆ

ኣዋጃት ኢሳያስ ኣፈወርቂ ንልኡላውነት ኤርትራ ይጥሕሱ ዶ?[1]

ናይ ከፍላ-ሓጋይ 2018 ሃንደበትነት

ነቶም ኣብ ገጾም ፍስሃ ዓሲልዎም ትስፉዋት ዝመስሉ ዝነበሩ ዕስለ
ኢትዮጵያውያን፡ ብኣንጻር ናይ 'ቲ ኤርትራውያን ከም ንቡር ዝወስድዎ -
ቄጡዕን ጸዋግን ገጽ - ባህታ ብዝተመልአ ከምስታ "ንሕና ሓደ ህዝቢ ኢና፡
ድሕሪ ሎሚ ክልተ ዝተፈላለያ ኤርትራን ኢትዮጵያን ኣይከህልዋን 'የን፡ ነዚ
ዝጠራጠር ሰብ እንተደአ ሃልዩ ጥዑይ ኣእምሮ የብሉን፡ ከምርመራ ኣለዎ"
ከብል 'የ ገሊጹሎም። ሓደ ንከኾኑ ዘውክለሎም 'የ ዝመስል። እዚ ንኣእዛን ናይ
'ቶም ተኣኪቦም ዝነበሩ ጭፍራ፡ ሙዚቃ 'የ ነይሩ። እቲ - ብሰይጣን ዝተቐብአ
- ቀዳማይ ጸላኢ ናይ ኢትዮጵያ ጌርም ዝወስድዎ ዝነበሩ ኢሳያስ ኣፈወርቂ እዩ
እምበኣር፡ ነዚ መግለጺ 'ዚ ብዘየወላውል ቃላት፡ ንሱ ሓደ ካብኣቶም ምኳኑ
ብወግዒ ገሊጹሎም። እቲ ዝጠፍአ ቆልዓ ካብ ቄሪ ወጺኡ ናብ ቤቱ ተመሊሱ።
እቲ ዝተኸስተ ኩነታት ደንጽዩ ዝተደናገረ እኩብ ህዝቢ ድማ ብሓጎስ
ተመልሰ።

እቲ ናይ ኣይከሰርናን ኣዋጅ፡ ኣብ 'ቲ ናይ ኢሳያስን ኣብዩን ኣዝዩ ጥቡቅ
ዝኾነ ምሕዝነት ዝተራእየሉ እዋን ኣብ ኣስመራ እዩ ተጌሩ። እቲ "ሓደ ህዝቢ
ኢና" ዝበል መግለጺ 'ውን ኣብ ሓምለ 2018 እዩ ኣብ ኣዲስ ኣበባ ተባሂሉ።

---

1 ሓበሬታ ንኣምባቢ

እዚ ኣብ 'ዚ መቐድም ተጌሩ ዘሎ መወከሲ፡ ብገለ ፍሉጣት ኤርትራውያን ልሂቃን
ዝተደርሰን ዝረትዔን መጽሓፍ 'የ።

ኣርእስቲ ናይ 'ታ መጽሓፍ፡

ኤርትራ፡ ሃገረ-መንግስቲን ልኡላውነትን

Eritrea: ERITREA: NATIONHOOD AND SOVEREIGNTY

እንተ ኾነ፡ ኢሳያስ በዚ ኣዝዩ ዘደንጹ ሓድሽ ናይ ሃጸያዊ ትካል ኣዋጅ ጥራሕ ኣይተሓጽረን፡ ኣብ 'ቲ ኣንጻር ሃጸይነት ተባሂሉ ዝተሰግረ ተሞክሮ፡ ኣብ 'ቲ ብግምጃ ዝተሸፈነ ናይ ሬሳ ሳንዱቕ 'ውን መስማር 'ዩ ሸኺሉ። እዞም ኣብ ቅድሚ 'ቲ ሃጸያዊ ትካል ቀሪቡ ንማሕላ ዝተጠቕመሎም ሓደስቲ ቃላት፡ ብጥንቃቐ ዝተመርጹን ፈጺምካ ዘየጠራጥሩን እዮም ነይሮም።

ኣይከሰርናን . . . . ኣይጠፍኣናን! ክብል 'ዩ መዲሩ።

እዞም ቃላት እዚኣቶም ነቶም ንክቕበልዎ ወይ ክኣምንዎ ዘሸግሮም ናይ ኢትዮጵያ ጭፍራ ይኹን፡ ብፍላይ ድማ ነቲ ንናይ ቅድም ኣዛዚኡ - ስዒቡ ጸላኢኡ ዝተቐየረ - (ነብስሄር መለስ) ምእዙዝ ዓስከር ኮይኑ ክሳብ ኣብ ናይ ኤርትራን ኢትዮጵያን ኣብ "ናይ ባድመ ኲናት" ከም ወተሃደራዊ ሰላይ ኮይኑ ዘገልገለ መሻርኽቱ ብዙሕ ትርጉም ዘይዋሃቦ ክመስል ይኽእል ይኸውን።

እንተ ኾነ እዚ ሕልና ኣልቦ ዝኾነ ናይ "ኣይከሰርናን" ኣዋጅ ብሕልና ናይ 'ቲ ኣብ ናይ ባድመ ኲናት ብዙሓት ኣሽሓት ኤርትራውያን ተሰዊኦም ቀለብ ኣራዊት ከም ዝኾኑ ዝፈልጥ "ወንጌላዊ ኣብዪ" ብኸመይ ከም ዝትርጎም ክይገረመኒ ኣይተረፈን። ምናልባት 'ውን ከም 'ቲ ኢሳያስ ዝብሎ፡ እቲ ኲናት ርትዓውን ክኸውን ዝነበሮን እዩ ኢሉ ከመኽንየሉ ክፍትን ይኽእል ይኸውን። እንተ ኾነ ርትዓውነት ካልእ 'ዩ፡ ኣይከሰርናን ኢልካ ምእዋጅ ድማ ካልእ ዝተፈልየ ነገር 'ዩ።

ኣብ 'ዚ ነጥቢ 'ዚ ዉሑዳት መስመራት ንከንብር ዝደረኸኒ ምኽንያት፡ ኣብዪ ናይ ኢትዮጵያ ጠቕላሊ ሚኒስተር ኮይኑ ኣብ ዝተመርጸሉ እዋን ኣብ ዘቕረቦ መደረ፡ ብፍላይ ብዛዕባ ምፍታሕ እሱራት ይኹን ብዛዕባ ኣብ መንጎ ኤርትራን ኢትዮጵያን ዝነበረ ዘይርጉእ ኲነታት ብሰላማዊ መንገዲ ንምፍትሑ ዘሕለፎ ውሳኔ፡ ኣዝዩ ተንካፊ ብምንባሩ ንብዙሓት ሰባት ተስፋ ኣስኒቑን ኣደናጊሩን 'ዩ። እታ ትንቢታዊት ሚለንዩም ኣብ ቀረባ ምህላዋ 'ውን ኣእሚኑና። ኣዓሸዩና! ንሱ ጥራሕ ግን ኣይኮነን፡ ነቲ ዓለምለኻዊ ሕብረተሰብ 'ውን ቀሺሽዎ 'ዩ። እቲ ኣደናጊሩን መልክዑ ቀይሩን ንናይ 2018 ናይ ኖበል ንሻን ሽልማት ኣብነታዊ ክብሪ ንክወስድ፡ ውሳኔ ንክሓልፍ ዝጎስጎሱን ካልኦትን 'ውን ዘይወጽእ ጣዕሳ ኮይንዎም ኣሎ።

እንተ ኾነ እዚ ብሃጸያዊ ጥሙሕን ጽላለን ዝተደረኸ ናይ ምምዝማዝ ሓይሊ፡ ዋላ 'ውን ነቶም ኣቐዲሞም ጥዑያት ዝመስሉ ዝነበሩ ሰባት፡ መልክዖም ቀይሮም - ንገዛእ ነብሶም ዘይናቶም ምስሊ ገኒዞም - ከይሓፈሩ ኣብ 'ቲ ህቡብላ ናይ ሃጸያዊ ሃረርታ ክውጥሑ ይገብሮም 'ዩ። ኣብዪ ዋላ ኣቐዲሙ ዘይተለኽፈ ይንበር፡ ሕጂ ግን እታ ሃጸያዊት ሕንዚ ወጊኣቶ ኣላ። ኣብ ጉዳዩ እታ ናይ ንጉሳዊ ቤተ ሰብ ሕንዚ ዝያዳ ካብ ጽቡቕ ድሌት ዝተበገሰት ክትመስል ትኽእል፡ እንተ ኾነ ሓደ መዓልቲ ንጉሳዊ ዘውዲ ክደፍእ ምኳኑ ወላዲቱ ሓቢራቶ ምንባራ ገሊጹልና 'ዩ።

ናይ ኢሳያስ ኣፈወርቂ ዕብዳን ንነጻያዊ ሃረርታ

ዝኾነ ኣምባቢ ከመይ ኢሉ 'ዩ ሓደ ኣብ ዝተወሰነ እዋን ናይ ሓርነት ተቓላሳይ - ሰውራዊ - ዝነበረ፡ ሃጸያዊ ሃረርታ ከንግድ ዝኽእል ኢሉ ከግረም ይኽእል ይኸውን፡ እቲ መልሲ ድማ ኣብ ጥምረት ናይ ሕክምናን ናይ ታሪኻዊ ባህላዊ ኩነት ክርከብ ይክኣል። ነዚ ኣርእስቲ 'ዚ፡ ኣብ 'ታ "ንቅዱስ እምነት ዘርከሱ . . . (2020)" "Desecrators of the Sacred Trust . . ." (2020) እትብል መጽሓፈይ ዳህሲሰዮ ኣለኹ።

ከም 'ቲ ኣብ 'ታ ተወኪሰያ ዘለኹ መጽሓፍ ጠቒሰዮ ዘለኹ፡ ኢሳያስ ኪኖ እታ ንእሽቶን ድኽምትን ኤርትራ ሓሊፉ፡ ነይታን ርእሰን ናይ ግዝኣታት ክኸውን ሕልሚ ነይርዎ 'ዩ። ትንቢታውያን ዝኾኑ ሓሳባት ከኣንግድ 'ውን ፈቲኑ ነይሩ 'ዩ። ገለ ካብ 'ቶም ኣድነቕቱ (ገለ ህልዋት ገለ 'ውን ዝሓለፉ) እንተ ኾኑ 'ውን፡ ኪኖ ኤርትራ ሓሊፉ ኣርሒቹ ከገዝእ ዝግብለ ምኳኑ ይኣምኑሉ ነይሮም 'ዮም። ከምኡ እንተ ኾይኑ ደኣ ስለምንታይ ሰውራውን ናይ ኤርትራ ናይ ሓርነት ተቓላሳይን ክኸውን ሃቀነ ከገርመና ይኽእል 'ዩ። ጽቡቕ ሕቶ 'ውን 'ዩ። እቲ ከፈልጥ ዝህቅን ሓንጎል ግን፡ ዋላ 'ውን ንኮንፈሽ ጠቒሱ ነዚ ኣዋጣሪ ሕቶ ከምልሰ ይግባእ። እቲ መልሲ 'ውን ኣዝዩ ቀሊል 'ዩ፡ ንሱ ድማ ጉዳይ ህንጡይነትን ህንጡይነትን ጥራሕ 'ዩ፡ ንማርክ ኣንቶኒ ናይ ሸክስፐር ጆልየስ ሴዛር ምጥቃስ ይክኣል፡ እዚ ድማ እቲ ካብ "ሓዲን ዓረ ዝተረረ" ሃንቀውታን እቲ ንብዙሓት ኣሰዋእካ ባህግኻ ናይ ምፍጻም ድሌት ዘበገሰ ኣይከሰርናን ኢሉ ዝኣወጀ መንፈስ 'ዩ።

ኢሳያስን እቲ ሓርነታዊ ቃልስን

ስለዚ ኢሳያስ (እንተኾነ ከሳብ ሕጂ ብርግጽ ክገብር ዘይክኣለ) ንናይ ኤርትራ ልኡላውነት ኣብ ትሕቲ መሰዋእያ ናይ ሃጸያዊ መደብ ዕዮኡ ገንሸል ክገብራ ድሌት ኣለዎ። ቅድሚ ሓምሳ ዓመታት (ኣብ ታሕሳስ 1: 1970) ናይ ኢትዮጵያ ሰራዊት ኣብ ኤርትራ ኣዝዩ ዘስካክሕ ጃምላዊ ቅትለት ፈጺሙ 'ዩ። ኣስታት 1000 ዝኾኑ ንጹሃት ሲቪል ነበርቲ ዑናን በስኪደራን ብህወቶም ከለዉ ኣብ ውሽጢ ዓዶም ብሓዊ ሓሪሮም 'ዮም። ሕጂ ድማ ልክዕ እቲ ሰራዊት 'ቲ እዮ፡ በቲ ንትግራይ ናይ ምጥቃዕ ናይ ኢሳያስን ኣብዱን ናይ ሓባር ስትራተጂ፡ ብዕድመ ናይ ኢሳያስ ኣፈወርቂ ናብ ኤርትራ ተመሊሱ፡ እቲ ንትግራይ ብኸበድቲ ኣጽዋር ንምውቃዕ ብኣብዱ ዝፎርብ ምኽንያት፡ መራሕቲ ህ.ወ.ሓ.ት. ገበን ስለ ዝፈጸሙ ንክኣሰሩን ኣብ ሕጊ ንክቐርቡን ዝብል 'ዩ።

ሕጂ ካብ 'ቲ ናይ ትግራይ ኩናት ኣርእስቲ ከይወጻእናን ካብ ቅኑዕ ሕልና ተበጊስናን ነቲ ኩናት መን ጀሚርዎን ስለምንታይን ከ? ኢልና ንሕተት። ብኣገላልጻ ናይ ኣብዱ፡ መሪሕነት ህወሓት ነቲ ማእከላይ (ፈደራላዊ) መንግስቲ ብምኽንያት ናይ ኮቪድ 19 ዘስጋገር ምርጫ ብቅሉዕ ተቓዊሞም፡ ኣብ ክልሎም ምርጫ ከካይዱ ወሲኖም። ብኡ መሰረት ድማ ነቲ ናይ ፈደራላዊ መንግስቲ

ውሳኔ ተቓዊሞም ነቲ ምርጫ አካይደም 'ዮም። እተን ካልኦት ክልላት ምስ 'ቲ ናይ ፈደራላዊ መንግስቲ ናይ ምርጫ ምስግጋር ውሳነ ብምስምማዕ ነቲ ምርጫ አየካየዳን። ንሳቶም ግን ነቲ ምርጫ ብምኽያድ ተቓውሞኦም ርጉጽ ጌሮም። እቶም ናይ ህወሓት መራሕቲ፡ ብመሰረት እቲ ቅዋም ዘፍቅዶ፡ ነቲ ናይ ምርጫ ምስግጋር ተቓዊሞም ምርጫ ከም ዘካየዱን እቲ ቅዋም 'ውን ምስግጋር ናይ ምርጫ ዘፍቅድ ም'ኳ ምጥቃሶም አገዳሲ ነጥቢ ም'ኳ ምዝካር አገዳሲ 'ዩ።

እዞም ክልተ ዝተፈላለየ መርገጺ ዘለዎም ወገናት፡ ብመሰረት እቲ ቅዋም መኖም 'የ ቅኑዕ ንዝብል ም'ጉት ንጎድኒ ገዲፍና፡ ብዓይኒ ቅኑዕ ፍርድ'ን ልቦና'ን ከመይ ንመዝኖ? ብመንጽር እቲ ኩናት ከኽትሎ ዝኽእል አዝዩ ገዚፍ ናይ ሂወትን ንብረትን ዕንወት። እዚ መሰረታዊ ዝኾነ ናይ ፖለቲካ ፍልልያት፡ ዓቢ ሚዛን ተዋሂብዎ፡ ንዓለማዊ ማሕበር ሰብ ተወኪስካን ሓገዝ ረኺብካን ክፍታሕ ዝነበሮ ጉዳይ 'ዩ። እቲ ብአብዪ አሕመድ ዝምራሕ ፈደራላዊ መንግስቲ፡ ነቲ ብኩናት ክስዕብ ዝኽእል ጥፍአት ንከወግድ፡ ንህወሓት አእሚኑ አብ ዝርርብ ንክአትው። ዝአክል ግዜን ጸዓትን ተጠቒሙ ድዩ? ብወገን አብዪ፡ ሰላማዊ ፍታሕ እቲ ካልኣይ ዘይርከቦ አማራጺ ስለ ዝኾነ፡ ነዚ ንምግባር ንህወሓት አአሚንካ እቲ ጉዳይ ብሰላማዊ መንገዲ ንክፍታሕ፡ ከሳብ ሽምግልቲ ናብ መቐለ ብምልአኽ ከነዕርፎ ፈቲና ህወሓት ግን ዋጋ ዕዳጋ ክገብሩ አይመረጹን ከብል 'የ ዝጠቅስ። ህወሓት 'ውን ናይ አብዪ መንግስቲ ንትግራይ ከወርርን ከጥፍኦን ወሲኑ 'ዩ። እዚ ስትራተጂ 'ዚ ምስ 'ቲ ናብ ኩናት ከአቱ ናቱ ም'ኽንያት ዘለዎ ኢሳያስ እናተማኸሩ ንልዕሊ ሓደ ዓመት ከጦጅእዎ ዝጸንሑ መደብ 'የ ክብል ይገልጹ።

አብዪ ነዚ ብታንክታትን ከበድቲ አጽዋራትን ዝተሰነየ፡ 100,000 ሰራዊት ዘአንገደ ናይ ዕጥቂ ኩናት፡ ከም ሓደ ንገበኛታት ንምህዳን፡ ሕግን ስርዓትን ንም'ኽባር ዝተገብረ ወፍሪ ጌሩ 'የ ክገልጾ ፈቲኑ። ናይ ህ.ወ.ሓ.ት. መልሲ ድማ እዚ ንዓታቶምን ንመላእ ህዝቢ ትግራይን ንም'ብራሲ ዝተኻየደ ናይ ዓሌት ም'ጽናት ኩናት 'የ እዮም ዝብሉ። እንተ 'ኾነ በዚ ይኹን በቲ፡ እዚ አብ ትግራይ ዝተኻየደ ኩናት አዝዮም ዓበይቲ ከሳራታትን ናይ ንብረት ዕንወታትን ምስዓቦም ብሩህ ኮይኑ አሎ።

ናይ ትግራይ ኩናትን ሳዕቤናቱን

እቲ ናይ ፖሊስ ስርሒት ዝተሰምየ ወፍሪ ንናይ ትግራይ ርእሲ ከተማ ዝኾነት መቐለ ብመሓዝ ተዛዚሙ። እንተ'ኾነ እቲ ገበነኛታት ናይ ም'ሓዝ ዕላማ ግብራዊ አይኮነን። አይተታሕዙን፡ ስልጣኖም ም'ንስሓብ ጌሮም ነታ ከተማ ገዲፎም 'ዮም ናብ ጎቦታት አዝሊቖም። ናብ 'ቲ ናይ ቀደም አገባብ አቀላልስኦም ናብ ናይ ደባይ ኩናትን ስልጣ 'ዮም ተመሊሶም። ስለ 'ዚ መቐለ ብናይ ኢትዮጵያ ፈደራላዊ ሰራዊት ተታሒዛ፡ አብ ትሕቲ ቁጽጽር ፈደራላዊ መንግስቲ ትእቶ እምበር እቶም ብናይ አብዪ መንግስት "ጉጅለ ገበነኛታት" ተባሂሎም ዝተሰምዩ ናይ ህወሓት መራሕቲ አብኡ ዘይምጽንሓም ከተሓዙን አብ ሕጊ ክቐርቡን አይተኻእለን።

ብርግጽ ድማ፡ ምትሓዝ ናይ መቋለ - እቲ ብሕብረት ናይ ኢትዮጵያ ሓይልታትን፡ ብሕብረት ናይ ብኢሳያስ ተኣዚዘን ኣካል ናይ 'ቲ ናይ ሓባር ወፍሪ ዝኾና ገለ ናይ ኤርትራ ክፍላተ ሰራዊታትን ዝተኻየደ ወፍሪ- መፈጸምታ ናይ ትግራይ ኩናት ክኸውን ኣይከኣለን ጥራሕ ዘይኮነ ኣይክኸውንን እዩ 'ውን።

ናይ ትግራይ ኩናት ዝፈጠሮ ካልእ ሳዕቤን

1. ናይ ኤርትራውያን ስደተኛታት ጭውውያ

ኣብ ርእሲ 'ቲ ኣብ ናይ ትግራይ ኩናት ዘረጋገጸ ናይ ሓነ ምፍዳይ ስጉምቲ፡ ኢሳያስ ነዚ ምትእትታው 'ዚ ተጠቒሙ ንሰራዊት ኤርትራ ናብ መዓስከራት ስደተኛታት ኤርትራውያን ኣብ ትግራይ ከም ዝኣትዉ ብምግባር፡ ኣስታት 6000 ዝኾኑ ኤርትራውያን ስደተኛታት ከም ዝጨወዩ ጌሩ፡ ናብ 'ቲ ቅድሚ ነዊሕ እዋን ሃዲሞም ዝገደፍዎ ቦታ ናብ ኤርትራ ከም ዝምለሱ ብምግባር ካልእ ናይ ሓነ ምፍዳይ ስጉምቲ ከም ዝወሰደ ተጸብጺቡ 'ዩ። እዚ ተግባር 'ዚ እንድሕሪ ተረጋጊጹ፡ ብቐሊሉ ሽለል ኢልካ ዘይሕለፍ ዓለም ለኸዊ ናይ ሓጊ ጥሕሰት ኮይኑ፡ ኢሳያስ ከም ፈጻሚ ናይ 'ቲ ገበን ከምኡ 'ውን ኣብዩ ነቲ ጭውውያ ንክፍጸም ብምምሕዳርን፡ ብባለምለኸዊ ሕጊ ተሓተቲ ዮም። ገለ ሓላፍነታውያን ዝኾኑ ጸለውቲ ሰባት ድማ ነዚ ዝተፈጸመ ጭውውያ ኣብ ትሕቲ ጽላል ሕቡራት ሃገራትን ሕብረት ኣፍሪቃን ኮይኑ ብዝነጥፍ ነጻ ኣካል ንክጸረ ሓቲቶም ኣለዉ።

እቲ ብቐጥታ ከውሰድ ዘለዎ ስጉምቲ ድማ፡ ሓደ - ንኸልተ ዕላማ - ዝዓዪ፡ ኣብ ትሕቲ ናይ ሕቡራት ሃገራት ላዕለዋይ ተጸዋዒ ስደተኛታት (UNHCR) ኮይኑ ዝሰርሕ ኣጋሩዬ ሸማግለ ናብ ኢትዮጵያን ኤርትራን ምልኣኽ 'ዩ።

እቲ ቀዳማይ ዕማም፡ ብመሰረት ዓለምለኸዊ ሕጊ ሰብኣዊ መሰላት ኣብ ልዕሊ 'ቶም ዝተጨወዩ ስደተኛታት፡ ብኢሳያስን በቶም ጨካናት ናይ ጸጥታ መሓውራቱን ዝኾነ ይኹን ጉድኣት ከይወርዶም ምርግጋጽ 'ዩ። ኤርትራ ናይ ቤት ማእሰርቲ ሃገር ኮይና፡ ኣማኢት ኣሽሓት ህዝቢ ኣብ ኮንተይነራት ተጓጽዮም፡ ብናይ ቀትሪ ሀሮርማ ዋዒን ብናይ ለይቲ ቀዝሒን ብዝተፈላለዩ ኣሽገርቲ ሕማማትን ዝሳቐዩላ ዓባይ ቤትማእሰርቲ 'ያ።

እቲ ካልኣይ ዕማም ናይ 'ታ መርማሪት ሸማግለ ድማ፡ ነቲ ናይ ጭውውያ ኩነታት ብደቂቕ ፈቲሻን መረድኢታን ኣኪባን፡ ነቲ ብኢሳያስን ስርዓቱን ተፈጺሙ ተባሂሉ ዝተረጋገጸ ታሪኽ ምቋራብ 'ዩ። ቀጺላ 'ውን ነቲ ተረጋጊጹ ኣብ ኢትዮጵያን ኣብ ኤርትራን ተፈጺሙ ዝተባህለ ናይ ጭውውያ ተግባራት ንምምርማር፡ ነቶም ኣብ 'ቲ ናይ ጭውውያ ተግባር ተሳቲፎም ዝበሃሉ ጥርጡራት ምምርማር 'ዩ። እቲ ናይ ምጽራይ ጸብጻብ ድማ ናብ ሕቡራት ሃገራትን ሕብረት ኣፍሪቃን ከምኡ 'ውን ብሰፊሑ ናብ ማሕበረ ሰብ ዓለምን ጋዜጠኛታትን ተመራመርትን ከም ዝቐርብ ክግበርን ስፍሕ ሸፈነ ክካየደሉን ይግባእ። እንተ

ኾነ፡ እቲ ቀንዲ ምኽንያት ንገለ አገደስቲ ዝኾኑ ነጥብታት ምንጻር ኮይኑ፡ ዓለም ድማ ብብሩህ ከትርድኦን ከትፈልጦን ይግባእ፡፡

ቀዳማይ፡ ናይ ኢሳያስ አፍወርቂ ሃጸያዊ ሃረርታን ዝተሓላለኸ ውዲታትን ብዘየገድስ፡ ኤርትራና አይትሸየጥን 'ያ፡ እቲ ብናይ ስዉአትና ከቡር ደም ዝተረኸበ ኤርትራዊ ልኡላውነት እንተ ኾነ 'ውን ብናይ ስልጣን ጽምኣት ዘለም ዓንዳሪ ኢሳያስን ኢትዮጵያዊ ናይ ገበን መሻርኸቱ ናብ ዕዳጋ አይከወርድን 'ዩ፡፡

ካልአይ፡ እቶም ካልኣት ናይ ኤርትራ ናይ ሓርነት ተቃላስትን፡ እቶም አብ 'ዚ ናይ 'ዛ መጽሓፍ መደብ ዕዮ እቱዋት ዝኾኑ ኤርትራውያን ከኢላታትን፡ ነዚ ኢሳያስን አብዩን ተዓጢቖምሉ ዘለዉ ዝተሓላለኸ ሃጸያዊ መደባት ንምቅላስ ተዓጢቖም አለዉ፡፡ እቲ እዋናዊ ቴማን አርእስትን ናይ 'ዛ መጽሓፍ መደብ ዕዮ ድማ፡ "ኣዕኑድ ናይ ልኡላዊት ነጻ-ሃገር ኤርትራ" The Pillars of Eritrea's Sovereign Statehood. እዩ፡፡

ሳልሳይ፡ ኩሎም ኤርትራውያን፡ ብፍላይ ድማ እቲ ግዳይ ናይ ባርነት ኮይኑ ገለ ካብኣቶም 'ውን ንረብሓ ናይ ኢሳያስ ምስጢራዊ ውዕላት መሳርሒ ዝኾነ ሓድሽ ናይ መንእሰያት ትውልዲ፡ ክሳብ 'ታ ናይ መጨረሽታ ትንፋስ (ብናይ ቀደም ናይ ሰውራ ኤርትራና አገላልጻ - ናይ መጨረሽታ ጥይትን ናይ መጨረሽታ ሰብን) ከዋደቕ 'ዩ፡፡

ራብዓይ፡ ህዝቢ ኤርትራ አብ ውሽጢ ይኹን አብ ወጻኢ፡ ንኢሳያስ አፈወርቂ ይኹን ነቶም ናይ ምጽናት መሳርሕቱ ብሞልጋቡ፡ ብሓድሽን ብዲሞክራስያዊ አገባብ ብዝተመርጹ አባላት ባይቶ ንምትካአምን ሓድሽ መብጽዓ ዝአተወሉ ሓድሽ ናይ ትንሳኤ እዋን በጺሑና አሎና፡፡

"እቶም ናይ ኤርትራ ልኡላዊ ሃገራውነት አዕኑድ" መደብ ዕዮ መጽሓፍ

እዚ ናይ 'ዛ መጽሓፍ መደብ ዕዮ፡ ንተወፋይነት ናይ 'ቲ ንሓርነት ናይ ኤርትራ አብ ምምጻእ አንጻር እቲ መጽነቲ ስርዓት ዝካየድ ዘሎ ከኢላዊ ክፋል ናይ ቃልሲ ተወሳኺ ናሪ አብ ምፍጣር ዘንጸባርቕ ክኸውን 'ዩ፡፡ ዕላምኡ ድማ አብ 'ቲ **"ምርግጋጽ ኤርትራዊ ልኡላውነት"** ዝብል አርእስቲ ተገሊጹ አሎ፡፡

አብ 'ቲ ስዒቡ ዝቐጽል፡ እቲ አንባቢ ነቲ ባህርን ዕላማን ናይ 'ቲ መደብ ዕዮ ይኹን ንዝርዝር ናይ ተሳተፍቲ አብ መጨረሽታ ክፋል ናይ 'ቲ ጽሑፍ ከረኽቦ እዩ፡፡ አብ 'ቲ ናይ መእተዊ ምዕራፍ እንገብሮ አፈናዊ ትዕዝብቲ ድማ ነዚ መደብ ዕዮ ንክሕሰብ ዝደረኸ ምክንያት እንታይ ምዃኑ ክሕብረና 'ዩ፡፡ ጽሟቕ ናይ ነብሲ ወከፍ ምዕራፍ ድማ አብ መደምደምታ ምዕራፍ አሎ፡፡

252

እቲ ኣብ 'ዚ መደብ ዕዮ ናይ 'ዚ መጽሓፍ ዝተገብረ ጻዕሪ፡ ነቲ መዳርግቲ ዘይርከበ መስዋእቲ ዝተኸፍሎ ናይ ሃገርና ልዑላውነት ንምዕቃብን ንምክልኻልን ዘሎና ልዑል ተገዳስነት ዘገሮ ኮይኑ፡ ንሱ ድማ ነጸብራቕ ናይ ዘሎና ዓሚቝ ሓርበኛዊ ሓልዮት 'ዩ። እቲ ናይ ኢሳያስ ሃጸያዊ ሃርርታን ዝተሓላለኸ ውዲታትን፡ ንኤርትራዊ ሓርበኝነት ብኣንጻር ናይ 'ቲ ተስፋ ንሙቝራጽ ዝስራሑ ዝያዳ ንተገዳስነትና ዘዐሙቝ 'ዩ። እዛ ናይ ጀጋኑን ሰማእታትን መሬት፡ ሕጂ ይኹን ዝዘንተ ዕለት ኣይከትሽየጥን 'ያ። እቲ ቆጺርካ ዘይውዳእ መስዋእቲ ዝተኸፍሎ ልኡላውነት ብኹሎም ኤርትራውያን ሓርበኛታትን ብዘለዎም ኩሉ ዓቕምታትን ምክልኻል ክግበረሉ ይግባእ።

እቲ እዋናውን ብሩህን ዝኾነ ሓደጋ (ከምቲ ሓደ ካብ ምዕራፍትና ገሊጽዎ ዘሎ) እቲ በቲ ዘይተመርጸን ዓንዳርን ንልኡላውነትና ብምዕፋን ገበን ናይ ምፍጻም ድሌት ዘለዎ ኣንጸላልዩና ዘሎ ሓደጋ፡ ግድነት ከም 'ቲ ዘለዎ 'ዩ ክረአ ዝግባእ። - ነቲ በቲ ክሱስ ዝተፈጸመ ዝለዓለ ክድዓት ሃገር፡ ኣብ ቅድሚ ሕጊ ቀሪቡ እቲ ሕጊ ዝፈቕዶ መቕጻዕቲ ከውስነሉ። ሕጂ እቲ ጉዳይ ነጺሩ 'ዩ፡ ኤርትራውያን ነዚ እዋናው ንጹርን ሓደጋ ኣልልዮም ከውስኑ ንዕኡ መጨረሽታ ከገብሩሉን ኩሉ ዝኽኣሎም ከገብሩ ይግባእ። ነዚ ክንገብር ዘይምኽኣል ማለት ድማ ነቲ ዝደለብናዮ ልኡላውነት ምስኣን ማለት 'ዩ። ነብስና ናብ 'ቲ ናይ መጨረሽታን ዝመረረን ቅልስ፡ ንናይ ሂወትን ቅልስ ክንቅርብ ኣሎና። ንናይ ኢሳያስ ኣፈወርቂ ገበን ናይ ምፍጻም ድሌት ንምብርዓንን ዘሎና ዘበለ ኩሉ ኣገባባት ተጠቒምና ኣብ መጨረሽታ ከነብጽሖ ይግባእ።

እቲ ቅልውላውን ብድሆታቱን

ቻይናውያን ንቅልውላው ናይ ሓደጋን ትዕድልትን ምግጣም እዩ ኢሎም ይገልጽዎ። ሕጂ ንሕና፡ ኣብ ናይ ሂወት ጉዕዞ ቃራና መንገዲ ብድሆ ንርከብ ኣሎና፡ እዚ ኣብ ትግራይ ተኸሲቱ ዘሎ ኩናት፡ ንኽንጠፍእ ወይ 'ውን ነዚ ናይ ኢሳያስ ኣፈወርቂ ጨፍላቒ ስርዓት ኣሊና ንኽንሰርር ናይ ብድሆ ትዕድልቲ ገጢሙና ኣሎ። ከመይ ጌርና ንትግብሮ ብዙሖ ዘካትዕ ሕቶ ኣይኮነን፡ ዝኾነ ይኹን ኣብለጭላጭ ምራል ናብ 'ቲ ናይ መጨረሽታ ዘየብጽሕ ኣገባብ ወሲዱ ከዐንቅፈና ኣይግባእን። እቲ ናይ መጨረሽታ፡ ነቲ ኣጽናቲ መንግስቲ ናይ ኢሳያስ ንኽኒልግስ ዝሕብረና ኣገባብ ጥራሕ 'ዩ ከኸውን ዘለዎ። እቲ ኣብ መጨረሽታ ሃገርን ህዝብን ንምድሓን ን30 ዓመታት ንምሰል ርእስ ውሳነ ተቓሊሱ ንሃገሩ ነጻ ዝገበረ ኣገባብ ጥራሕ 'ዩ ንህላወኡ ኣረጋጊጹሎ። ናይ ሓደ/ሓንቲ ኣብ ኣፍደገ ሞት ኮይኑ/ና እናእንቀጥቀጠ/ት ኣብ ኩርናዕ ዝተቐረረን/ትን ዝስግኣን/ትን ፍጡር/ፍጥርቲ ምስሊ ኣብ ኣእምሮኹም ቅረጹ። ከም 'ዚ ዝኣመሰለ/ት ፍጡር/ፍጥርቲ እንታይ ት/ይገብር? እቲ መልሲ ቀሊል 'ዩ - እቲ ኣብ ሓደጋ ዝወደቐ/ት ፍጡር/ፍጥርቲ ኣይ/ት/ጠራጠርን 'ዩ/ያ። ናቱ/ታ ናይ ሓደጋ

ህዋሳት ነቶም ምንጪታት ናይ ሓደጋ ሓይሊ ይኹልዕዎም። ድሕነት ምርግጋጽ እቲ ንሕና ደቂ ሰባት ምስ ካልኦት ፍጡራት እንካፈሎ ቀዳማይ ሕጊ ናይ ፍጥረት 'ዩ። ስለ 'ዚ ኣብ ታሪኻዊ መድረኽ ናይ "ግበር ወይ ድማ ሙት"! ኢና ዘሎና።

ብሩህን እዋናውን ሓደጋ -- ቅምስልቲ ኤርትራ?

ጽሑፋት ናይ 'ዞም ተሳተፍቲ ናይ 'ዚ መደብ ዕዮ ኣእምሮኣዊ/ከኢላዊ መዘና ናይ 'ቲ ደባያዊ ቅዲ ኩነት፡ መቐጸልታ ናይ 'ቲ ድሕሪ ናይ ሰላሳ ዓመት ንሃገር መንግስቲ ኤርትራ ንምፍጣር ዝፈሰሰ ደምን ዘንጠብጠበ ረሃጽን ንብዓትን 'ዩ። እቶም ኣብ 'ዚ ቅጺ ሰፊሮም ዘለዉ ዝተፈላለዩ ምዕራፋት እቶም ከም ኣዕኑድ ኮይኖም ንሓሳባት ናይ ልኡላውነትና ዝድግፉ 'ዮም። ኩሉ ኤርትራዊ - ንልኡላውነት ናይ ሃገር ዝምልከቱ ኣገደስቲ ኣዕኑድ ምህላዎም - ብቐጻሊ ምዝኽኻር ከግበረሉ ኣዝዩ ኣድላዪን ኣገዳስን ዝኾነ ሃገራዊ ዕማም 'ዩ።

እቶም "ብሩህን እዋናውን ሓደጋ ...." ከምኡ 'ውን "ቅምስልቲ ኤርትራ ....." ዝብሉ ቃላት ኣብ 'ዚ ቅጺ 'ዚ፡ ኣርእስታት ናይ ክልተ ምዕራፋት ኮይኖም ቀሪቦም ኣለዉ። እዚ ድማ ነቲ ንሃገር መንግስትና ገጢምዋ ዘሎ ብድሆታት ይኹን፡ ከለዓሉ ኣለዎም ዝበሃሉ ኣገደስቲ ሕቶታት ኣልዒሉ መልሲ ንምርካብን፡ ሓንቲ ዲሞክራስያዊትን ልዑል ምዕባለ ዘለዋ ሃገር ኤርትራ ንክትህሉ፡ ሃገርና ኤርትራ ኣብ ዓለም ኣብ ናይ ሃገራት ስድራቤት ግቡእ ከብራ ንክትረክብ ተባሂሉ 'ዩ። ንሱ ድማ እቲ ንሃገርና ዝጽበያ ዘሎ ተኸእሎታት፡ ኣዝዩ ጥንቁቕ፡ እንተኾነ ግን ምስ 'ቲ ኤርትራ እትውንኖ ሰራሕተኛ፡ ቀልጢፉ ከሓዊ ዝኽእል፡ ንዓይ ይጥዓመኒ ዘይብል ብናይ ሓርበኝነት መንፈስ ዝተቓጸለ ህዝቢ፡ ነዚ ኣጋንፉ ዘሎ እዋናዊ ሓደጋ ጥራሕ ዘይኮነ፡ ኪኒኡ ስጊረ ነቲ ናይ ሓርነት ተቓላስቲ ከዉን ንክኸውን ዝተተምነይ ቅዱስ ሓሳብ ከዉን ንምግባርን ነቲ ዝኸፈልዎ ከቢድ መስዋእቲ ከተረጋግጾ ጽኑዕን ትስፉውን እምነት ኣለዎ። እቲ ነዞም ተሳተፍቲ ናይ 'ዛ መጽሓፍ ኣብ ሓደ ንክመጹ ዝገበረ ሓባራዊ እምነት፡ እቲ ንሓርነትናን ልኡላውነትናን ኣብ ምምጻእ ዝተኻየደ ነዊሕ ቃልሲ፡ ከም ምስክርነት ናይ ተስፋ ኮይኑ ስለ ዝጠመሮም 'ዩ።

ኣብ መጨረሽታ፡ ከም 'ቲ ኣብ ልኡላውነትና ኣዚና እንቖጅስ፡ ንሕና 'ውን ንንጠባብትን ሓዊስና ንናይ ካልኦት ሃገር መንግስታት ልኡላውነት ከነኽብር ይግባእ። ስለ 'ዚ፡ ኣብ ናይ ካልኦት ሃገራት ጉዳያት ኢድና ከነእቱ ዘይንኣምነሉ ምኽንያ ንኹሎም ዝምልከቶም ኣካላት ከነፍልጥ ይግባእ፡ እንተላይ ነዚ ኣብ 'ዚ እዋን ኣብ ትግራይ ዝኸይድ ዘሎ ኩነት ከይተረፈ። እዚ ድማ፡ እቲ ኣብ ልዕሊ ጎረቤትናን ሓውናን ዝኾነ ህዝቢ፡ ትግራይ ዝኸይድ ዘሎ ብሕብረተሰብ ዓለም ኩነኔ ዝግብኦ ኩነት ዘውረዶ ናይ ሞትን ዓመጽን ምዝንባል ህዝብን ካብኡ ሓሊፉ 'ውን ናይ ኩነታት ገበናትን ገበናት ኣንጻር ሰብኣውነትን ዘጠቓለለ ኣዕናውን ቀዛፍን ኩነታት ካብ ልቢ ከም ዝተሰምዓና እና ኣፍለጥን ሓዘና እናገለጽናን።

تقدمة

تصريحات أسياس أفورقي تعد انتهاكاً للسيادة الإرترية

برخت هبتي سلاسي

مفاجأة منتصف صيف 2018م

بوجه تعلوه ابتسامة مشرقة لم يعهدها الإريتريون من قبل في وجه رئيسهم، الذي عرفوه طيلة سنوات حكمه عابساً متجهماً، وقف أسياس أفورقي مبتهجاً أمام حشد إثيوبي، ليقول لهم بحميمية غير معهودة: من الآن فصاعداً لن تكون هناك إرتريا وإثيوبيا، "نحن شعب واحد"، وكل من يشكك في ذلك عليه التأكد من قدراته العقلية. كان لهذه العبارات وقع الموسيقى في آذان الحشد المبتهج، كيف لا وهو الشخص الذي ظنوا لسنوات مضت أنه العدو اللدود لإثيوبيا المتجسد في صورة الشيطان، ها هو الآن يقف أمامهم ويعلن بعبارات لا لبس فيها أنه واحد منهم، أنه طفلهم الضائع العائد الى الأهل والدار لاتقاء البرد، كان الحشد منتشياً من الفرح أشد الإنتشاء.

إن الاعلان بأننا (لم نخسر) كان قد تم التصريح به سابقاً في أسمرا عندما بدأت العلاقة الوثيقة بين أبي أحمد وأسياس تتكشّف للعلن، وقد تبع هذا التصريح، تصريحاً أخر في وقت لاحق في يوليو 2018م في أديس أبابا مضمونه (نحن شعب واحد).

لم يتوقف أسياس عند حد هذا الإعلان الوحدوي المذهل ضمن المشروع الإمبراطوري الجديد، بل تعمد أن يدق المسمار الأخير في نعش تجربة التحرير الإرترية المناهضة للمشروع الامبراطوري الوحدوي، ولهذا اختار الكلمات التي استخدمها بعناية لا تترك مجالاً للشك في أن ولائه للمشروع الإمبراطوري الجديد ولاءً لا يتزعزع، عندما قال (ما خسرنا وما ضاع لنا شيئاً).

ربما لم تكن هذه الكلمات الأخيرة للرئيس الإرتري تعني الكثير للجمهور الإثيوبي، وربما لا تعني الكثير لشريكه الجديد أيضاً، والذي كان قبل كل شيء مساعداً مخلصاً لعدوه السابق الراحل ملس زيناوي (تنكر له الآن)، ولعب دوراً مهماً في الحرب الارترية الاثيوبية، التي يطلق عليها (حرب الوياني)، من موقعه في قسم الاتصالات في جهاز الاستخبارات العسكرية الإثيوبية إبان هذه الحرب.

لقد ظللت أتساءل كيف "استوعب" عقل وضمير آبي الإنجيلي إعلان "ما خسرنا شيئاً" القاسي، بالنظر إلى حقيقة أنه يعرف أن عشرات الآلاف من الشباب الإرتري الأبرياء قد تم التضحية بهم كوقود فيما يسمى حرب بادمي. ربما اعتبرها

نتيجة منطقية فرضتها حقيقة الحرب كما فعل أسياس، ولكن تقبل الحقيقة شيء، والتصريح بأننا "ما خسرنا" شيءٌ آخر تماماً.

أنني أركز على هذه النقطة تحديداً، لأن خطاب آبي أحمد الواعد عندما أُنتخب رئيساً للوزراء، وقيامه بإطلاق سراح جميع السجناء والمعتقلين، وقبول الحل السلمي للتوتر بين إرتريا وإثيوبيا، كان مؤثراً لدرجة أنه خدع البعض منا وأعطانا الأمل أن الألفية المنتظرة والتي يضرب بها المثل قد أصبحت قاب قوسين أو أدنى. والحقيقة أن خداعه لم يقتصر علينا بل خدع المجتمع الدولي والذي ساهم في تلميع صورته بتتويجه بجائزة نوبل للسلام لعام 2018م، وهو قرار ندم عليه الكثيرون لاحقاً بما فيهم بعض الذين ضغطوا لصالحه وسوقوه للحصول على هذا الشرف الرمزي في ذلك الوقت.

لكن الواضح أن هذا هو جنون الطموح الإمبراطوري الذي يجعل حتى من اعتقدنا أنهم عقلاء في السابق ينغمسون في دوامة الاشواق الإمبراطورية، ويبدو أن الجرثومة الامبراطورية قد أصابت آبي أحمد هذا إن لم يكن مصاباً بها من قبل، وهنا تبدو الجرثومة الامبراطورية استعارة ملائمة جداً لحالة آبي أحمد، خاصة وأنه أخبرنا أن والدته تنبأت له أنه سيكون يوماً ما الملك السابع لإثيوبيا.

جنون الاشواق الإمبراطورية لأسياس أفورقي

بالنسبة للقارئ الذي يتساءل كيف يمكن لمقاتل من أجل التحرير (ثوري) أن يمتلئ بالأشواق الإمبراطورية؟ الإجابة على مثل هذا السؤال متاحة في كتابي (منتهكوا الأمانة المقدسة – الصادر في عام 2020م) والتي تستصحب الابعاد الطبية والتاريخية، والثقافية. لقد فصّلت في الكتاب المذكور كيف أن أسياس كان يحلم بأن يصبح امبراطوراً متوجاً لما هو أبعد من إرتريا الصغيرة التي لا تلبي طموحاته، ليس هذا وحسب، بل كان ينتابه شعوراً بأنه يمتلك خصائص وصفات الأنبياء، وكان بعض المعجبين به (بعضهم على قيد الحياة والبعض الآخر غادرها)، يصدقون ذلك ويعتقدون أنه يستحق أن يحكم ما هو أكبر من إرتريا. وهنا قد تتساءل، لماذا إذاً ظل يتظاهر بأنه ثوري ومقاتل من أجل تحرير إرتريا؟ إنه سؤال جيد ومحير في ذات الوقت حتى بالمنطق الكونفوشيوسي، ويأمل العقل المتطلع الحصول على إجابة شافية له. الجواب بسيط، جوهر الأمر يتعلق بـ (الطموح والطموح ولا شيء غير الطموح)، وعلى حد تعبير مارك أنطوني في رواية شكسبير عن يوليوس قيصر، عندما قال (يجب أن يكون مصنوعاً من عنصر شديدة الصرامة، حتى يكون مستعد للتضحية بآلاف الأروح، ومن ثم يعلن في الملأ "نحن لم نخسر".

أسياس وحرب التحرير

الواضح أن أسياس مستعد (لكنه بالتأكيد غير قادر بعد) على التضحية بسيادة إرتريا على مذبح مشروعه الامبراطوري، وهنا لابد أن نتذكر أنه قبل خمسين عاماً -في الأول من ديسمبر 1970- ارتكب الجيش الإثيوبي واحدة من أفظع المجازر في إرتريا، حيث تم حرق حوالي ألف من المدنيين الأبرياء وهم أحياء في قريتي عونا وبسكيدرا، واليوم عاد نفس الجيش إلى إرتريا، ولكن هذه المرة بدعوة من أسياس أفورقي كجزء من استراتيجية أسياس/أبي المشتركة لمهاجمة التيغراي. لقد كان السبب الذي قدمه آبي للهجوم على تيغراي بأسلحة ثقيلة هو الادعاء بأن قادة الجبهة الشعبية لتحرير تيغراي قد ارتكبوا جرائم ولذا يجب القبض عليهم وتقديمهم للعدالة، الآن بينما نتحدث عن موضوع الحرب في تيغراي، يجب علينا بكل تجرد النظر في مسألة من بدأ الحرب ولماذا؟ إن تفسير أبي هو أن قادة الجبهة الشعبية لتحرير تيغراي تحدوا الحكومة المركزية -الفيدرالية- من خلال اتخاذهم قرار تنظيم الانتخابات في الاقليم، بالرغم من قرار الحكومة الفيدرالية بتأجيل الانتخابات بسبب جائحة كورونا (COVID-19) ومن ثم مضوا قدما في إجراء الانتخابات في تحد صريح لقرار الحكومة الفيدرالية وفرض الأمر الواقع، بينما التزمت الحكومات الإقليمية الأخرى بقرار تأجيل الانتخابات، بالمقابل قادة الجبهة الشعبية لتحرير تيغراي من جانبهم قد أعتدوا بحقهم الدستوري في إجراء الانتخابات زاعمين أن تأجيل الانتخابات انتهاك لما نص عليه الدستور، وبذا وجد الجانبان نفسيهما في مواقف متعارضة، وهو ما يقود إلى التساؤل -بغض النظر عمن هو على الجانب الصحيح دستورياً- هل بذلت جهود حقيقية لحل هذه الاختلافات السياسية المتعارضة والتفسيرات الدستورية المتناقضة بحكمة ومرونة، بما في ذلك طلب المساعدة والمشورة من المجتمع الدولي؟ هذا سؤال مهم للغاية في ضوء حقيقة أن الحرب تنطوي على خسائر غير ضرورية في الأرواح وتدمير للممتلكات، وهل كرست الحكومة الفيدرالية بقيادة آبي أحمد وقتاً وطاقة كافيين في محاولات إقناع الجبهة الشعبية لتحرير تيغراي بالتفاوض لإيجاد حل سلمي وتجنب الحرب؟ آبي أحمد من جانبه يدعي إنه بذل ما في وسعه للقيام بذلك، بما في ذلك إرسال وسطاء للسفر إلى مقلي لمحاولة إقناع قيادة الجبهة الشعبية لتحرير تيغراي بالحل السلمي وأنه الخيار الأفضل، ولكن قيادة الجبهة الشعبية لتحرير تيغراي لم تكن على استعداد لتقديم أي تنازلات، من جهتها تدعي الجبهة الشعبية لتحرير تيغراي أن حكومة أبي أحمد كانت قد قررت غزو تيغراي مسبقاً تنفيذاً لاستراتيجية تم التخطيط لها منذ أكثر من عام بالتشاور والتنسيق مع أسياس، والذي لديه أسبابه الخاصة لخوض الحرب مع الجبهة الشعبية لتحرير تيغراي. آبي أحمد وصف الحملة العسكرية التي شارك فيها حوالي مائة ألف جندي مسلحين بالدبابات والمدفعية الثقيلة بأنها حملة لإنفاذ القانون والنظام، مثلها مثل أي عمل تقوم بها الشرطة بهدف اعتقال المجرمين، بالمقابل اعتبرت الجبهة الشعبية لتحرير تيغراي أن الحملة العسكرية هي حرب إبادة جماعية تهدف إلى محوهم وكذلك شعب تيغراي ككل من الوجود، ولكن أياً كانت النتيجة النهائية، فمن الواضح بالفعل أن الحرب في تيغراي قد كلفت الجميع خسائر فادحة في الأرواح ودماراً في الممتلكات.

257

الحرب في تيغراي وتبعاتها

لقد انتهت العملية البوليسية المزعومة بالسيطرة على مقلي عاصمة الإقليم، لكن الهدف المعلن للعملية وهو إلقاء القبض على الجناة لم يتحقق، لم يتم القبض عليهم لأنهم انسحبوا تكتيكياً إلى الجبال، لقد عادوا عملياً لاستراتيجيتهم القديمة وهي حرب العصابات. إذاً سيطرت القوات الفيدرالية على مقلي، ولكن لم يتحقق هدف إلقاء القبض على "المجلس العسكري الإجرامي - الجونتا"، وهي الصفة التي أطلقتها حكومة آبي أحمد على القيادة العليا للجبهة الشعبية لتحرير تيغراي، وعليه من الواضح أن الاستيلاء على مقلي لم ولن ينهي الحرب في تيغراي، والتي كما ورد تم التخطيط لها وتنفيذها بواسطة قوات مشتركة بين الحكومة الفيدرالية والعديد من الفرق الإرترية التي أمرها أسياس بأن تكون جزءاً من العملية المشتركة.

عاقبة أخرى من عواقب حرب التيغراي- اختطاف اللاجئين الإرتريين

بالإضافة إلى الانتقام الذي سعى إليه أسياس من حربه على التيغراي، هنالك أيضاً تقارير عن أنه استغل فرصة توغل القوات الإرترية في إقليم تيغراي لتحقيق هدف انتقامي آخر وهو اختطاف حوالي ستة ألف إرتري من مخيمات اللاجئين الإرتريين في تيغراي ومن ثم إعادتهم إلى إرتريا التي فروا منها في السابق وفق ما ورد في بعض التقارير، وإذا ثبت بالفعل صحة هذه التقارير، فإن هذا يعد انتهاكاً خطيراً للقانون الدولي، وكلا من أسياس بصفته مرتكب الفعل، وكذلك آبي أحمد لأنه متواطئ يفترض أن يخضعا للمساءلة أمام القانون الدولي، وقد دعا بعض المسؤولين في المنطقة والمجتمع الدولي إلى إجراء تحقيق شفاف وشامل في حوادث الاختطاف من قبل لجنة محترفة محايدة تحت رعاية الأمم المتحدة والاتحاد الأفريقي، وعليه يجب أن يكون الإجراء الفوري هو إرسال لجنة تحقيق دولية محترفة تحت رعاية مفوضية الأمم المتحدة السامية لشؤون اللاجئين إلى كل من إثيوبيا وإرتريا لمهمتين أساسيتين وهما: الأولى ضمان عدم وقوع أي أذىً للاجئين المختطفين من قبل أسياس وأجهزته الأمنية البغيضة والمعروفة بارتكاب أعمال يحظرها القانون الدولي الإنساني، ومعلوم أن إرتريا هي دولة سجون من الطراز الأول، حيث يتم حبس مئات الآلاف في حاويات مزدحمة، يعانون فيها من حر النهار القائظ وبرد الليل القارس، وأغلبهم يعاني من أمراض خطيرة، بينما المهمة الثانية للجنة هي التحقيق والبحث بجدية في أوضاع المختطفين وجمع الأدلة المتعلقة بدور أسياس وحكومته في عملية الاختطاف إذا ثبتت صحة هذه التقارير، وهو ما يقتضي أيضاً قضاء اللجنة لبعض الوقت في كل من إرتريا وإثيوبيا واستجواب جميع الأشخاص المشتبه في تورطهم في عملية الاختطاف، ومن ثم إتاحة نتائج هذا التحقيق للأمم المتحدة والاتحاد الأفريقي وكذلك للمجتمع الدولي ككل بما في ذلك الصحفيين والباحثين.

إن هذه الظروف المعقدة والمصيرية التي يمر بها وطننا والتي بدأت تتكشف من خلال مشاركة إرتريا في هذه الحرب هي مناسبة لتوضيح بعض الحقائق المهمة والحاسمة والتي يجب أن تكون مفهومة للجميع بشكل واضح لا لبس فيه وهي:

أولاً: أن إرتريا ليست للبيع بالرغم من مكائد وأشواق أسياس أفورقي الامبراطورية، وأن سيادة إرتريا، التي تم تحقيقها بدماء الشهداء الغالية، لن يتم مقايضتها من قبل مغامر متعطش للسلطة وشريكه الإثيوبي في الجريمة.

ثانياً: الإرتريون الذين قاتلوا من أجل تحرير بلادهم، بما فيهم المثقفون الإرتريون المشاركون في هذا الكتاب، مصممون على المضي قدماً في التصدي للمكائد والأشواق الإمبراطورية، التي أنخرط فيها كل من أسياس أفورقي وآبي أحمد، وفي إطار هذه الجهود المتواصلة يأتي مشروع هذا الكتاب بعنوان (تأكيد السيادة الإرترية).

ثالثاً: جميع الإرتريين ولا سيما الجيل الجديد من الشباب الذين تعرضوا للاستعباد، وتمت محاولة استخدامهم من قبل أسياس في محاولته لتحقيق أجندته وصفقاته السرية، سوف يقاومون طموحات أسياس الإمبراطورية بكل قوة متمثلين شعار الثورة الإرترية إبان مرحلة الكفاح المسلح (المقاومة حتى آخر نفس وآخر رصاصة).

رابعاً: هنالك صحوة عامة في أوساط الجماهير الارترية داخل إرتريا وخارجها، صحوة جددت فيها الجماهير الارترية عهدها لإزالة أسياس ونظامه واستبداله بنظام ديمقراطي وحكومة منتخبة ديمقراطياً.

مشروع كتاب (إرتريا: الأمة والسيادة)

مشروع هذا الكتاب يعكس تفانياً واخلاصاً لإضافة فكرية في مسيرة الكفاح المستمر من أجل تخليص إرتريا من قبضة هذا النظام الذي يعمل بشكل متواصل على تقويضها، وقد تم تلخيص هدف الكتاب في عنوانه (تأكيد السيادة الإرترية). وفيما يلي من فصول، سيتعرف القارئ على طبيعة وأهداف مشروع الكتاب وأسماء المساهمين فيه الموجودة في نهاية الكتاب. الفصل التمهيدي يعطي فكرة عن دوافع وتصورات مشروع الكتاب، كما يتضمن الكتاب فصلاً ختامياً يحتوي على ملخص لكل فصل من فصوله. إن الجهد المبذول في مشروع هذا الكتاب هو انعكاس لعمق ولائنا الوطني وعزمنا على الحفاظ وحماية وتعزيز سيادة بلادنا، وهي السيادة التي تم الحصول عليها بتضحيات لا تعد ولا تُحصى، علماً أن مكائد أسياس وأشواقه الإمبراطورية غير قادرة على تثبيط عزيمة الوطنيين الإرتريين، بل تزيد من عزيمتنا وتصميمنا، وليكن في علم الجميع أن إرتريا أرض الأبطال والشهداء ليست ولن تكون مطلقاً للمساومة، وهي التي تم الحصول عليها بتضحيات لا تقدر بثمن، وعليه فمن المؤكد أنه سيتم الدفاع عنها بواسطة جميع الوطنيين الإرتريين وبكل الموارد المتاحة لهم.

الخطر الواضح والماثل (وهو توصيف ورد في أحد فصول هذا الكتاب) للإشارة إلى الخطر الذي يشكله أسياس على وطننا وهو الشخص المغامر وغير المنتخب ذو النوايا الإجرامية الساعية لإجهاض سيادة بلادنا، ولابد أن تتم تعريته وفضحه ليظهر على

حقيقته، وأنه قد قام بارتكاب الخيانة العظمى التي لابد وأن يواجه بسببها العقوبة القانونية المناسبة المنصوص عليها في القانون، لقد أصبح واضحاً الآن أن الإرتريين لابد وأن يتخذوا قرارهم باستدراك هذا الخطر الواضح والماثل وأن يفعلوا كل ما يتطلب وضع حد له بشكل نهائي، وإن عدم القدرة على القيام بذلك يعني فقدان سيادتنا العزيزة، وعليه لابد من أن نرتب قوانا للمعركة الأخيرة وهي معركة نكون فيها أو لا نكون، وفي سبيل ذلك لابد من استخدام كل الوسائل المتاحة لوضع حد للنوايا الإجرامية لأسياس أفورقي.

الأزمة الماثلة وتحدياتها

يعرّف الصينيون الأزمة بأنها تزامن الخطر والفرصة في وقت واحد، نحن الآن على مفترق طرق في مواجهة التحدي المصيري، ومع الحرب الحالية في تيغراي، فنحن بالتأكيد نواجه تحدياً، ولكنه يمكن أن يشكل فرصة حاسمة في ذات الوقت، فرصة لوضع حد لنظام أسياس أفورقي الاستبدادي. إن كيفية تحقيق ذلك يجب ألا تكون قضية محل اختلاف، ولا يمكن أن يتم تشتيت تركيزنا بادعاء تصورات أخلاقية عن الغاية التي لا تبرر الوسيلة، ذلك أن وضع حد لنظام الإبادة الذي أسس له أسياس كفيل بتحديد الوسائل المناسبة التي يجب استخدامها، ذلك أن غاية إنقاذ بلادنا وشعبها الذي ناضل لثلاثين عاماً من أجل تقرير المصير وتحقيق الاستقلال الوطني يبرر في حد ذاته كافة الوسائل التي تساعدنا في إنجاز ذلك، ولندرك ذلك علينا أن نتخيل أن مخلوقاً محاصراً ومهدداً بالقتل وهو يرتعش ولا سبيل له للفرار، ماذا الذي يمكن أن يفعله مثل هذا المخلوق المهدد بالفناء؟ الجواب بسيط – أنه لن يتردد في مهاجمة مصدر الخطر، لأن ذلك رد فعل غريزي، وغريزة البقاء هو القانون الأول للطبيعة، وهو القانون الذي نتشاركه نحن البشر مع المخلوقات الأخرى، لذلك نحن في لحظة تاريخية نكون فيها أو لا نكون.

خطر واضح وماثل – أين إرتريا؟

إن كتابات المشاركين في هذا المشروع هي المعادل الفكري لحرب العصابات، الحرب التي استمرت لثلاثين عاماً من الجهد والدم والعرق والدموع والتي في نهاية المطاف أثمرت دولتنا المستقلة، إن الفصول العديدة الواردة في هذا المجلد تسعى بشكل أو آخر لتعزيز الأركان العديدة التي تدعم فكرة سيادة بلادنا، وأنه واجبنا الوطني تذكير الإرتريين بشكل مستمر بهذه الركائز الأساسية التي تدعم سيادة إرتريا.

العبارات "خطر واضح وماثل "و "أين إرتريا" هي عناوين لفصول في هذا المجلد - عبارات تلخص التحديات التي تواجهها دولتنا وتثير أيضاً أسئلة مهمة يجب أن تجد إجابات في إطار سعينا لأن تكون إريتريا دولة ديمقراطية ومتطورة على النحو الأمثل وتحتل مكانة دولية نفاخر بها بين الأمم. إنه التفاؤل الحذر، ولكن الواثق في ذات الوقت بشأن مستقبل إرتريا واضعين في الاعتبار إمكانيات إرتريا وشعبها الجاد بكل ما يتصف به

من المرونة والوطنية المتجردة والبعد عن الأنانية وهو ما يمكنه ليس فقط من تجاوز الأخطار الماثلة، ولكن أيضاً من بناء المستقبل المزدهر، وهو مستقبل غرس أساسه مقاتلو الحرية عبر تضحياتهم الجسيمة. إن الإيمان المشترك الذي يوحّد المساهمين في هذا الكتاب هو بارقة الأمل الذي مكننا من المحافظة على شعلة كفاحنا مشتعلة طوال هذه المدة حتى تحقق استقلالنا وترسخت سيادته وطننا.

وأخيراً، بقدر حرصنا على سيادتنا، يجب علينا احترام سيادة الدول الأخرى بما في ذلك الدول المجاورة لنا، لذلك يجب أن نكون واضحين أننا لا نؤمن بالتدخل في شؤون الدول الأخرى بما في ذلك الحرب الجارية في تيغراي. وفي ذات الوقت نعبر عن حزننا العميق لرؤية إخواننا وأخواتنا من التيغراي في حرب مدمرة - حرب اتسمت بتفشي القتل والاغتصاب والتشريد الجماعي، وهو جرائم تستدعي فرض عقوبات دولية وتحرير لوائح الاتهام بارتكاب جرائم الحرب، والجرائم ضد الإنسانية في مواجهة الجناة.

261

NOTE ON CONTRIBUTORS

Abdulrazig K. Osman is a PhD holder in Political Science-Democratisation, from Deakin University-Australia. Obtained a master's degree in Globalisation from the Australian National University, Master's degree in International Relations from Khartoum University and a degree in Journalism. He is a registered Journalist in Sudan, Co-founder of the Eritrean Centre of Media Services and worked as a director for an Eritrean broadcast called "Al-Sharq". He is a regular contributor to Eritrean debates on the Arabic domain.

Dr. Anghesom Atsbaha is an Associate Professor of African History and the Chair of the Department of Social and Behavioural Sciences. He teaches colonial Africa, modern African history and social science. Appointed by the Mayor of Chicago, Anghesom served as member of the Commission of Human Relations-Advisory Council on African Affairs and served as a member of the African advisory group for Congresswoman Jan Schakowsky. Professor Atsbaha is the recipient of the City of Chicago's 2010 Superior Public Service, Truman College 2010 Distinguished Professor Award and 2019 DePaul University Lifetime Achievement in Education. He is a regular contributor and participant on "The Professors" - WYCC-TV Channel 20 program and has presented and moderated several conferences including the 2000 United Nations video conferences with African ambassadors. Currently he is serving as 2020-2022 President of Association of Eritrean Studies.

Dr. Assefaw Tekeste Ghebrekidan was born in Eritrea and earned his medical degree at Haile Selassie I University in Addis Ababa, Ethiopia, and later served as a physician in the Eritrean Popular Liberation Front (EPLF), which led the country's thirty-year war for independence from Ethiopia. From 1982 to 1991, Dr. Ghebrekidan served as Head of Medical Services for the EPLF and Head of Civilian Health Services for Eritrea. He crafted the National Health Policy of the Transitional Government of Eritrea after independence in 1991.

In 1992, Dr. Ghebrekidan became Secretary (Minister) for the Department of Social Affairs in the Provisional Government of Eritrea. In 1994, he returned to academia as the Dean of the Faculty of Health Sciences at the University of Asmara. Since 1999, he had been a Research Fellow in the School of Public Health at University of California, Berkeley and earned a Doctor of Public Health degree for his study on corruption and its effect on health in sub-Saharan Africa. In May 2005 he joined the Touro University in California as the Director of Public Health Program. He is currently serving as global health professor.

Over the last two decades, along with the calm but brave Eritrean women and men, he served and is still serving as part of the resistance against the brutal dictatorship in Eritrea.

Awet T. Weldemichael is Professor of History at Queen's University in Kingston, Ontario. He has authored/edited several books and journal articles on the history and politics of Eritrea and the Horn of Africa, among others. He is a member of the Royal Society of Canada, College of New Scholars.

Bereket Habte Selassie is currently the William E. Leuchtenburg Distinguished Professor of African Studies and Professor of Law at the University of North Carolina at Chapel Hill. Prior to this he served as Chairman of the Constitutional Commission of Eritrea between 1994 and1997. In recognition of his tireless work for democracy and human rights, Dr.

Bereket was awarded the Honorary Doctor of Laws by Simmons College in May 2009. The internationally renowned jurist, academic and Pan-African activist continues to receive invitations to deliver keynote addresses in various forums in America, Europe and Africa.

Daniel Teklai is a writer and activist who is a co-founder and Chairman of *One Nation*, a grassroots-based organization seeking to bring democratic change in Eritrea. In 2011, he also co-founded the cyber-based *Eritrean Youth Solidarity of Change (EYSC)* which served as a springboard for forming many decentralized, pro-democracy forces around the world. A bank marketer by profession, Daniel has over 20 years' experience in commercial and investment banking. He holds a bachelor's degree from the University of Delaware and lives in California with his wife and two children.

Dr. Ghirmai Negash is a Professor of African Literature, and the Director of the African Studies Program at Ohio University, where he teaches postcolonial and decolonial literatures and critical theory. He is the author, editor, and translator of seven books of criticism, fiction, and poetry including: *A History of Tigrinya Literature in Eritrea* (1999); *At the Crossroads: Readings of the Postcolonial and the Global in African Literature and Visual Art*, Lead Ed., (2014); *The Conscript*, a translation of Gebreyesus Hailu's Tigrinya novel (1927, 1950) into English (2012); *African Liberation Theology: Intergenerational Conversations on Eritrea's Futures* (co-written with Awet Weldemichael, 2018); and *Megedi Adinaa* (2017). Prof. Negash is a recipient of the National Endowment for the Humanities NEH (2015) and Stellenbosch Institute for Advanced Studies (STIAS, 2019) Fellowships. He is also a permanent member of the African Academy of Sciences (AAS) and the 2020-21 President of the African Literature Association (ALA).

Ismail Omar-Ali, is a prolific writer/columnist at awate.com who has written hundreds of articles & critiques on a variety of subjects ranging from nationalism, dictatorship, democracy, religion, philosophy to politics among other things. After several visits to Eritrea shortly after independence, he became increasingly convinced that Eritrea was moving headlong towards dictatorship & became a fierce critic of the Eritrean regime ever since. In numerous debates with pro-government intellectuals in the dehai Eritrean forum, he repeatedly warned against the regime & its brutal crackdown of former ELF/EPLF warriors, innocent Muslims & Jehovah witnesses under various pretexts. In 1997, he led a petition by Diaspora Eritrean Muslims to protest the regime's insensitivity towards Muslims & to urge it to fulfill its promise of democracy & pluralism. Ismail is a PMP certified IT professional with master's in information systems & lives with his family in Virginia.

Mohamed Kheir Omer, PhD, is an Eritrean-Norwegian researcher and political activist with a passion for history. He runs a digital archive on Eritea, hegait.blogspot.com. With a degree in Veterinary Science, Dr. Omer, was the Dean of the College of Agriculture and Aquatic Sciences at the Univ. of Asmara, Eritrea (1992-1996) and later joined the G-13 to work for change and reform in his homeland.

A former member of the central committee of General Union of Eritrean Students, affiliated to the ELF (1977-1979), Omer is a published author: "The Dynamics of an Unfinished African Dream: Eritrea: Ancient Times to 1968", 2020 and co-author to "Asmara: Pictorial Book 1890-1938.", 2018.

Samuel Emaha Tsegai is a Ph.D. Candidate in History at Queen's University in Kingston, Ontario. Prior to joining the graduate program at Queen's University Department of History, he taught history at the Eritrean College of Arts and Sciences in Adi Keyeh. He holds a BA degree in History from Eritrea, and MA degree in History from Queen's, where he also teaches.